AGAINST THE LAW

CRIME, SHARP PRACTICE

AND THE CONTROL OF PRINT

PUBLISHING PATHWAYS

PREVIOUS TITLES IN THE SERIES

EDITED BY ROBIN MYERS & MICHAEL HARRIS

Development of the English Book Trade 1700–1899. OPP, 1981

Sale and Distribution of Books from 1700. OPP, 1982

Author-Publisher Relations in the Eighteenth and Nineteenth Centuries. OPP, 1983

Maps and Prints: Aspects of the English Booktrade. OPP, 1984

Economics of the British Booktrade 1605–1939. Chadwyck-Healey, OPP, 1985

Bibliophily. Chadwyck-Healey. OPP, 1986

Aspects of Printing from 1600. OPP, 1987

Pioneers in Bibliography. St Paul's Bibliographies, 1988

Fakes and Frauds. Varieties of Deception in Print and Manuscript. St Paul's Bibliographies, 1989

Spreading the Word. The Distribution Networks of Print 1550–1850. St Paul's Bibliographies, 1990

Property of a Gentleman. The Formation, Organisation and Dispersal of the Private Library 1620–1920. St Paul's Bibliographies, 1991

Censorship and the Control of Print in England and France 1600–1910. St Paul's Bibliographies, 1992

Serials and their Readers 1620–1914. St Paul's Bibliographies, 1993

A Millennium of the Book: Production, Design & Illustration in Manuscript and Print (900–1900). St Paul's Bibliographies, 1994

A Genius for Letters: Booksellers and Bookselling from the 16th to the 20th Century. St Paul's Bibliographies, 1995

Antiquaries, Book Collectors and the Circles of Learning. St Paul's Bibliographies, 1996

The Stationers' Company and the Book Trade 1550–1990. St Paul's Bibliographies, 1997

Medicine, Mortality and the Book Trade. St Paul's Bibliographies, 1998

Journeys through the Market: Travel, Travellers and the Book Trade. St Paul's Bibliographies, 1999

EDITED BY ROBIN MYERS, MICHAEL HARRIS & GILES MANDELBROTE

Libraries and the Book Trade. Oak Knoll Press, 2000

Under the Hammer: Book Auctions since the Seventeenth Century. Oak Knoll Press & The British Library, 2001

Lives in Print: Biography and the Book Trade from the Middle Ages to the 21st Century. Oak Knoll Press & The British Library, 2002

The London Book Trade: Topographies of Print in the Metropolis from the Sixteenth Century. Oak Knoll Press & The British Library, 2003

AGAINST THE LAW

CRIME, SHARP PRACTICE
AND THE CONTROL OF PRINT

Edited by
Robin Myers, Michael Harris
and Giles Mandelbrote

OAK KNOLL PRESS
&
THE BRITISH LIBRARY
2004

First published 2004 by
Oak Knoll Press
310 Delaware Street
New Castle
DE 19720
and
The British Library
96 Euston Road
London NW1 2DB

Cataloguing in Publication Data
A CIP Record for this book is available
from both The British Library and
the Library of Congress

ISBN 1-58456-153-X (Oak Knoll)
ISBN 0-7123-4896-4 (BL)

Typeset by Ella Whitehead
Jacket design by Bob Elliott
Printed in England by St Edmundsbury Press, Bury St Edmunds

Contents

Introduction

THE BOOK, WHETHER in manuscript or print, has often been a battleground for the opposing interests of dissent and authority, or for rival commercial interests. The original essays grouped under the title *Against the Law* are all concerned with historical aspects of the book trade's role as one of the gatekeepers to social status, reputation, money and power. From one side, the book trade and its products are considered as an opportunity for criminal activity, either by means of sharp practice or by deception, fraud and theft. Another perspective is offered by the attempts of the authorities to control the medium of print itself through forms of censorship, or to dominate the cultural shape of communities through its application and use. The contributors to this volume explore the underside of the book trade, revealing the ways in which laws and regulations relating to books have been exploited and manipulated, or evaded and broken, over many centuries.

Beautiful and precious objects of all kinds have always been the target of thieves and crooks. Books are no exception: **Christopher de Hamel** writes of a period when men and women feared hell-fire and eternal damnation, when an anathema inscribed in a book might stand as good a chance of protecting it as stout locks, or threats of imprisonment or worse. He cites a number of examples of mediaeval book thefts and the measures taken by owners and monastic librarians to try to protect their property from these depredations.

At a much later date, in the mid-nineteenth century, Count Libri abused his official position and scholarly reputation to steal some of the greatest treasures of French and Italian libraries, often covering his tracks by destroying fine bindings, obliterating manuscript annotations and other identifiable marks of ownership. His is an extraordinary story, combining brazen greed and political intrigue, elegantly and amusingly told by **Anthony Hobson**.

Forms of sharp practice which were designed to circumvent established practices and create an unfair, if not illegal, commercial advantage were evident in all periods. One example of this kind of bibliodeception is described by **Nicholas Pickwoad** in his highly technical paper on the history and construction of false raised bands. To what extent this always amounted to sharp practice is a moot point. In some cases it undoubtedly was, but it was also accepted trade practice by the nineteenth century. The majority of bibliophiles perhaps knew and cared too little about book structure to tell the genuine article from the false, so binders regularly followed the fashion of sewing on false raised bands. This was much less time-consuming and therefore more profitable for the binder (and sometimes perhaps also cheaper for their customers). The practice gave the customers what they wanted and few owners were any the wiser.

Helen Berry explores the sharp practices of the late seventeenth- and early eighteenth-century book trade through the eyes of the bookseller John Dunton. Dunton was the victim of a good deal of skulduggery practised by his fellow booksellers and auctioneers in London and Dublin, but he seems also to have been haunted by the recollection of deceptions which he himself had contrived at an earlier stage of his career. In particular, as an apprentice Dunton had deceived his master, Thomas Parkhurst, by over-valuing his late father's library and selling it to Parkhurst at an inflated price. In an extraordinarily long and detailed will, Dunton pours out his sense of guilt and his desire to make amends. Dunton's *Life and Errors* and *Dublin Scuffle* have long been important sources for those researching the book trade of the period, but this chapter draws attention to new and less familiar material.

Maureen Bell's 'Offensive Behaviour in the English Book Trade' draws on the long-awaited *Chronology and Calendar of Documents relating to the London Book Trade, 1641–1700*. She attempts, with a wealth of illuminating and lively examples, to define what 'offensive behaviour' meant to the later seventeenth-century authorities, ranging from rudeness and insubordination to deliberate malpractice and theft. We are introduced to a wide cast of characters on the fringes of the book trade, and of legality — such as Mrs Breach, the 'fat woman who keeps a bookselling shop at the foot of the stone stairs going up to the Court of Requests'. This chapter forms a bridge between those papers on skulduggery, crime and sharp practice and those more concerned with legal requirements and copyright.

Adri Offenberg's 'The Censorship of Hebrew Books in Sixteenth-Century Italy' is another world, focusing on the efforts to control print by the papal authorities, who persecuted Jewish printers and owners of Hebrew books for ideological religious reasons. Much of his evidence comes from censored copies of Hebrew books surviving in the British

Library and elsewhere, which sometimes give the names of the censors. These were often renegade Jews or apostates, who were the only people who could read Hebrew and therefore knew what to censor. They were, however, often careless to the extent of censoring names which seemed to them to have a heretical meaning and thus making complete nonsense of a text.

Alastair Mann discusses the changing meaning and interpretation of copyright in Scotland, with a brief comparison with England. A large part of his chapter is concerned with the repressive actions and sharp practice of the King's Printer in Scotland, with counterfeiting and duplicity in the book trade, and the defence of local privileges in opposition to English imports and Dutch pirates. He also provides some valuable case studies to illustrate the complex and often chaotic publishing history of bibles and almanacs in Scotland.

Finally, **Bill Bell**'s 'What did the nineteenth-century convict read?' gives a wholly different slant to the subject of crime and those operating against the law. An increasing state interest in crime and the mechanisms for its control was reflected in new uses for the medium of print. By the end of their long voyage, convicts transported to Australia were often more literate than immigrants within the law. This sociological case study is based on a variety of sources, including surviving diaries and letters.

These papers are the published proceedings of the 26th annual book trade history conference held at the St Bride Printing Library and Birkbeck College.

Michael Harris
Giles Mandelbrote
Robin Myers

London
August 2004

Contributors

BILL BELL lectures in the School of Literature, Languages, and Cultures at the University of Edinburgh. He is General Editor of the *History of the Book in Scotland* and is Director of the Centre for the History of the Book.

MAUREEN BELL lectures in the Department of English at the University of Birmingham. She has written extensively on the seventeenth-century English book trade and is currently completing a chronology and calendar of documents relating to the London trade, 1641–1700.

HELEN BERRY is Senior Lecturer in History at the University of Newcastle. She is the author of *Gender, Society and Print Culture in Late-Stuart England. The Cultural World of the Athenian Mercury* (Ashgate, 2003).

CHRISTOPHER DE HAMEL is Donnelley Fellow Librarian of Corpus Christi College, Cambridge. Formerly in charge of the sale of medieval manuscripts at Sotheby's, he has published extensively on manuscripts and the history of book collecting.

ANTHONY HOBSON has published books about Italian Renaissance collectors and Italian bookbindings. He is a former President of the Bibliographical Society and has given the Sandars lectures in Cambridge and the Lyell lectures in Oxford.

ALASTAIR MANN is Lecturer in Scottish History at the University of Stirling, co-editor and research consultant for the History of the Scottish Parliament Project at the University of St Andrews and co-editor of the *History of the Book in Scotland, vol. I: medieval to 1707* (in progress). He is the author of *The Scottish Book Trade, 1500 to 1720* (Tuckwell Press, 2000).

ADRI K. OFFENBERG has recently retired as curator of the Bibliotheca Rosenthaliana, University of Amsterdam. Formerly editor-in-chief of *Studia Rosenthaliana*, he has completed a substantial catalogue of the Hebrew incunabula in the British Library (HES & De Graaf, 2004).

NICHOLAS PICKWOAD is a freelance book conservator who is in charge of the St Catherine's Monastery Library Project. He is adviser on book conservation to the National Trust and teaches courses in Europe and America on European bookbinding.

List of those attending the Conference

Lisa Arlott
St Bride Printing Library

Barry Benster
Huddersfield Children's Bookshop

Thomas Berger
St Lawrence University, Canton, New York

Laurel Brake
Birkbeck College, London

Roger Cline
Treasurer, London Topographical Society

Andrew Cook
India Office Records, British Library

Carlo Dumontet
National Art Library, Victoria & Albert Museum

Judy Edwards
18th-century theatre studies

Christine Ferdinand
Fellow Librarian, Magdalen College, Oxford

Amy Flanders
D.Phil. student, Lincoln College, Oxford

Richard Ford
Manuscript dealer

Jane Francis
Retired librarian

Oliver Gerland
University of Colorado, Boulder

Moira Goff
British Library

John Goldfinch
British Library

Susan Gregory
Researcher

Matthew Groom
Archivist, Worshipful Company of Stationers

William Hale
Parker Library, Corpus Christi College, Cambridge

David Hall
Deputy Librarian, University Library, Cambridge

John Hewish
Librarian, retired

John Hinks
Research Fellow, University of Birmingham

Jonathan Hopson
National Art Library, Victoria & Albert Museum

Ashley Huish
Librarian, retired

Kristian Jensen
British Library

Patricia May Jurilla
Postgraduate student, SOAS

Christopher Lee
Independent scholar

Colin Lee
Book collector

David Lee
Bibliographer and indexer

B. Levy

Yvonne Lewis
National Trust

Karen Limper
British Library

Christina Mackwell
Lambeth Palace Library

Alexander Malcolm
Book collector

Keith Manley
Institute of Historical Research, University of London

Howard Mather
Bookseller

Charlotte Miller
Sotheby's book department

Miriam Miller
Postgraduate student, University College, London

Massimiliano Morini
Post-doctoral student, University of Bologna

Leslie Morris
Houghton Library, Harvard University

Alan H. Nelson
University of California, Berkeley

Sheila O'Connell
Department of Prints and Drawings, British Museum

Margaret Payne
Retired librarian

Michael Perkin
Retired Special Collections Librarian

Julian Pooley
Archivist, Surrey History Centre; Nichols Archive Project

Christelle Rabier
Ph.D. student, University of Paris I

Sheila Rainford
Book dealer

Julian Roberts
Retired librarian, Bodleian Library, Oxford

Dorothy Sinson
The Caxton Club, Chicago

Junie Sinson
The Caxton Club, Chicago

Eric Stockdale
Author; retired judge

David Stoker
Department of Information Studies, University of Wales, Aberystwyth

Patrick Streeter
Book dealer

John Symons
Wellcome Library, London

Jean Tsushima
Archivist Emeritus, Honourable Artillery Company

Lisa Vine
Independent scholar

John Walwyn-Jones
Antiquarian bookseller

Anne Watts
Freelance editor

Veronica Watts
Independent

David Wickham
Private collector; retired Archivist, Worshipful Company of Clothworkers

Priscilla Wrightson
Book collector

Romana Zacchi
Professor of English Literature, University of Bologna

Book Thefts in the Middle Ages

CHRISTOPHER DE HAMEL

TWO PHYSICAL FEATURES of medieval institutional manuscripts which commonly catch the popular imagination are chained bindings, and those dramatic ownership inscriptions inside the covers which invoke the curses of God and the saints against anyone stealing or selling the book. Chains or chain-hasps are especially characteristic of volumes which formed part of institutional libraries where at least some of the other books were available on loan, often medieval college or university collections. Chains usually indicated something like 'reference only' in a modern library. They date mostly from the end of the Middle Ages or even later, and they must have been disincentives to theft rather than fool-proof security. It is not difficult to twist off a chain. Curses are rather different. From time to time at Sotheby's I had to catalogue for sale manuscripts with thousand-year-old anathemas, calling down perpetual damnation in the name of Almighty God on any person who should ever at any time sell or attempt to sell the book, and I have to confess I sometimes found the experience of selling such manuscripts distinctly creepy. European book curses go back to at least the seventh century.[1] They say things like 'He who steals or sells this book or removes its inscription may he be cursed'; or 'May he who takes this book be killed by the sword of anathema'; or 'If anyone dares to carry it off, either secretly or publicly, let him incur the curse of the twelve apostles'; or '... let him lie under the malediction of Jesus Christ and the most glorious Virgin his mother and the blessed Thomas the martyr' (that one is from Canterbury); or '... may he receive eternal damnation with Judas the traitor and Annas and Caiaphas'; or '... hang by the throat as ravens pick out his eyes' — that one is German, and so is this: 'let him die the death, let him be fried in a pan, let the falling sickness and fever seize him, and let him be broken on a wheel and hanged, Amen.' A twelfth-century monk stole a fragment of the wrapper of the sacred Gospel of Saint Cuthbert in Durham Cathedral and hid it in his shoe; his leg immediately swelled up and his crime was discovered.[2] Such stories were doubtless reported avidly. It must have taken some bravado in the Middle Ages to steal or trade in a book if you really anticipated the curse of God for doing so. There is a thirteenth-century Augustine in the Bodleian with the ownership inscription of Robertsbridge Abbey in Sussex ('Liber sancte Marie de Ponte Roberti') and a double anathema against stealing the book, beside which Bishop John Grandison (d. 1369), has then added, in Latin, 'I, John, bishop of Exeter, do not know where the said house is; and I did not steal this book but acquired it by legal means.'[3]

The fact of chaining books and the fact (especially) of writing curses implies the very real possibility that books might actually be stolen. It suggests too that there was a market for second-hand books with unclear title, and also, of course, that the expected thieves were literate enough to understand the inscriptions. While many people have written about chains and indeed about curses, I am not aware that anyone has ever collected references to actual thefts of books in the Middle Ages.

My first example is a fictional one, from a collection of *exempla* or popular moral tales from late medieval Germany.[4] It concerns a Saint Anastasius who, according to the story, owned a complete Bible on parchment, said to be worth at least 18 florins. He showed it to a lay-brother who was visiting him in his monastic cell, and who subsequently stole it. The saintly Anastasius did not report the loss of the manuscript for fear that if he was accused, the lay-brother would deny it and would thus add the sin of perjury to that of theft. The thief took the stolen Bible to the next town to sell it. He asked a discounted price of 16 florins for it, but his potential client still hesitated and took the manuscript on approval, wanting a second opinion on its value. This would-be buyer then consulted none other than Anastasius, who merely said 'It is a good book and worth the price.' When this was reported to the lay-brother, he was so moved that the saint had not exposed him as a thief, that he converted at once and became a monk.

The story had an obvious moral purpose to its medieval hearers, but to us it is a good image of a situation necessarily familiar and credible to the audience, whereby a book is stolen furtively from a monastery and is immediately offered for sale in a nearby town.

An authentic example of a theft of a Bible took place in Reading Abbey in 1253.[5] On approximately 27 July that year, a small manuscript Bible went missing from the cloister. It had been acquired by the library at Reading about five years earlier with the bequest of Alwred of Dover. In fact, another volume is still extant from Alwred's same bequest and it contains the injunction: 'Whoever steals or makes off with this book will be cursed.' Doubtless the missing Bible also contained a similar threat. First of all, the monks searched the monastery and the book was not found. Then the bishop of Salisbury was informed, and he published a decree of excommunication throughout the archdeaconery of Berkshire against the unknown culprit or anyone knowingly receiving the missing book. Still no result. Finally, after five months, a circular letter was sent by the sacrist round to other monasteries describing the manuscript in some detail, both in size (it was stated to be 1½ palms high) and in its precise components, begging that if the book was unwittingly purchased by another institution, or was offered as security for a loan, the abbey would refund the price without question as long as the volume was returned to Reading. This tells us that it had a commercial value. As far as we know, the manuscript never turned up.

There was a happier outcome at the Abbey of St-Hubert, in Luxembourg, in about 1012.[6] The monastery's Golden Psalter, which had been given to them by the emperor Lothair, was stolen. As at Reading, an anathema was issued in the local province, and so the thief took the book into France and sold it in Toul, far to the south. It was bought by a woman called Heilewide as a present for her ten-year-old son, named Bruno, who, to his mother's disappointment, was unable to read it. In the meantime, the decree of excommunication against possession of the stolen book was promulgated throughout the empire, and Heilewide learned of it. She hurried with her son to the abbey, and begged forgiveness for unknowingly buying the Psalter, and she returned it. In exchange the monks presented her with a Sacramentary, which she later gave to the abbey of Givet. We know of the story because the boy, Bruno, grew up to become Pope Leo IX.

The reason why the Golden Psalter had been stolen from St-Hubert was undoubtedly because of its treasure binding, described then as being inset with precious pearls. The stealing of books for the bullion value of their jewelled bindings probably accounts for many of the earliest references we have to book thefts. A party of Viking raiders stole a purple and gold Gospel Book in England, and the ransom for its return was paid in gold in the second half of the ninth century by two local benefactors, Alderman Aelfred and his wife Werberg, who gave it to Christ Church in Canterbury, with an inscription in Old English imploring the help of God and all his saints that no one should alienate the book from Christ Church as long as Christianity may endure.[7] By a coincidental twist of fate, the volume is now actually back again in Norse possession, for this is the *Codex Aureus* in the Royal Library in Stockholm. The original thieves were pagan and presumably had no interest in the text. Doubtless they were attracted to a precious binding of gold or silver. A Gospel Lectionary of similar date now in Arras has notes in runes, which shows it too to have been in Scandinavian hands.[8]

It seems possible that the value of the bindings lies behind one of the most extensive book thefts in medieval England. The town of Abingdon was a monastic borough, which meant that the monks of the abbey there had privileges and rights of taxation deeply resented by the local population. In May 1327 a crowd of some 3,000 insurgents, many of them from Oxford, stormed the abbey and looted it of 262 manuscripts, and they forced the chapter to sign a charter acquitting them of blame, for perhaps those books too contained ownership curses.[9] After three years, however, the abbey revoked the charter and demanded compensation for what had been lost. They then listed what had gone missing: 100 Psalters, 40 Missals, 100 Graduals, 12 books of civil law and 10 of canon law, together with many church vestments, 10 chalices, 40 silver candelabra, 46 gold and silver cups, 40 spoons, and so on, as well as 100 sides of beef, 1,000 of mutton and 300 of bacon, all valued at the huge total of a thousand pounds. It sounds as though the rioters were raiding the sacristy and the kitchens, not the library. Probably all insurance claims throughout history are exaggerations but they must necessarily be within the bounds of plausible credibility, and here is a rare glimpse of huge numbers of multiple copies of liturgical books as well as vast quantities of meat. The aggressors were poor and very hungry. David Knowles, who reports the story, says that the books were doubtless picked up by Oxford stationers in the crowd: I suspect that the volumes may have also been stripped of their bindings for sale to goldsmiths.

In the same year, 1327, a mob stormed the abbey of Bury St Edmunds. The chronicle record is less detailed there than at Abingdon, but the books stolen were reported as including 20 Missals, 24 Breviaries, 12 Bibles, 20 Psalters and 10 Diurnals.[10] Once again it sounds as though these were books from the sacristy and that they were more likely to have been valuable for the covers than for the content. A hundred years later, the precentor's roll for Ely Cathedral records an expenditure of 8*s*.8*d*. in

1422–3 to replace an altar Missal which had been stolen:[11] it too may well have had a jewelled binding.

Other peasant uprisings took place in Germany in the 1520s. The abbey of Amorbach was raided on 1 May 1525 by a mob led by Goetz von Berlichingen and Jorg Metzler of Ballenberg. Seven years later the monastery was still seeking compensation for the losses incurred that day, including a Gospel Book in a decorated cover. In this case, they did eventually get it back, for what is almost certainly the actual volume is in the Grey Collection in Cape Town, with a contemporary inscription describing how it was looted from Amorbach in 1525 by George of Ballenberg, 'a butcher by trade' (it says) 'a man treacherous in his actions and deeds ... the destroyer and most vile annihilator of churches and places of worship' and that the book was returned without its binding which (it says) was once covered with gold, silver and gems.[12]

The liberating of books during warfare is a more complicated moral question, for whether or not you call this theft or legitimate spoil depends on which side you are on. Book looting goes back to classical antiquity. When the Roman consul Emilius Paulus defeated Perseus of Macedon in 168 B.C. his own share of the plunder included the Macedonian royal library. The Duke of Bedford, regent of France after its conquest by his brother Henry V, acquired no fewer than 843 manuscripts from the library of the Louvre in 1424–5 and he sent them back to England. One of them, in fact, is in my care in the Parker Library.[13] I do not suppose its acquisition by the duke would stand up under modern rules of military occupation, but perhaps after nearly 600 years we can assume that any claims may now have lapsed. This was not the opinion of the papal legate Marino de Fregeno who in 1461–3 travelled through Sweden and Norway laying claim to books which he said had been looted by the Goths at the time of the sack of Rome in 510, almost a thousand years earlier.[14] There is a marvellously illuminated French picture Bible in the British Library which was among the spoils of the Battle of Poitiers on 19 September 1356, when it was stolen from the tent of the king of France. The looter sold it to the Earl of Salisbury for £33.6*s*.8*d*., and subsequently the earl's widow instructed her executors to sell it on for not less than £40.[15] In the library of Lord Bath at Longleat is a Middle English chronicle of Hector Boece. It has a note on the flyleaf that it was looted from Edinburgh Castle 'at the wyninge and burninge therof' (as it says, in quaintly-spelled English) in 1544.[16] That, to me, simply shows sensible bibliophilic opportunism. While most of the victorious English army were doubtless raping Scottish maidens and drinking whisky in the Royal Mile, Sir John Thynne, of Longleat, was evidently in the library, helping himself to the books. In 1500 Avis Godfrey was prosecuted in London for stealing a Book of Hours belonging to Elizabeth Sekett. In her own defence she said that she found it in the street in Pudding Lane, and the case was dropped.[17] Even then it was accepted that this was hardly theft.

Instances of stealing books for the sake of profit occur throughout the Middle Ages. An early reference is in a letter of Lupus of Ferrières writing to Archbishop Hincmar in 858. Lupus says that he has been reluctant to send a copy of Bede's *Collectanea* because the book is too large to conceal on one's person or to hide in a bag and, even if it could be, he says, 'one would have to fear an attack of robbers who would certainly be attracted by the beauty of the book.'[18] It implies that there was already a market for stolen books in the mid-ninth century. That is an important point. Oderic Vitalis records that in about 925 two guests at the abbey of St-Evroul in Normandy stole from the monks some charters and a book — '*librum*', not named — and we even know the miscreants' names, Raoul de Drachy and Herluin, chancellor of the duc d'Orléans, who kept the book when the pair divided up their spoils.[19] When the fourteenth-century poet Petrarch was a boy, his father gave him a romanesque manuscript of Isidore, and in about 1325, when he was about 21, his father helped him commission a magnificent manuscript of Virgil. In November 1326 these books were both stolen. By extraordinary chance the Virgil was recovered in April 1338 and the Isidore in 1347, and both survive, one in Milan, one in Paris.[20] To celebrate the return of the Virgil, Petrarch commissioned a magnificent frontispiece by Simone Martini, no less, and so the theft led indirectly to one of the very great *quattrocento* illuminations. In 1390–1 most of the books in the library of King's Hall, Cambridge, were chained to discourage theft. However, the catalogue records that an unchained copy of the Decretals of Gregory IX was stolen, carried off (the catalogue notes indignantly) by one 'Howard', who sold it, apparently, for 2 marks.[21] The most plausible candidate for the culprit seems to be Walter Howard, a fellow of King's Hall in 1397, dead or gone by 1404.[22]

Many medieval book thefts were probably inside jobs. Chains and book curses would have been more of a warning to regular users of libraries than to outside burglars in the night. The commonest way of losing books (and one not unique to the Middle Ages) must have been when people borrowed volumes and failed to return them. The abbot of Fulda lent a Missal around the year 1000 to the bishop of Würzburg and the monastery negotiated in vain for its return after the bishop's death.[23] In 1337 the monks of Christ Church in Canterbury compiled a list of 44 books which had been borrowed and never brought back to the abbey, including a life of Thomas Becket which had been lent to Edward II, no less, who had died ten years earlier without ever returning it.[24] The abbey of Spalding lent twelve books to a student in Oxford, Alan Kyrketone, in the early 1430s; and in 1438, three years after he had left university, the books had still not been recovered.[25]

The safe-keeping of books in libraries must have depended greatly on the vigilance or efficiency of their custodians. The chronicle of the abbey of Fécamp in Normandy records the theft of books from the library apparently in 1284, when the abbot, Richard de Treigos, was absent on the crusades.[26] Charges of selling books illegally were common accusations against unpopular monastic office-holders. There is the famous case of Richard of Wallingford, abbot of St Albans, who died in 1336. He was clearly charmed by Richard de Bury, author of the *Philobiblion*, into giving him four books from the library of St Albans and then into selling him 32 more volumes from the abbey for the considerable sum of £50.[27] The chronicle reports (perhaps unfairly) that the abbot himself kept half the money from the book sale and that he used the other half for feasting, 'a deed', the chronicler writes, 'infamous to all who agreed to it, so to make the only nourishment of the soul serve the belly.' Wallingford's successor, Michael of Mentmore, was actually able to buy many of the books back from the estate of Richard de Bury in 1346, including a twelfth-century copy of John of Salisbury. This volume still survives, now among the royal manuscripts in the British Library,[28] and it contains two original curses, one of about 1180, 'whoever removes it or commits fraud with it or deletes the inscription or changes it will be anathema' and again, added about 30 years later, 'whoever takes it away or deletes or alters the inscription will be cursed, Amen, Amen, Amen.' These two inscriptions were certainly there when the book was taken from the abbey in the 1330s and they clearly did little to discourage either the seller or the buyer.

Instances of monks accused of selling their institution's books illegally are surprisingly common. In 1320 the abbot of St Ulrich in Augsburg disposed of manuscripts as old as the twelfth century and these were not recovered until 1344, on payment of £27 and 15 pfennigs.[29] There were internal disputes resulting in accusations of illicit book sales at St Frideswide's in Oxford in 1378, at St Werburgh's in Chester in 1409, and at Michelham Priory in Sussex in 1478.[30] An ordinance of William Curteys, abbot of Bury St Edmunds in the 1430s, assigned different punishments for stealing books: if monks took them, the miscreants would be confined to the cloister and deprived of various privileges; but if any secular person from outside the abbey should steal or appropriate a book, they would be subject to the greater excommunication.[31]

The idea that monks themselves might misappropriate books is probably not as strange as it sounds at first. In 1330 the king sent a writ to the sheriff of Oxford requiring him to ensure that a member of the Oxford Franciscan house, Friar Walter de Chatton, should immediately return two books, valued at 40 shillings, which he had unjustly taken from one John de Penreth; in default of which, the friar and the warden of his convent would be summoned to appear before the king's justices at Westminster. The sheriff forwarded the writ to the mayor of Oxford, who declared that he could do nothing about it, since the Franciscans were outside his jurisdiction.[32]

This touches on a point which was immensely complicated and controversial, which is that there was a distinction in medieval law between laymen (for whom theft was a criminal offence, ultimately punishable by death), and monks and clerics, who could claim the benefit of clergy, which gave them the right to trial by the ecclesiastical courts. That is really the distinction being made by the ordinance of William Curteys at Bury, for members of the church and laymen were subject to different systems of justice. Proving benefit of clergy in a medieval law court often required no more than to demonstrate literacy: a Psalter would commonly be passed to the defendant and he would be asked to read a few lines.[33] It seems quite likely that most competent medieval book thieves would be able to read, at least a bit, and so most probably escaped civil punishment. This gives extra relevance to the anathemas and religious threats of the book curses, for there was nothing else. I have searched in vain through the *Decretum* of Gratian and the indexes of medieval canon law for guidance of punishing book thieves, and the only specific references to books that I have found relate to authorship and heresy.

Sometimes the ownership of books was in doubt, even at a high level. Thomas de Cobham, bishop of Worcester, bequeathed a substantial library to the university of Oxford but the building planned for them was not ready when the bishop died in 1327. His executors pledged the manuscripts as security for a loan to meet the expenses of the estate. The founder and provost of Oriel, Adam de Brome, however, redeemed the pledge himself and installed the books in his own college. The proctor and a great crowd broke in and removed the books by force from Oriel in the name of the university; and the dispute as to their legal ownership dragged on until 1410 when Archbishop Arundel finally refunded Oriel with the £50 which Brome had paid 83 years earlier.[34] The irony is that the university rapidly proceeded to lose all the books, through negligence and theft, whereas the medieval library of Oriel is at least partly intact.

Something very dodgy took place after the death of Henry IV in 1413. The royal librarian, Robert Bradfelde, '*custos librorum*', as he is called, seems to have sold nine important books from the King's estate to the well-known London bookseller, Thomas Marleburgh. In 1419 a legal case came before the King's Bench for their recovery or for reimbursement, and the missing volumes were listed. They were obviously highly commercial, including a *Polychronicon* worth 10 marks; a Bible in Latin, also valued at 10 marks, and another in English, worth £5; a Gower valued at £5; two Psalters; and so on. The considerable total claimed on behalf of the heir, Henry V, was £58.6*s*.8*d*.[35] It is actually one of the earliest glimpses we have of an English royal library, and we know of it only because of the reported theft. A rather similar lawsuit was brought in Paris in the mid-fifteenth century when the Parisian bookseller, André le Musnier, was charged with attempting to sell a Bible which, it was alleged, had been removed illegally from a college library.[36]

The mention of booksellers such as Thomas Marleburgh and André le Musnier brings us to the final part of this paper, and indeed to the central theme of sharp practice in the book trade. There is absolutely no reason to suggest that Marleburgh and le Musnier were thieves, for they were both well-known booksellers, but they were accused of benefiting from what would certainly have to be called sharp practice. We will come back to André le Musnier a bit later. Throughout this paper there has been a recurrent theme, which is that theft of books goes hand-in-hand with a book trade. The former has little benefit without the services of the latter. Nearly every one of the medieval book thefts which I have alluded to was not so much because the culprit wanted a text but because the manuscript was perceived to be valuable and saleable; and the rapid increase in the twelfth century in curses against thieves corresponds precisely with the rise of a secular lay book trade giving opportunities for manuscripts to be bought and sold. The second-hand book market is older than the trade in newly-made books. The earliest unambiguous reference to a Paris bookseller, probably in the 1170s or 80s, castigates him as a rascal who had double-crossed Peter of Blois, our authority for the encounter.[37] Allegations of sharp practice therefore go back to the very first mention of the trade. We know many of the names of people involved in the late medieval book trade only from documents of legal proceedings for unpaid rent or tax, failed contracts, broken promises, or other civil offences. I do not believe that the book business involves a larger element of skulduggery than any other occupation, but certainly if we want examples of swashbuckling medieval low-life, the records of the book trade will supply all we could ask. Let us take the Paris trade in a single year, 1488–9. I owe all these to the extracts from prosecutions unearthed by Richard and Mary Rouse.[38] A parchmenter was charged that year with breaking the curfew and carrying a dagger at night. A bookseller was charged with assaulting a prostitute called Perrette Martine. A bookbinder, Crespin Daillart, was arrested for assault on another prostitute on Christmas Day, 1488, and was let out on the 28th, presumably when he had sobered up. A second bookbinder was arrested for stealing a silver *chasse* and attempting to sell it. A printer, Pierre le Dru, was imprisoned for beating up a clothworker; and another bookbinder, Thomas le Croisier, was imprisoned four times that year for assault and for smashing down the door of the illuminator Henri Ploumion and stealing from him. The items taken may or may not have included books. These are just samples from a single year. What sounds like another book-trade dispute took place in London three years earlier, in 1485, when an attorney reported the theft from his house of 60 copies of Caxton's *Reynard the Fox*, printed in 1481.[39] There can have been no point in taking them unless for re-sale.

There are two famous cases of thefts between members of the book trade. In 1398 the manuscript illuminator Jacquemart de Hesdin, who worked for the Duc de Berry, accused a rival illuminator in Poitiers of stealing his colours and his pattern sheets, and, with the help of his brother-in-law, Jean Petit, they murdered him. They were tried, and pardoned.[40] What may be the actual pattern book is now in the Morgan Library in New York. The second case took place in Lombardy, about 1490. The illuminator Giovan-Pietro Birago was then working on a complex and richly illustrated manuscript Book of Hours for Bona Sforza, dowager duchess of Milan. Part of the unbound book had already been delivered to the client when a substantial part of the rest was stolen from Birago's workshop by one Fra Gian-Jacopo, who was arrested and imprisoned. Birago, making the complaint, valued the missing leaves at 500 ducats. (Mark Evans, in reporting this story, compares Leonardo da Vinci's valuation of his own *Virgin of the Rocks* at only 100 ducats.) It transpired that the stolen leaves had already been sold to Juan Maria Sforzino, future bishop of Milan. One of them turned up in 1941, and two more in 1984.[41]

Finally, let us come back to the Parisian bookseller André le Musnier. This is a story of sharp practice, certainly, but whether or not it was theft depends rather on whose side you believe. It involves incunabula, from the first printing presses of Mainz. Peter Schoeffer, former employee of Gutenberg and the son-in-law and successor of Johann Fust, sold many books in Paris. Fust had died there on a business trip in 1466; Schoeffer was in Paris in 1468; and by 1470 the firm had their own agent in Paris, one Herman of Stratboen. Both Peter Schoeffer and Conrad Henkis (the printer who had married Fust's widow) used to send books from Mainz on consignment to Herman, and clearly this was a profitable outlet. Unfortunately Herman died suddenly in late August 1474. A Parisian lawyer immediately arrived and confiscated all books in Herman's possession, under the ancient *droit d'aubaine*, which was the king's right to the goods of a foreigner who died in the royal domain. A law suit was lodged at once by the university, objecting that the seizure was illegal on the grounds that the archbishopric of Mainz was a free state in league with Louis XI and that the books were not the property of Herman. Some, indeed, had actually been sold to members of the university of Paris, including the influential Johann Heynlin von Stein, who with Guillaume Fichet had brought the first printing press to Paris. Schoeffer and Henkis claimed compensation of 2,425 *écus d'or* for their losses. Now the trial revealed sharp practice, for the lawyer who had seized the books and who was summoned to appear as defendant in court, proved to be Philippe le Musnier, the son (no less) of our old friend the bookseller, André le Musnier, who had by then already disposed of all the contested books, doubtless on a huge commission. Eventually the king agreed to reimburse the Mainz printers for their loss, at a rate of 800 *livres* a year, beginning in August 1475, until the total should be reached. Predictably, it was never paid, and as late as 1515 Schoeffer's descendants were still seeking compensation.[42]

What should we make of these various tales of book losses and book thefts throughout the Middle Ages? It is notable, first of all, how many disputes on ownership dragged on for decades, if not centuries. There was no statute of limitation in medieval civil law, and such a concept was unknown in England until 1623: if an item was stolen, the loser never lost the right to hope for its recovery. Anathemas were sometimes the only weapon for discouraging theft, and there is no time limit for eternal damnation. Monastic ownership inscriptions in books very often state that a book belonged to the saint of a monastery rather than to its monks, 'the book of Saint Cuthbert of Durham', 'this book belongs to Saint Mary of Fountains', and so on, and of course a saint is everlasting and to steal from one is sacrilege as well as theft.

A second theme is that for theft to be profitable, a book has to be a commercial commodity. The book trade, consciously or unwittingly, was the greatest accomplice of the thieves. The fact of constant thefts is itself unexpected evidence of an active market in books, much earlier (in fact) than any other documentary evidence for the beginnings of the European book trade.

Thirdly, it is quite clear that theft or unilateral redistribution of books from libraries was a problem throughout the Middle Ages. It seems a wonder that any medieval libraries survived at all and, of course, most of them did not. The whole library of Humfrey, Duke of Gloucester, was evidently pilfered from Oxford in less than a hundred years. So was that of the Franciscan convent in Oxford. I have not even touched on the scattering and looting of libraries at the Reformation or in the Wars of Religion, which, even by the mildest interpretation, would not be considered legal in modern terms. The late bookseller, H. P. Kraus, used to say that 'you expect every great manuscript to have been stolen at least once.' I have used medieval library catalogues frequently in constructing this story. Some show evidence of heart-rending losses. Let me conclude with the library catalogue of Stoneleigh Priory in Warwickshire in 1385–6.[43] Here is the entire text, in full, in Latin: 'In libraria abbatis, nichil' — in the library of the abbot, absolutely nothing.

References

1. M. Drogin, *Anathema! Medieval Scribes and the History of Book Curses*, Montclair (New Jersey), 1983, from which most of the examples here are taken.
2. T. J. Brown, ed., *The Stonyhurst Gospel of Saint John*, Oxford, 1969, p. 3.

3. Oxford, Bodleian Library, MS. Bodley 132.

4. L. S. Thompson, 'Notes on Bibliokleptomania', *Bulletin of the New York Public Library*, LXXXVIII, 1944, pp. 723–60, esp. p. 730.

5. R. Sharpe, J. P. Carley, R. M. Thomson and A. G. Watson, eds., *English Benedictine Libraries, The Shorter Catalogues*, London, 1996 (*Corpus of British Medieval Library Catalogues*, 4), pp. 448–51.

6. A. Derolez, B. Victor and L. Reynhout, eds., *Provinces of Liège, Luxembourg and Namur*, Brussels, 1994 (*Corpus Catalogorum Belgii, The Medieval Booklists of the Southern Netherlands*, II), p. 180.

7. R. Gameson, ed., *The Codex Aureus, An Eighth-Century Gospel Book, Stockholm, Kungliga Bibliotek, A.135*, Copenhagen, 2001 (*Early English Manuscripts in Facsimile*, XXVIII), I, pp. 75–7.

8. R. McKitterick, *The Carolingians and the Written Word*, Cambridge, 1989, pp. 135–6.

9. H. E. Salter, 'Chronicle Roll of the Abbots of Abingdon', *English Historical Review*, XXVI, 1911, p. 734; D. Knowles, *The Religious Orders in England*, I, Cambridge, 1948, reprint 1974, pp. 267–8, a reference I owe originally to John Collins.

10. M. R. James, *On the Abbey of Saint Edmund at Bury*, Cambridge, 1895, p. 108.

11. Sharpe, *et al.*, as above, n. 5, p. 449.

12. C. Steyn, *The Medieval and Renaissance Manuscripts in the Grey Collection of the National Library of South Africa, Cape Town*, Salzburg, 2002 (*Analecta Cartusiana*, 180), pp. 11–13. The manuscript is Grey Collection, MS. 4.b.3.

13. J. Stratford, *The Bedford Inventories, The Worldly Goods of John, Duke of Bedford, Regent of France (1389–1435)*, London, 1993, pp. 95–6. This is presumably the source for Cambridge, Corpus Christi College, MS. 324, a *Mirroir des Dames*, still at the Louvre in 1413 but in England by the mid-fifteenth century.

14. G. H. Putnam, *Books and their Makers during the Middle Ages*, 1896–7, reprint, New York, 1962, I, pp. 229–30.

15. G. F. Warner and J. P. Gilson, *Catalogue of Western Manuscripts in the Old Royal and King's Collections*, London, 1921, II, pp. 341–2, Royal MS. 19.D.II.

16. J. Collins, *A Short Account of the Library at Longleat House, Warminster, Wilts.*, London, 1980, p. 6.

17. M. C. Erler, 'Devotional Literature', *The Cambridge History of the Book in Britain*, III, *1400–1557*, ed. L. Hellinga and J. B. Trapp, Cambridge, 1999, pp. 495–525, at p. 497.

18. McKitterick, as above, n. 8, p. 135.

19. G. Nortier, *Les bibliothèques médiévales des abbayes Bénédictines de Normandie*, Paris, 1971, p. 98.

20. A. C. de la Mare, *The Handwriting of Italian Humanists*, I, i, Oxford, 1973, p. 1.

21. P. D. Clark and R. Lovatt, *The University and College Libraries of Cambridge*, London, 2002 (*Corpus of British Medieval Library Catalogues*, 10), p. 343, no. 95.

22. A. B. Emden, *A Biographical Register of the University of Cambridge to 1500*, Cambridge, 1963, p. 317.

23. Putnam, as above, n. 14, p. 229.

24. M. R. James, *The Ancient Libraries of Canterbury and Dover*, Cambridge, 1903, pp. 146–9.

25. D. N. Bell, 'Monastic Libraries, 1400–1557', *The Book in Britain*, III, as above, n. 17, pp. 229–54, at p. 234.
26. Nortier, as above, n. 19, pp. 12–13.
27. E. A. Savage, *Old English Libraries, The Making, Collection, and Use of Books during the Middle Ages*, 1911, reprint, 1970, p. 50.
28. London, British Library, Royal MS. 13.D.IV.
29. Putnam, as above, n. 14, p. 232.
30. W. Page, ed., *The Victoria History of the County of Oxford*, II, 1907, reprint, Folkestone, 1987, p. 99; Savage, as above, n. 27, p. 61.
31. James, *St. Edmund*, as above, n. 10, pp. 108–11.
32. A. G. Little, *The Grey Friars in Oxford*, Oxford, 1892, p. 60.
33. J. Bellamy, *Crime and Public Order in England in the Later Middle Ages*, London, 1973, p. 152.
34. M. B. Parkes, 'Book Provision and Libraries at the Medieval University of Oxford', *Scribes, Scripts and Readers, Studies in the Communication, Presentation and Dissemination of Medieval Texts*, London and Rio Grande (Ohio), 1991, pp. 299–310, at p. 308.
35. C. Meale, 'Patrons, Buyers and Owners: Book Production and Social Status', in J. Griffiths and D. Pearsall, eds., *Book Production and Publishing in Britain, 1375–1475*, Cambridge, 1989, pp. 201–38, at p. 203; J. Stratford, 'The early royal collections and the Royal Library to 1461', *The Book in Britain*, III, as above, n. 17, pp. 255–73, at p. 261. For Marleburgh, cf. C. P. Christianson, *A Directory of London Stationers and Book Artisans, 1300–1500*, New York, 1990, pp. 131–2.
36. R. H. Rouse and M. A. Rouse, *Illiterati et uxorati, Manuscripts and their Makers, Commercial Book Producers in Medieval Paris, 1200–1500*, Turnhout, 2000, II, p. 15.
37. W. Wattenbach, *Schriftwesen im Mittelalter*, Leipzig, 1896, p. 558.
38. Rouse and Rouse, as above, n.36, II, pp. 43, 65, 23, 99, 111 and 51.
39. J. H. Baker, 'The books of the common law', *The Book in Britain*, III, as above, n. 17, pp. 411–32, at p. 430.
40. J. J. G. Alexander, *Medieval Illuminators and their Methods of Work*, New Haven and London, 1992, pp. 411–32, at 130.
41. M. Evans and T. Kren in T. Kren, ed., *Renaissance Painting in Manuscripts*, New York and London, 1983, pp. 113–22; W. M. Voelkle and R. S. Wieck, *The Bernard H. Breslauer Collection of Manuscript Illuminations*, New York, 1992, pp. 216–17.
42. Rouse and Rouse, as above, II, n. 36, pp. 320–3.
43. N. R. Ker, *Medieval Libraries of Great Britain, A List of Surviving Books, Supplement to the Second Edition*, ed. A. G. Watson, London, 1987, p. 64.

The Censorship of Hebrew Books in Sixteenth-Century Italy

ADRI K. OFFENBERG

THIS PAPER IS derived from my work on Part XIII of the *Catalogue of Books Printed in the XVth Century Now in the British Museum* (BMC), which describes the Hebrew incunabula in the British Library. Part I appeared in 1908; the latest part (to date) in 1985. In fact, from the time I came into the field of Hebrew incunabula in the 1970s, I could not help remarking how incomprehensible and unforgivable it was that in this monumental catalogue Hebrew books had been entirely overlooked, even though, until after the Second World War, the British Museum collection of Hebrew incunabula was the largest and most beautiful in the world. Hebrew incunabula constitute but a fraction of the output of fifteenth-century presses, probably totalling about 140 editions, less than half of one percent of the total production of the incunable period. Hebrew books were printed only in Italy, Spain and Portugal, with a solitary edition in Constantinople.

It seems as if my criticism did not go completely unnoticed, because to my surprise, in 1991, I was invited to do the job myself and produce a separate volume of the Hebraica. It is not entirely satisfactory to put all the Hebrew editions together in a single volume, separating like from like, for all incunabula, whether Hebrew or non-Hebrew, were printed on the same sort of press by the same technique and using the same kind of paper. The only difference was the typefaces, but the same is true of the Greek, which, in previous parts of BMC were catalogued with the Museum's incunabula in Roman and Gothic type. This separation of the Hebrew books obscures the many interesting connections between the Christian and Jewish presses, especially in Italy, but also to a lesser extent in Spain and Portugal.

Nevertheless, it was a great pleasure and an enormous challenge to me to spend seven years, starting in October 1992, working on this project for six weeks twice a year. In addition, I spent many hours of my spare time working up my notes and preparing camera-ready copy of the catalogue. During these years in London I was made a temporary member of the

British Library staff, given a house key, and allowed to look behind the scenes of that respectable institution, first in the old building in Great Russell Street, of which I have many fond memories, and later in the controversial new building in Euston Road. I had first-hand experience of the move from the old building to the new.

Studying early Hebrew books one comes across something which hardly plays any part in general incunable literature or in sixteenth- and seventeenth-century bibliography, but which is important in the description of Hebrew early printed books and manuscripts. This is the expurgation of parts of the text — obliterated with horizontal brush strokes, even entire pages torn out, or parts of the page cut off.

In the wake of the Counter-Reformation of the mid-sixteenth century the Church sought to prevent the circulation of books which might undermine the foundations of the Catholic faith: all Hebrew manuscripts and printed works in Italy ran the risk of being expurgated. The Church had various reasons for its war on Hebrew literature. The Jews were perceived as dangerous, because they were unbelievers, assisted the spread of Humanism and refused to convert to Christianity, holding fast to their faith and even attacking Christianity in their books openly or by implication.[1] All these 'blasphemiae, errores aut haereses' had to be corrected. In principle the revisers appointed by the Inquisition signed their work of destruction with their signature, and in some cases put the date and place, sometimes in perfectly legible humanistic handwriting, but very often in almost unreadable scrawl.

Systematic research into this form of censorship started, like so many aspects of Hebrew bibliography, with the great Moritz Steinschneider, who published a translation from the Italian of M. Mortara in 1862.[2] It appeared in the journal *Hebräische Bibliographie*, with a long and reasoned introduction by Steinschneider. Abraham Berliner continued this research in 1891.[3] Moritz Stern's *Urkundliche Beiträge* (1893), is very useful, a mine of background information on the organization and decrees concerning the censorship of Hebrew books in Italy.[4] *The Censorship of Hebrew Books* of 1899, the classic history of the subject by the American scholar William Popper (1874–1963), was the culmination of this research and has enabled the identification of individual revisers over a period of consecutive years.[5] It has also helped us to reconstruct, at least in part, the routes that individual copies travelled, especially where early owners' inscriptions add to revisers' data. Nathan Porges did further research into the 'Index

Expurgatorius' and, amongst other things, observed that the Church, contrary to its attitude to non-Jewish books, never gave its approval to Hebrew books and those who expurgated them were not permitted to call themselves censors, only revisers or expurgators. The Church did not completely trust them and did not take full responsibility for their work.[6] Isaiah Sonne, a Polish-American authority on the history of the Jews in Italy, gave a new turn to the subject in an extensive study of 1942, in which he concentrated on press censorship and looked particularly at the phenomenon of Jewish self-censorship in Italy from the middle of the sixteenth century: 'Indeed, the expurgation of single printed volumes, accomplished partly under the supervision of neophytes was sporadic, without any continuity, and in consequence devoid of systematic performance. Entirely different was the censorship exercised in the preparation of new editions. The publisher had to consider the needs and desires of his clientele, that was hardly willing to purchase books which were either liable to confiscation by the Inquisition or arbitrarily altered and mutilated.'[7]

To give a few simple examples of expurgation: a word like 'idolatry' (*avodah zara*) was absolutely forbidden, since it might hint at the Christian church and was required to be altered to 'worshippers of the stars and the planets'. The same had to be done whenever the words 'gentile' and 'gentiles' (*goy* and *goyim*) were used; these had to be changed to 'Samaritan(s)'. Even in a reference to a biblical text, for example in Psalm 2, 'Why do the people imagine a vain thing?', the Hebrew word for 'people' was forbidden. 'Rome', even if the reference was to Ancient Rome, had to be changed to 'Babylon', 'Persia', or 'Aram', which often made complete nonsense of the text; the name of the city 'Basle' was forbidden, since it was a heretic city. Of course the word 'talmud' was strictly taboo, even if it had the simple meaning of 'knowledge', as in the prayer 'Let us heed all the knowledge of Thy law'.[8] 'Heretic, sectarian' (*min*) was forbidden, but was expurgated even when it simply meant 'species, kind', as in 'a kind of peas'. But these are simple examples — often the expurgation was much more far-reaching. Numerous blunders were made by the generally ignorant sixteenth-century revisers, who automatically expurgated any forbidden word.

The following information about the Hebrew incunabula in the British Library can be given:[9] 43 copies of the British Library's copies bear traces of Italian censorship between 1556 and 1688, years of the offensive against

Hebrew literature; 36 of these copies are actually signed by one or more revisers, although nine have no signs of expurgation.

I have not made any attempt in my catalogue to analyse the kind of expurgation in the books described. Later owners have often restored the expurgated passages in the margin or between the lines, and sometimes the reviser's ink is so faded that the printed text can easily be read today; on other occasions there is loss of text where the ink has corroded and damaged the paper.

Cardinal Giampietro Caraffa, whom Popper calls 'the very spirit of the Dominican Inquisition incarnate', became Pope Paul IV on 22 May 1555 and at once set about placing the Jews in a ghetto and restricting their personal liberty in many other ways. He also imposed a levy of ten ducats per annum on every synagogue in Italy for the support of the Collegio dei Neofiti, an institution at which Jewish converts received Christian instruction. In 1559 the Roman Office of the Inquisition issued the *Index librorum prohibitorum* on the Pope's instructions. More than 583 authors were banned. But this index was considered unduly harsh, and in 1564, under the next Pope, Pius IV, the Council of Trent issued a more moderate revision of the *Index* which remained the model for all later editions. Although the Talmud, its glosses, annotations, interpretations and expositions are mentioned, the prohibition was somewhat modified by the additional stipulation, that if the title 'Talmud' was left out, and there were no calumnies or insults to the Christian religion, these would be tolerated. Because the inquisitors and bishops were too ignorant of Hebrew to carry out their censorship decrees, the Popes employed the Neophytes as searchers for forbidden works in Jewish homes (searches such as that undertaken in Rome on 12 July 1555), and to act as correctors and expurgators of permitted works.

The revisers proceeded as follows: the Hebrew books were demanded from their Jewish owners in the name of the Inquisition, and were handed over to the local office. Concealment was rigorously punished, not only by seizure of the books and large fines, but also, in certain circumstances, by imprisonment and confiscation of property. The books collected were examined by the appointed revisers, who destroyed the prohibited ones and punished those who owned them. The offensive books were then expurgated and restored to their owners with a certificate of censorship. The Jews had to defray the costs of the censorship — that is, the revisers' fees. It was forbidden, on pain of heavy punishment, to restore the expurgated words, or to supply the missing passages between the lines or in the margins.[10]

The most important of the prohibited works was the Talmud, the enormous, encyclopaedic corpus of Jewish religious knowledge, a folio often bound in twelve to twenty volumes. In 1553 the confiscation and burning of the Talmud was announced in a special papal decree. Within eight days those who possessed a Talmud had to deliver it at the office of the Inquisition on pain of two years' imprisonment. In Rome, on the very day of the Jewish New Year, 19 September 1553, agents of the Inquisition searched the houses of the Jews. In October, the same happened in Venice.

In 1553–4, thousands of copies of the Talmud, both manuscript and printed, were confiscated and burned, and further printing of talmudic treatises was strictly forbidden. As already mentioned, the Talmud was again condemned in Pope Paul's *Index librorum prohibitorum* (1559). Pope Sixtus V's *Index* of March 1589 banned all 'books of the Jews', which were believed to be anti-Catholic. In 1595 the apostate Dominico Irosolomitano issued the *Index Expurgatorius* or *Sefer ha-zikkuk*, which survives in a number of manuscript copies. It lists hundreds of Hebrew books to be revised before they were allowed to be read. The *De correctione librorum*, which set out the rules for revision, was appended to Pope Clement VIII's *Index* of 1596. In total, the *Index* was issued 42 times, last appearing in 1948. Only in 1966 was the *Index* finally abolished. Thousands of extant Hebrew books still bear the marks of the revisers.[11]

The first reviser of Hebrew books was Jacob Geraldino. As 'Apostolic Commissioner' of censorship he was given general charge over the whole papal territory. His orders were to examine every manuscript and book already printed or to be printed, and to correct and expurgate as he thought fit anything contrary to the Catholic faith of the Church of Rome, or contrary to good principles and morals; and it was the Jews, it appears, who paid his salary. His duties took him from place to place and, judging from one book he examined, he seems to have been in Bologna in September 1555. The papacy began to extend its jurisdiction beyond its own territories, and in March 1556 Jacob Geraldino appears as 'Apostolic and Ducal Commissioner'. This seems to indicate that he had visited some places outside papal territory, perhaps Ferrara, then subject to the house of Este.

Three copies in the British Library, bearing Geraldino's name and that of his notary Jacobus Menotius, were all inspected on the same day, 18 March 1556, probably in Ferrara, according to Popper.

Information on copies of early Hebrew books bearing revisers' signatures is far from complete. I know of fifteen catalogues or inventories of Hebrew incunabula with data of that kind,[12] four catalogues in which later editions have also been listed,[13] and twelve catalogues of Hebrew manuscripts with material on censorship in the copies described.[14] But I also know of about 150 other catalogues or inventories of Hebrew incunabula, which give no information on the subject. Catalogues lacking information on censored copies include some relatively large collections, like those of the Hebrew incunabula in the Bodleian Library at Oxford, the Bayerische Staatsbibliothek at Munich, the New York Public Library and the Mendel Gottesman Library, Yeshiva University, New York, the Library of Congress at Washington, the National Library of Canada at Ottawa, the Biblioteca Palatina at Parma, the Biblioteca Apostolica Vaticana, the National and University Library at Jerusalem, the Zentralbibliothek at Zürich and many more. Consequently there is no record as to whether two thirds of all known copies have been expurgated or not. It goes without saying that our knowledge of medieval manuscripts and of books printed after 1501 is even less complete.

Returning to the desk of Geraldino's notary at Ferrara on 18 March 1556, we learn from the catalogues mentioned above that three other Hebrew incunabula, now kept in other collections, were there on the same day: a copy now in the State Library at Moscow; a copy now in the Stadt- und Universitätsbibliothek, Frankfurt am Main; and another, mentioned by Popper, at Columbia University, Butler Library, New York.[15]

Three more books in the British Library have an exact date of expurgation. The first was expurgated by Alexandro de Caii, location unknown, on 18 August 1559. The second was expurgated by Zomegnius at Turin on 16 November 1589. The third by Luigi da Bologna, probably at Mantua, on 23 August 1597 (this book had been corrected by the reviser Hippolitus Ferrarensis three years earlier on 23 February 1594, probably at Cremona). A fourth book, also signed by Luigi da Bologna, gives location, month and year: this time Carpi, in March 1599.[16] In March 1599 he also revised at Carpi a vellum copy of the first Hebrew prayer book in folio, printed at Soncino-Casalmaggiore in 1485–6, now in the Bibliothèque Nationale de France in Paris; in the same month he expurgated another copy of this

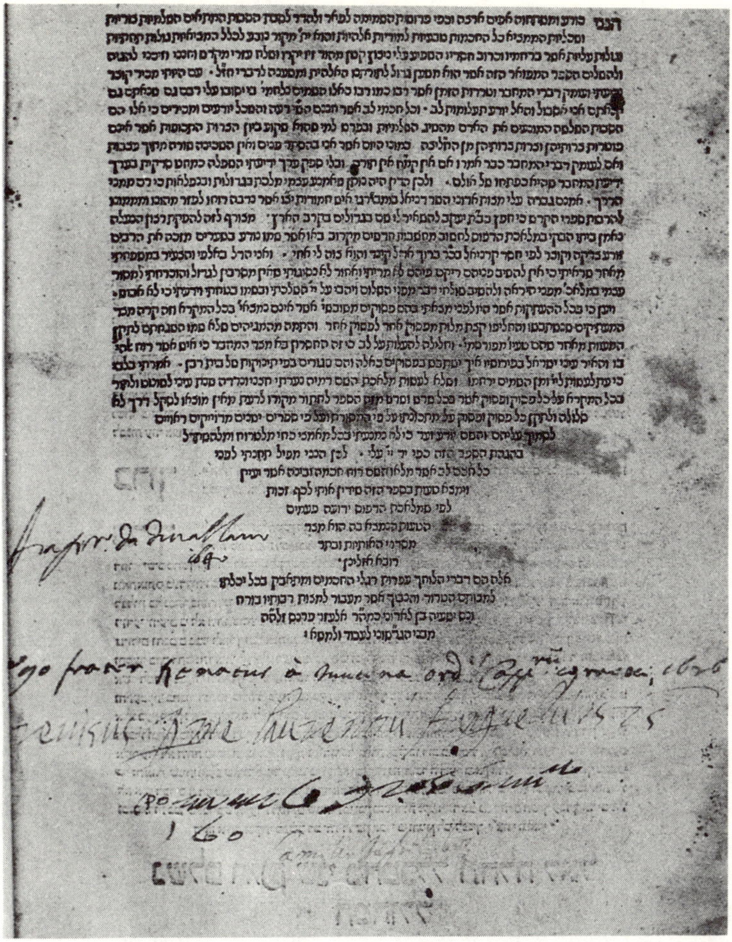

Fig. 1. Signatures of five revisers between 1575 and 1640 on the verso of the final leaf of David ben Joseph Kimhi's *Sefer ha-shorashim* ('Book of roots' — Hebrew dictionary), Venice: Daniel Bomberg, 1529.

Fra[ter] gir[olamo] da duralano 1640

Ego frater Renatus à Mutina ord[i]nis Capp[ucino]ru[m] correxi 1626

Revisus p[er] me Laurentiu[m] Franguellu[m] 1575

Dominico Irosolomi[ta]no 160[0]

Camillo Jaghel 1613

(*Courtesy Bibliotheca Rosenthaliana, Amsterdam University Library. Shelfmark 15 B 36*)

edition, now in the Russian State Library at Moscow.[17] Two sixteenth-century books, revised by him in the same month, are also known.[18] In all, Luigi da Bologna signed nine Hebrew incunabula now in the British Library during the years 1597–1602.

The names of fourteen other revisers are found in the British Library's collection, often in conjunction with earlier or later signatures. The name of Laurentius Franguellus, who was probably at Ferrara in 1575 and at Mantua in 1597, appears six times. I found the name of Dominico Irosolomitano (*c.*1552–1621) eight times — at Mantua, in 1594, 1597 and 1598. His Hebrew name is not recorded but he was, like most revisers, an apostate. Born in Jerusalem, he was given a Talmudic and kabbalistic education at Safed, and also studied mathematics and medicine. His early career was as a rabbi before he began to practise medicine in Cairo, later becoming physician to the sultan in Constantinople. In 1593 he converted to Christianity and served the Inquisition as reviser of Hebrew books, first at Mantua and nearby towns, then at Monferrato, Milan and Rome. He became a member of the Collegio dei Neofiti in Rome, where he taught Hebrew in addition to his work as a reviser. Domenico's writings, mostly surviving in manuscript, include an *Index Expurgatorius*, or *Sefer ha-zikkuk*, listing every passage in Hebrew literature to which the Inquisition objected, a translation of the New Testament and the Apocrypha into Hebrew, and anti-Jewish, pro-Christian sermons in Italian.[19] The signature of Camillo Jaghel, who is not to be confused, although he often is, with the Italian Jewish philosopher and author Abraham ben Hananiah dei Galicchi Jaghel, occurs nine times. Camillo was active at Ancona, Lugo and Urbino and signed Hebrew incunabula now in the British Library in 1611, 1613, 1619 and 1620. Popper finds no proof of where Camillo Jaghel was working in 1611, and speculates that he might have been in the province of Urbino.[20] But it seems much more likely that he was based in Lugo in the province of Ravenna in 1611, since his name occurs three times in the British Library's collection of Hebrew incunabula in the combination '1611 in Lugo', as well as twice in volumes in the Stadt- und Universitätsbibliothek in Frankfurt am Main, once in the former library of the Israelitische Kultusgemeinde in Vienna, three times in the incunabula of the Hebrew Union College in Cincinnati and six times in sixteenth-century Hebrew books in libraries in Emilia Romagna (Parma, Bologna, Ferrara and Reggio nell'Emilia).[21] In early printed Hebrew books in the Bibliotheca Rosenthaliana in Amsterdam his name also occurs six times

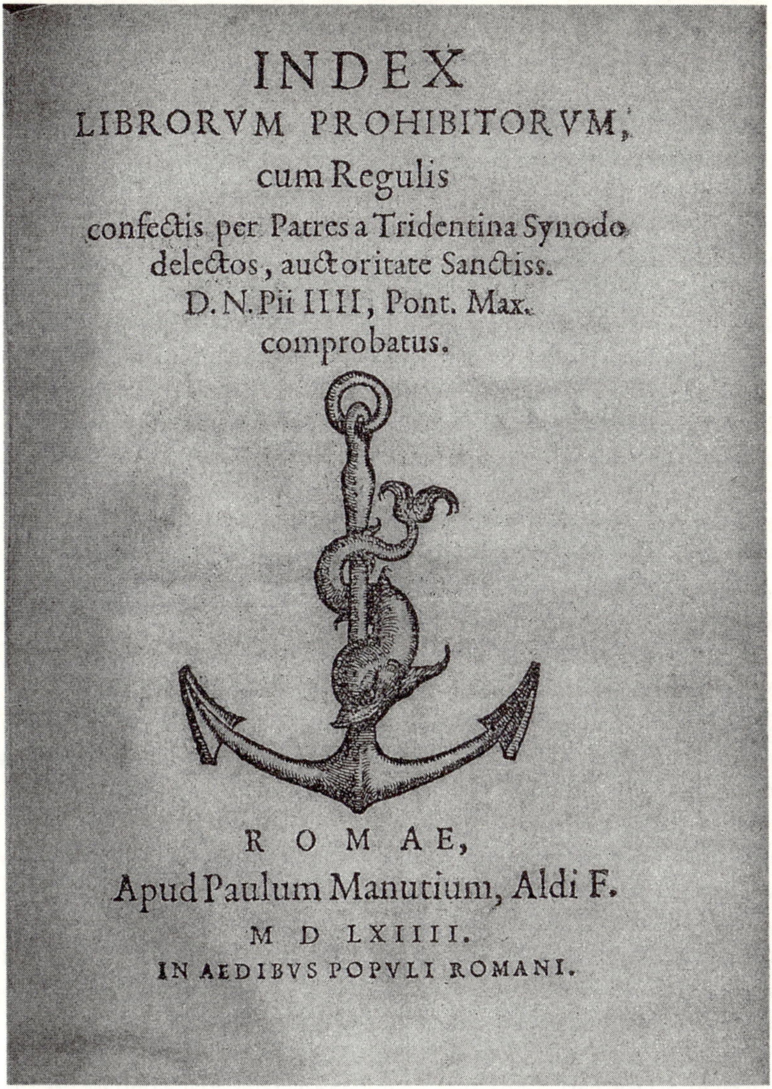

INDEX
LIBRORVM PROHIBITORVM,
cum Regulis
confectis per Patres a Tridentina Synodo
delectos, auctoritate Sanctiss.
D. N. Pii IIII, Pont. Max.
comprobatus.

ROMAE,
Apud Paulum Manutium, Aldi F.
M D LXIIII.
IN AEDIBVS POPVLI ROMANI.

Fig. 2. Titlepage of the Tridentine index of 1564, which was printed in several Italian cities. (*Courtesy Royal Dutch Book Association, Amsterdam University Library. Shelfmark KVB 6481*)

together with the place-name Lugo and the year 1611. Jews had enjoyed considerable prosperity when Lugo belonged to the duchy of Ferrara, but conditions deteriorated in 1598 when it came under direct papal rule.

The other names and dates of revisers can be looked up in the index to BMC XIII. The signature in 1688, of Antonio Franceso Enrique, who revised one book at Urbino, is the last evidence of censorship of these books. But church censorship went on to the middle of the eighteenth century, continuing with great intensity in East-European countries until the end of the nineteenth century.

I have selected one out of about 50 Italian censors (or rather revisers) of Hebrew books between the middle of the sixteenth and the middle of the eighteenth century to examine his activities in this period as closely as possible. I have looked at all the literature known to me, for references to the apostate Alessandro Scipione, whose original Jewish name is unknown. I selected him because he was active for a relatively short and continuous period of about ten years, from 1589 to 1598, most of the time in the same place, the Duchy of Mantua. By contrast nearly all the other revisers worked in several regions, not always mentioned, either for a very short space of time, or else at irregular intervals over very long periods. But the most important reason for selecting Scipione was that we have crucial, even unique information about censorship in Mantua in the 1590s. Some 40 years ago Professor Shlomo Simonsohn discovered a group of 430 inventories in the Jewish Community Archives at Mantua which contained private booklists compiled by the Jews of Mantua in 1595.[22] When Clement VIII was elected Pope in 1592, the Church again began to put restrictions on Hebrew books. On 28 February 1593 the Pope edited a bull, entitled 'Cum Hebraeorum malitia', which forbade the possession of the Talmud, 'the Kabbalah' and other Hebrew works. This led the Bishop of Mantua, Francesco Gonzaga, to order the Jews of the Duchy to bring their books to the Inquisition building in 1595 to be examined and expurgated. The Mantua Jewish community numbered about two thousand, who enjoyed relative religious freedom and good relations with the Duke, Vincenzo I Gonzaga. Only one Jewish book (and that contrary to the wishes of the Duke) was ever burnt in Mantua. In August the Jews began bringing their books to the Inquisition building, which was soon full to overflowing, and the bishop realized that it was almost impossible to examine so many books. He issued a decree ordering the Jews to take their books home, where each family was to prepare an accurate inventory of the books in its possession. The bishop appointed a commission of three expert revisers, Alessandro Scipione from Mantua, Laurentius Franguellus from Ferrara and Dominico Irosolomitano from Venice, all three Jewish converts. Franguellus and Irosolomitano have already been mentioned. The Jews had to pay them the great sum of 400 scudi to come and check the books in their homes. These were the 430 inventories which Simonsohn discovered and which Shifra Baruchson analyzed in the 1990s.[23] So now we know almost exactly what and how many books the Mantuan Jews possessed in 1595. There were over 23,000 printed volumes of 1,234 different editions (of which about five per cent were printed outside Italy), and about 3,000 manuscripts.

Simonsohn and Baruchson did not pay much attention to the reviser Alessandro Scipione, so after I had completed my work on BMC XIII I did a certain amount of research on him. His name occurs in one of the Hebrew incunabula in the British Library.[24] The collection of sources edited by Moritz Stern in 1893 contains a document dated 13 June 1590, from the municipal archives of Mantua. From this document it appears that Scipione received twenty scudi in gold from three Jewish scholars for the revising of Hebrew books during the year from June 1589 to June 1590. The second document which Stern published related to the appointment on 27 August 1595, already mentioned, of the three expert revisers.[25] I think I have seen almost every bibliographical record of the printed works and manuscripts in which the name of Scipione occurs — that is, 96 times in 26 printed books and 70 manuscripts. Of course this is in no way representative if set against the 25,000 copies or more which were in the possession of the Jews of Mantua in 1595. Most of the manuscripts bearing Scipione's signature were copied in Italy, between 1293 and 1587. Five manuscripts were made in Spain or Provence, six in Germany and one in Crete. Among the 26 printed books, thirteen are incunabula, which is not surprising, since it is Hebrew incunabula which have been most intensively studied in relation to censorship. One incunable was printed at Lisbon, the other twelve in Italy. It is remarkable that of the remaining sixteenth-century books almost 50 per cent were printed abroad, in Salonika, Constantinople, Cracow and Safed, which suggests a brisk book trade at Mantua. The latter observation is partly confirmed by the proportion of expurgated books in the collection — about 35 per cent of 800 or so sixteenth-century Hebrew books in the Bibliotheca

Rosenthaliana at Amsterdam, where we are in the process of re-cataloguing the early printed Hebrew books. Almost all areas of Hebrew literature are represented: the Bible, Bible commentaries, liturgy, philology, mathematics, with rather more emphasis on philosophy and kabbalah. Kabbalah was especially suspect to the Church, so this kind of text was rigorously expurgated.

I will conclude with a closer examination of the activities of Alessandro Scipione. In the 96 cases where I found his name, his signature was *always* accompanied by that of Dominico Irosolomitano, the former rabbi and court-physician from Palestine, Cairo and Constantinople, usually but not always in the same year. The name of Laurentius Franguellus, who flourished in Ferrara, *c.*1575, also occurs a few times with the other two. He was probably an old man in 1595, when his name occurs in conjunction with Scipione, and he was soon succeeded by the reviser Luigi da Bologna. The significance of this observation is not yet completely clear to me. From the document of August 1595, published by Stern, it appears that Scipione, Irosolomitano and Franguellus formed a commission of three in Mantua. The signature of Irosolomitano (mostly without a date) also occurs regularly with Scipione's in the years before 1595. Was Irosolomitano's name intended to give official weight to Scipione's signature? Did the Inquisition doubt Scipione's ability? I find Scipione's name for the first time in 1590 and for the last in 1598, most of these books being checked again some ten to twenty years later by the reviser Giovanni Dominico Carretto who also operated in Mantua (so we know that these books were still in Mantua then).

It is strange that, as Mortara established in 1862 in his seminal study of the subject, many Hebrew books were signed four or five times by different revisers in different years, without any expurgation of the text being visible. This brings me to a rather tame conclusion: in many cases Inquisitorial censorship of Hebrew books seems to have been motivated by nothing much more than a mixture of extortion and vexation.

References

1. Shlomo Simonsohn, *History of the Jews in the Duchy of Mantua*, Jerusalem 1977 (*Publications of the Diaspora Research Institute,* Book 17), p. 685.
2. M. Mortara, 'Die Censur hebräischer Bücher in Italien und der Canon purificationis', *Hebräische Bibliographie*, vol. 5 (Berlin) 1862, pp. 72–7, 96–101.
3. Abraham Berliner, *Censur und Confiscation hebräischer Bücher im Kirchenstaate. Auf Grund der Inquisitions-Akten in der Vaticana und Vallicellana dargestellt*, Frankfurt a. M. 1891.

4. Moritz Stern, *Urkundliche Beiträge über die Stellung der Päpste zu den Juden. Mit Benutzung des päpstlichen Geheimarchivs zu Rom*, Kiel 1893.
5. William Popper, *The Censorship of Hebrew Books*, Columbia University thesis, New York 1899. (Reprinted with an introduction by Moshe Carmilly-Weinberger, New York 1969.)
6. Nathan Porges, 'Der hebräische Index expurgatorius sepher ha-Zikkuk'. *Festschrift zum siebzigsten Geburtstage A. Berliner's gewidmet von Freunden und Schülern.* Herausgegeben von A. Freimann und M. Hildesheimer, Frankfurt a. M. 1903, pp. 274–95.
7. Isaiah Sonne, 'Expurgation of Hebrew books — the work of Jewish scholars. A contribution to the history of censorship of Hebrew books in Italy in the 16th century', *Bulletin of the New York Public Library*, vol. 46 (1942), pp. 975–1015. Published separately 1943. Reprinted in: *Hebrew printing and bibliography. Studies by Joshua Bloch and others, reprinted from the publications of The New York Public Library on the occasion of the seventy-fifth anniversary of the establishment of the Jewish Division of The New York Public Library. Selected and with a preface by Charles Berlin*, New York 1976, pp. 201–41.
8. Nathan Porges, 'Censorship', *The Jewish Encyclopedia*, vol. 3, New York & London 1906, pp. 642–50.
9. BMC XIII, pp. xxi–xxiv.
10. Nathan Porges, 'Censorship', p. 644.
11. For the sixteenth-century Italian indexes, cf. J. M. De Bujanda (avec l'assistance de R. Davignon et E. Stanek), *Index de Rome 1557, 1559, 1564. Les premiers index romains et l'index du Concile de Trente*, Sherbrooke, Québec 1990, and J. M. De Bujanda, U. Rozzo, P. G. Bietenholz, P. F. Grendler (avec l'assistance de R. Davignon, E. Stanek et M. Richter), *Index de Rome 1590, 1593, 1596. Avec étude des index de Parme et Munich 1582*, Sherbrooke, Québec 1994. (*Index des livres interdits*, vols 8 and 9).
12. I. Adler, 'Les incunables hébraïques de la Bibliothèque nationale'. *Le livre hébraïque. Incunables, publications israéliennes. Exposition organisée avec le concours de la Bibliothèque nationale*, Paris 1962, pp. [65]–119; *Catalogue des incunables [de la] Bibliothèque nationale*, vol. 2, fasc. 4: *S-Z et Hebraica.* [Réd. par U. Baumeister *et al.*], Paris 1985 (*CIBN*); E. S. Artom, 'Gli incunaboli ebraici della Biblioteca Nazionale Universitaria di Torino', *Soncino-Blätter. Beiträge zur Kunde des jüdischen Buches*, vol. 1 (1925), pp. 47–69; U. Cassuto, 'Incunaboli ebraici a Firenze', *La Bibliofilia*, vol. 12 (1911), pp. 349–56; 464–72; vol. 13 (1912), pp. 222–30; 384–94; A. Cohen, 'Hebrew incunabula in Cambridge', *The Jewish Quarterly Review*, vol. 19 (1907), pp. 744–50; L. N. Goldfeld, 'The Hebrew incunables at the Biblioteca Casanatense, Rome', *Yad la-kore*, vol. 18 (1979), pp. 223–40 (in Hebrew); S. M. Iakerson, *Hebrew incunabula. Description of publications kept in libraries of Moscow and Leningrad*, Leningrad 1988 (in Russian); V. Madsen, *Katalog over det Kongelige Biblioteks inkunabler*, 2 vols, København 1935–8. Vol. 3: *Accession 1938–1962, Inkunabler i andre biblioteker, Registre* (udgivet af E. Dal), København 1963. (Nrs 4298–4334 by R. Edelmann); M. Marx, 'A catalogue of the Hebrew books printed in the fifteenth century now in the library of the Hebrew Union College', *Studies in bibliography and booklore*, vol. 1 (1953–4), pp. 21–47 (Cincinnati, Ohio); J. C. T. Oates, *A catalogue of the fifteenth-century printed books in the University Library Cambridge*, Cambridge 1954; A. K. Offenberg, 'Catalogue of the Hebrew incunabula in the Bibliotheca Rosenthaliana', *Studia Rosenthaliana*, vol. 5 (1971), pp. 125–43; 246–67; vol. 7 (1973), pp. 128–50

(University Library, Amsterdam); A. K. Offenberg, *A short-title catalogue of Hebrew books printed in the fifteenth century now in the Bibliotheca Rosenthaliana*, Amsterdam 1990; K. Ohly & V. Sack, *Inkunabelkatalog der Stadt- und Universitätsbibliothek und anderer öffentlicher Sammlungen in Frankfurt am Main*, Frankfurt a. M. 1967; G. Tamani, 'Inventario degli incunaboli ebraici della Biblioteca Communale di Piacenza', *La Bibliofilia*, vol. 72 (1970), pp. 221–46; J. E. Walsh, *A catalogue of the fifteenth-century printed books in the Harvard University Library*. Vol. 4: *Books printed in France, the Netherlands, the Iberian Peninsula, England, and Montenegro. Hebraica and supplementary entries*, Binghamton 1996 (Harvard University Library, Cambridge, Massachusetts).

13. G. Busi, *Edizioni ebraiche del XVI secolo nelle biblioteche dell' Emilia Romagna*, Bologna 1987; S. M. Iakerson, *Ohel Hayim. A catalogue of Hebrew manuscripts of the Manfred and Anne Lehmann Family*. Vol. 3: *Printed books. Incunabula and sixteenth century books*, New York 1996 (in Hebrew); A. Toaff, 'Stampe rare delle Biblioteca della Comunità Israelitica di Roma scampate al saccheggio nazista', *La Bibliofilia*, vol. 80 (1978), pp. 139–49; B. Wachstein, *Katalog der Salo Cohn'schen Schenkungen. 2. Bücher aus der Sammlung S.H. Halberstam, Bielitz*, Wien 1914 (Bibliothek der Israelitischen Kultusgemeinde, Wien).

14. C. Bernheimer, *Codices Hebraici Bybliothecae Ambrosianae*, Florentiae 1933 (*Fontes Ambrosiani*, vol. 5); *Hebraica Ambrosiana*. 1. A. Luzzatto, *Catalogue of undescribed Hebrew manuscripts in the Ambrosian Library*. 2. L. Mortara Ottolenghi, *Description of decorated and illuminated Hebrew manuscripts in the Ambrosiana Library*, Milano 1972; G. Margoliouth, *Catalogue of the Hebrew and Samaritan manuscripts in the British Museum*. 3 parts, London 1899–1925 (with part 4: J. Leveen, *Introduction, indexes, brief descriptions of accessions and addenda and corrigenda*, London 1935); A. Neubauer, *Catalogue of the Hebrew manuscripts in the Bodleian Library and in the college libraries of Oxford*, Oxford 1886 (*Catalogi codd. mss. Bibliothecae Bodleianae*, pars XII); A. Neubauer and A. E. Cowley, *Catalogue of the Hebrew manuscripts in the Bodleian Library*, vol. 2, Oxford 1906; *Catalogue of the Hebrew manuscripts in the Bodleian Library. Supplement of Addenda and Corrigenda to vol. I* (*Neubauer's Catalogue*). Compiled under the direction of Malachi Beit-Arié. Ed. R. A. May, Oxford 1994; E. Róth & H. Striedl, *Die Handschriften der Sammlung H.B. Levy an der Staats- und Universitätsbibliothek Hamburg* (*Hebräische Handschriften*, Teil 3), Wiesbaden 1984. (*Verzeichnis der orientalischen Handschriften in Deutschland*, Band VI, 3); A. Z. Schwarz, *Die hebräischen Handschriften der Nationalbibliothek in Wien*, Leipzig 1925; A. Z. Schwarz, *Die hebräischen Handschriften in Österreich* (*ausserhalb der Nationalbibliothek in Wien*). Teil I: *Bibel-Kabbala*, Leipzig 1931; D. S. Loewinger & E. Róth, *SCHWARZ, Hebräische Handschriften II A, B*, New York 1973 (not consulted); G. Tamani, 'Elenco dei manoscritti ebraici miniati e decorati della "Palatina" di Parma', *La Bibliofilia*, vol. 70 (1968), pp. 39–136; *Hebrew manuscripts in the Biblioteca Palatina in Parma. Catalogue*. Ed. Benjamin Richler; palaeographical and codicological descriptions by Malachi Beit-Arié, Jerusalem 2001.

15. The six incunabula, bearing the signatures of Geraldino and Menotius, are nos 3 (Moscow), 28 (Frankfurt a. M.), 29 (B.L.), 35 (B.L.), 62 (B.L.), and 98 (New York), in A. K. Offenberg, *Hebrew incunabula in public collections. A first international census*. Compiled in collaboration with C. Moed van Walraven, Nieuwkoop 1990 (*Bibliotheca Humanistica & Reformatorica*, vol. 47). Abbreviated here Off*Census*.

16. These four books are respectively Off*Census* nos 91 (Naples 1488), 78 (Leiria, between 1492 and 1496), 1 (Lisbon 1489) and 16 (Hijar 1490).

17. Off*Census* no. 83.
18. G. Busi, *Edizioni ebraiche*, nos 61 and 72.
19. *Encyclopaedia Judaica*, vol. 6, Jerusalem 1971, 2nd edn 1973, col. 158.
20. W. Popper, *The censorship*, p. 139.
21. K. Ohly & V. Sack, *Inkunabelkatalog*, nos 351, 1848; B. Wachstein, *Katalog der Salo Cohn'schen Schenkungen*, no. 214; M. Marx, 'A catalogue of the Hebrew books', nos 18, 39 ('Lugano'), 42; G. Busi, *Edizioni ebraiche*, nos 39, 180, 331, 332, 344 and 363.
22. S. Simonsohn, 'Books and libraries of Mantuan Jews, 1595', *Kiryath Sepher*, vol. 37 (1962), pp. 103–22 (in Hebrew); Simonsohn, *History of the Jews in the Duchy of Mantua*, pp. 685–94.
23. Shifra Z. Baruchson, 'Jewish libraries: culture and reading interests in 16th century Italy', *Library History*, vol. 10 (London 1994), pp. 19–26. Idem, *La culture livresque des Juifs d'Italie à la fin de la Renaissance*, Paris 2001.
24. Off*Census* no. 104.
25. M. Stern, *Urkundliche Beiträge*, nos 148 (p. 156) and 158 (pp. 165–6).

'Some Property is Theft': copyright law and illegal activity in early modern Scotland

ALASTAIR J. MANN

THE STUDY OF the history of copyright in Scotland before the statute of 1710 has been largely ignored by British and Scottish book trade historians. Recently some new foundations have been laid, but much still needs to be done to further comparative studies and to investigate the vast records of Scotland's Court of Session where, from the Restoration onwards, a range of book trade disputes was heard.[1] Relevant historiography is thin on the ground, but this does not mean that the subject of copyright and literary property was unimportant to the book traders and authors of the first two centuries of Scotland's print history. The exploitation of property rights was vital to the early modern Scot, and literary property was no different from industrial patents and territorial rights in this respect. This economic imperative, as well as the essential role of print as the conduit of nonconformist religious and political ideas, made print culture the focus for illegal activity.

Early modern copyright in Scotland developed on different lines from that of England. There were practical, philosophical and legal reasons for this divergence. The actual term 'copyright' was equally alien to both countries at this early date; it is used here to denote the right to print (or reprint) a specific text. In sixteenth- and seventeenth-century Scotland, the typical licensee was granted the right to 'print, reprint, vend, sell and import'. Meanwhile in England, between 1556 and 1695, books had to be licensed by a government representative in order to acquire official permission to be printed. Ownership of copyright was formally recorded by the process of entry in the register of the Stationers' Company (established by royal charter in 1557), the form of words being 'Then entered for his copy under the hand of Mr Warden X a book called …'.[2] The owner of the right to 'copy' was almost always the printer or bookseller who entered the book for publication; the author was seldom even mentioned. In Scotland copyrights for individual books continued to spring directly from patents granted by the Crown; in England this practice also continued throughout the early modern period, though it declined, relatively though by no means completely, once registration at Stationers' Hall offered an alternative means of protection.[3] No equivalent to the Stationers' Company ever developed in Scotland. The smaller scale of the Scottish press and the tradition of burghs having equal status and rights to develop commerce independently prevented the formation of such a centralising society in Edinburgh. The right to print individual Scottish books was granted by the Crown, or its representatives, usually the Scottish Privy Council, for a limited number of years, either a specific period or the lifetime of the licence holder. In Scotland, as in France, Spain and the Low Countries, there was no notion of perpetual copyright, whereas in England the Stationers' Company English Stock and English booksellers and authors continued to claim perpetual copyright until it was quashed by the test case of 1774.

In Scotland the first royal patent was that given by James IV to Scotland's first printers Walter Chepman and Andro Myllar in 1507. This was to print a new national breviary, the *Breviarium Aberdonense* (1510), compiled by William Elphinstone, Bishop of Aberdeen, a text prescribed to replace 'Sarum use', the Salisbury breviary, though this was not strictly a patent for a single act of publication. The first such Scottish examples were the letters patent granted to Thomas Davidson in 1541 to print the acts of the Parliament of Scotland, and the eleven-title, educational book patent granted to the author William Niddrie in 1559, a bold but unrealised attempt at educational publishing in the twilight of pre-Reformation clericalism. These last two patents were for six and ten years respectively.[4] In fact, these Scottish examples mirror the two types of prerogative printing patent that operated in England: the Chepman and Myllar variety — general, usually for life and containing generic classes of books, bibles, prognostications and so on, and the Davidson and Niddrie type — 'particular' and limited in time, in England typically to licences of seven to ten years' duration, in Scotland set at nineteen years. Thus, before the Stationers' Company began to dominate the English book trade in the reign of Queen Elizabeth, the practicalities of copyright protection in England and Scotland were not too dissimilar. Notwithstanding the continuation of English prerogative patents in the seventeenth century, it was the 1710 copyright act which brought England back on a converging path with Scottish practice.

The legal and philosophical attitudes to copyright in Scotland come together in early modern Scottish law's interpretations of the nature of intellectual property. Although both Scots law and Roman law, the basis of the former, sustain the theory of 'incorporeal' rights, for example in noble titles without necessarily a territorial basis, Scots interpretation repudiated the concept of 'incorporeal' property in inventions and creations. For such property to have a certain legal basis it had to have physical form. A manuscript or a printed book was legal property, but not the text or its ideas. It was only illegal to copy such property, industrial or intellectual, if successful application was made to the appropriate authority for a patent or copyright licence. Following the number of cases concerning literary property before the Court of Session in the 1750s and 1760s, this view of copyright ownership led Scotland's judges to reject the notion of perpetual copyright — it was seen as unreasonable and foreign to Scottish copyright conventions. Meanwhile, in England, with its uncodified and statute basis for law, the author created property when he wrote a text and would then usually transfer ownership of that property by selling it to a member of the book trade. English common law assumed perpetual copyright, subject to qualifications imposed by statute — for example, in a rather opaque manner, by the 1710 act.[5] These contrasting approaches would become the constant backdrop to the 40 years of Anglo-Scottish legal conflict which started in the 1730s, but given the deepening commercial rivalry between England and Scotland since the advent of print it was a dispute waiting to happen.

In early modern England, both printed books and the Stationers' Company, a company of members of the book and allied trades with its own court and ordinances, had a special status. Throughout the seventeenth century the members of the Stationers' Company succeeded in accumulating rights as the Westminster Parliament and commercial interests continued to attack royal patents. The Statute of Monopolies of 1624 — which limited patents in inventions and industrial processes to twenty-one years for existing rights and fourteen for new rights, and also insisted they be tested by common law — excluded the royal printing patents and charters granted to corporations and societies.[6] In other words all English book patents were exempted. The licence to print was differentiated from the industrial patent. During his English reign James VI and I contributed to the rise of monopolies in English printing, though the trend was well established before 1603.[7] James has taken much of the blame for granting patents to individuals for particular book titles, he being 'less experienced, less well-respected and less politically astute' than Queen Elizabeth.[8] Yet this description takes no account of James's background in Scottish copyright traditions and practices, where copyrights were mostly granted directly by the Crown to individuals.

Scotland was not a complete 'island' in copyright terms, however. In the reign of Charles I the Stationers' monopoly reached into Scotland's public copyright system. The 'Scotch Patent', as it was known in London, was acquired as part of Miles Flesher's Stationers' Company monopoly which he built up from 1617 to 1638. This included a share in the office of Scottish royal printer, which he obtained in 1632 with his partner Robert Young. Ironically, Flesher had his dividend suspended by the Stationers in 1634 as a punishment for importing into England psalms printed at his Edinburgh press.[9] It would be 1670 before these English 'invaders' retreated across the border and returned the office of royal printer into Scottish hands.

But even when the patenting excesses of Charles I were swept aside in 1640 by the Long Parliament — Charles had exploited loopholes in the 1624 Act — book printing and publishing remained a special case in England. Meanwhile, although the Statute of Monopolies did not apply in Scotland before 1707, the Scottish convention of a restricted patent for an individual book title was well established before the Union of the Crowns. This did not stem from the expression of Scottish concern over monopolies during the Scottish reign of James VI. Indeed, with the encouragement of the King, the Scottish Privy Council set up a commission of grievances over monopolies in May 1623, and two months later a Standing Commission of Manufactories was established. In June of that year the commissioners of the Scottish burghs presented a petition protesting at monopolies which attacked natural trade and the interests of the people. Nearly two decades later, in 1641, the Scottish Estates halted some major monopolies 'because of the great hurt inflated on the lieges by monopolies, all patents purchased for the benefit of particular persons in prejudice of the public'.[10] But books were not on the agenda in Scotland in 1623 or 1641.

The fact that the main licensing and copyright-granting authority in Scotland was the Crown, working via its executive the Privy Council, gives the impression of a highly centralised copyright regime. Local Scottish copyright did, however, exist. This Scottish, 'local' variety was not so dissimilar to the copyright protection of the Stationers' Company. As we have seen, in England all printed matter not covered by royal grant was supposed to be passed by government licensers and then entered at Stationers' Hall in London; but there was no continuous and centralised registration regime in Edinburgh. In Scotland, although printing did not commence in Aberdeen, Glasgow and Dundee until 1622, 1638 and 1703 respectively, no centralised limitation was placed on the proliferation of presses, and local town councils were authorised, as with any other commercial activity, to license and manage their local presses.[11] In addition, those printing burghs with universities, Edinburgh, Aberdeen and Glasgow, built up financial, intellectual and print-licensing conventions that linked town and gown.[12] At this level local licensing and local copyright protection existed on a private basis under the authority of local magistrates. After the Restoration the 'printing burghs' took a special interest in a range of almanacs, diurnals, news-sheets and newspapers, and provided local copyright protection, as seen in Aberdeen town council's protection of the 'Aberdeen Almanack' from the 1660s, and the Edinburgh burgh licence granted to various newspapers, including that in 1709 to David Fearn to produce the 'Scots Postman'.[13]

The Crown was by no means a benevolent force as far as the liberty of Scottish copyright was concerned, especially with the range of rights and privileges it conveyed to the royal printers of Scotland, holders of the Scottish 'printing patent'. The wide supervisory and generalised copyrights granted in 1671 by Charles II and the Duke of Lauderdale to Andrew Anderson, royal printer from 1671 to 1676, and subsequently inherited by his remarkable widow Agnes Campbell, were the cause of major disputes in the book trade of Scotland in the 1670s and 1680s. James VII and II's strange appointment of James Watson, senior, to the anomalous post of 'household printer' in 1686, with a monopoly over all almanacs, created much consternation in the trade and especially for Agnes Campbell. The fact that Watson was a Catholic merely added the fuel of bigotry to the flames of the dispute. George I's absurd appointment of John Baskett, English royal printer, and Robert Freebairn as sole Printers to the King in Scotland in 1714, in spite of a valid 1711 warrant that existed in the names of Freebairn, Baskett and James Watson, the younger, led to such a level of litigation, reaching the Court of Session and eventually the House of Lords in 1718, that only the lawyers were the absolute winners. In fact the courts showed a remarkable degree of independence in the face of an irrational exercise of royal prerogative. The decision of Robert Freebairn to become printer to the Old Pretender in the autumn of 1715, and the subsequent forfeiture of his share of the gift, added another extraordinary twist to this seven-year legal saga.[14]

It is clear that James VI and I was not the only monarch nor the most inclined to interfere with and restrict the liberty of Scottish copyright. There was, however, one particular trade dispute that highlights both the Crown's tendency to facilitate monopoly control and the reluctance of the executive and legislature to place book trade monopolies into too few hands. In the 1590s and 1600s Andro Hart, the most significance printer and bookseller in Scotland before the Restoration, set up various partnerships and agreements with the London bookseller John Norton.[15] From about 1590 Hart and Norton began importing books directly from Germany and the Low Countries, and a decade later the partners agreed to import bibles from Dort to undermine the Bible patent in England held by the Barker family. By the time of Norton's death in 1612 Hart had become Scotland's largest book importer, and his scale of international trade was probably unsurpassed until the 1690s. Seeking to exploit his import business, in June 1614 Hart purchased from King James the exclusive right to print overseas and import into Scotland. This extraordinary right led to protests from the then royal printer Thomas Finlason, who excelled at accumulating copyrights which he shelved and left unutilised, and from the booksellers Richard Lawson and James Cathkin, ironically like Hart both staunch presbyterians and former prisoners of conscience. The subsequent case was heard before the Privy Council and the ruling delivered one of the most significant judgments in Scottish book history. Although Hart came armed with a letter from the King demanding that he must have his rights confirmed without delay, the Council rejected the privilege entirely. The words of the judgment provide a dramatic illustration of executive views about the licensing of the press, which in the 1670s and 1680s would be reflected in the opinions of Parliament:

> The fredome, libertie and previledge of prenting, homebringing and selling of all suche bookis and volumis quhilkis ar allowit and nowise forbidden … aught [to] be free to all His Majesties subjectis … and not conferrit and gevin to ony one persone without grite hurte and prejudice of the cuntrey, because every suche privat and plane fredome, libertie and privilege is not onlie a monopolie of ane evill preparative and example, bot will gif occassioun to alter and raise hicht, and change the pryces of all bookis and volumes at the appetite and discretioun of the persone and personis in whose favouris the said previlege salhappin to be conferrit; and for

this effect the saidis Lordis ordanis the gift and previlege purchest be the said Andro Hairt [from the King] to be stayed, and on nowise to be past nor exped.[16]

This important case shows that as far as book regulation was concerned the inclinations of the Crown (King and senior officers of state), executive (entire Privy Council) and legislature (estates of Parliament) were not always identical. Indeed both the Privy Council, Scotland's copyright agency, and Parliament, which when it did get involved took a generally liberal line in granting limited rights to licence holders, other that its ratification of Anderson's copyrights in 1672, sought to protect the book market of Scotland from excessive monopolism. In one respect, however, all three agencies shared the same sense of priorities: censorship mattered more than copyright, while government management of book dissemination rested on four not two familiar pillars: propaganda and licence as well as copyright and censorship. The last three of these are easily confused as simultaneous grants of copyright and licence to print were very common, and the control of licensing was, of course, an arm of censorship, even though *a priori* censorship would become impractical in the second half of the seventeenth century. Actual licence to print was obtained in a variety of ways: formally by a signed licence, sometimes printed in the work, indicating that a specific printing had been checked and approved by an agent of the Crown (an individual, a special committee or the Privy Council) and in some cases the Church, and also informally by mere act of open publication, with place, date, printer and author clearly stated. Neither of these licence types indicated copyright, even though the fact of and duration of copyright were frequently included within the text of a formal printing licence. Nonetheless, copyright and licensing had this in common: just as it was impractical for the authorities to license every small piece of printing ephemera so it was unnecessary or impractical for printers and authors to seek copyright protection for every small printing.[17] Doing what made sense was one of the endearing qualities of Scottish book regulation in the early modern period, with the exception of some phases when the bark of government outrage frequently failed to transform itself into the bite of effective censorship.

The Scottish authorities considered their copyright responsibilities to be two-fold: firstly to provide copyrights on application and secondly to mediate between aggrieved parties when disputes arose. Neither Parliament nor Privy Council believed that it was the responsibility of government to provide a copyright policing system: the customs searchers located at Scottish ports were entrusted with the public task of apprehending banned books on banned subjects, not printings that infringed private copyright. Copyholders were therefore left to police the trade themselves, and the wealth and greater resources of the royal printer often gave the incumbent a clear advantage. However, as seen in the details of copyright patents, the government did provide a range of sanctions for abuses of copyright. The need for compensation by confiscation of offending stock was recognised from the outset in the Chepman and Myllar patent of 1507. This warned that forbidden trafficking of titles within the gift would result in 'escheting [forfeiture] of the buiks'.[18] Such a sanction was included in almost every copyright patent for the next 200 years. In addition to confiscation, from the 1560s fines were introduced. The level of fine varied throughout the period — £200 (Scots) in the 1560s to a standard 500 merks (£333) from the late 1690s. Sometimes a reward was offered to the discoverer of copyright abuses, consisting of perhaps half the 'fine' and/or escheat value, as in the 1694 copyright given to John Binning for a range of works written by his father, the clergyman Hugh Binning.[19] Imprisonment was extremely rare and clearly not seen as an appropriate sanction for copyright abuse. The only instances of imprisonment, potential or actual, concerned the rights of the King's Printer or where Crown projects required protection. An example of such a threatened sanction can be found in the terms of the 31-year licence granted to Sir William Alexander in 1627 for the 'official' edition of the Psalms of David in metre. This was an especially 'official' edition with an 'official' copyright: the edition had been translated by Alexander with the help of the pen of the late King James. Where actual imprisonment resulted there were aggravating circumstances. In 1677 the Glasgow printer Robert Sanders was imprisoned for breaching the copyright of Agnes Campbell, King's Printer. The breach, according to the charges made before the Privy Council, involved a range of volumes: 'New Testaments and psalm books ... grammars ... many thousands of catechisms ... [and numerous] books of divinity and school books', all of which were technically part of the royal gift. But, in spite of the seriousness of the copyright breach, the main reason for Sanders' imprisonment was his failure to attend the second day of the hearing and to make his oath before the council. Special patents and special circumstances could produce the sanction of imprisonment, but in very few cases. Sanders could not, however, have been incarcerated for long.

Ten months later he was employed on official printing business by the council's commission of the west during its deliberations in Ayr. Although the proclamations he printed — including one that prohibited heritors from allowing tenants to settle on their lands if they refused to take an oath to keep the peace and to refrain from attending illegal field conventicles — were technically under the gift of the royal printer, the practicalities of the convenient Glasgow press were more important to the Privy Council.[20]

Governments also felt a responsibility to provide courts of arbitration which could step in and adjudicate on copyright matters. Breaches of trading regulations, and disputes between book traders over debts and premises, were usually resolved by the town councils and bailie courts of the Scottish printing burghs. Meanwhile, throughout the sixteenth and most of the seventeenth century, copyright disagreements came before the Privy Council. Given that the copyright system in Scotland depended directly, as we have seen, on royal or Crown prerogative, it was appropriate that all disputes concerning licences, rights and copyrights should come before the Privy Council, acting as a civil court.[21] But in spite of the best endeavours of the Privy Council in policing book trade disputes the level of litigation was growing beyond its competence by the 1680s. Matters such as apprenticeships, general book property rights and freedom of commerce came before the Court of Session. Some of the skirmishes were minor as when in 1681 the printer John Reid, senior, was incarcerated on the initiative of Agnes Campbell for apprenticeship absenteeism resulting in unlawful printing. A few weeks later the Lords of Session heard a process raised by Reid and his fellow apprentices, and although Reid was released it was on the understanding that he returned to his apprenticeship.[22] In fact there were three great book-trade cases before the Court of Session from the 1670s — the heirs of Archibald Hislop, bookseller v. Robert Currie and Agnes Campbell (1678–87); Robert Sanders, the younger, v. Bessie Corbett, his mother (1694–1705), and Watson, the younger v. Freebairn, Baskett and Campbell (1713–18), and these helped ensure that the Lords of Session developed an expanding competency over the legal basis of the business of books.[23] The background to these cases: the duties of Currie as a bookseller acting in the interests of his step-children; the nature and value of printing materials inherited by Sanders; and the legal validity of co-partnership agreements over the gift of King's Printer in the Watson case — show the new-found importance of the Session in book-trade law. Such cases provided the accumulated case law that legitimised the role of the Court of Session as a regulator of book commerce throughout the eighteenth century. Nonetheless, as it made perfect sense to appeal to the body that granted the right to print in the first place, it was before the Privy Council that most copyright disputes were heard. The demise of the Council in 1708, therefore, made it essential to find a British solution to a Scottish copyright vacuum.

***

Copyright and protection from pirates was vital to Scottish authors as well as Scottish printers. The attitude of the legitimate author seeking to protect his literary property is seen in the actions of the author and clergyman James Kirkwood, who at the turn of the eighteenth century would become famous for his remarkable and successful schemes to establish 'oasis' libraries in the poorest Highland parishes. It is, however, Kirkwood's earlier history as a grammarian that echoes typical copyright concerns. The history of grammar licensing and regulation in Scotland shows that the authorities did not take a consistent line in the licensing of school grammars. Prescription under James VI and I, with a set national grammar, was followed by recommendation under Charles I and then scholastic liberty under Charles II, although protecting copyright was no less important.[24] Kirkwood's grammar, published in three parts from 1674 to 1676, was subject to pirating, abridgement and copyright abuse in spite of the nineteen-year licence granted to him in 1674. He was so concerned that he delivered a supplication to the Privy Council in 1677 requesting a revised copyright with more rigorous punishments for abusers. That year he was granted fresh copyrights of nineteen years for a one-volume edition of his *Grammatica Facilis* and also for his *Rhetoricae Compendium,* each with the penalty of the very large fines of 2,000 merks (or £1,300) for pirates. In 1695, as the copyright terms were due to expire, Kirkwood was granted new nineteen-year licences for revised editions of both his grammar and his vocabulary. These were clearly new editions as the standard period of licence for a reprint was now eleven years. But the fact that no subsequent copyright breaches concerning Kirkwood are mentioned in the Council records suggests that these measures were effective. Being caught pirating such works could be potentially disastrous for most printers. The penalties protecting Kirkwood's copyrights, so severe that he may have had friends in high places, declare that contraveners 'make up whatever loss and damage [he] may sustain', as well as confiscation of the offending printed stock and the fine.[25] Indeed, in general there are indications that copyright protection was reasonably effective in Scotland by the seventeenth century, and not much inferior to the more formal English system, given estimates that perhaps 40% or 50% of all English printings were not registered with the Stationers' Company.[26]

Scotland's early modern case histories of illegal printing of copyrighted material are not without interest. The battle between the illegal and legitimate was continuous and sometimes dirty. As we have seen, under the terms of the Chepman and Myllar patent of 1507 the Aberdeen breviary was prescribed and Sarum use banned. However, in early 1510 the merchants William and Francis Frost, William Sym and Andro Ross were brought before the Privy Council charged with illegally importing the Salisbury breviary the previous year. The King's Printer Walter Chepman had made a complaint to the council and the council responded by making a general threat to the offending merchants to desist immediately or suffer confiscation of their stock, in a tone that suggested more serious sanctions were possible, perhaps a spell in prison.[27]

Liturgical litigiousness continued into the next century. In 1618 and 1619 Gilbert Dick, an episcopalian Edinburgh bookseller who was well connected, was granted copyrights on two catechisms and the Book of Common Prayer.[28] These copyrights coincided with a raft of liturgical reforms instigated by James VI and I and carried forward by three episcopalian-dominated general assemblies which met in 1616, 1617, the year James returned and presided over a Scottish Parliament, and 1618. In fact John Spottiswoode, Archbishop of St Andrews, and the new ecclesiastical High Commission, and not the Assembly, were responsible for instigating the copyrights obtained by Dick. The combination of these copyrights and the liturgical and ceremonial reforms, including the Five Articles of Perth that contained the 'papist' practice of kneeling, placed Dick in direct conflict with the strongly presbyterian book trade community of Edinburgh. In 1618 the printer Andro Hart and booksellers Richard Lawson and James Cathkin were brought before the Privy Council, following a direct instruction from King James, for breaching Dick's right to print catechisms.[29] The background of the defendants was clear enough. Hart and Cathkin were involved in Edinburgh presbyterian riots of 1596 and were imprisoned for their presbyterian views. In 1619 Hart, Lawson and Cathkin were all arrested and their booths searched and ransacked as the government sought to discover the distributors, printers and authorship of David Calderwood's anonymously published *Perth Assembly*, a tract which railed against the Five Articles.[30] Here we see the Crown enthusiastically using copyright law to support a loyal episcopalian, while cracking down on the presbyterian book trade 'activists', including the wealthy Andro Hart, a former 'Puritan' secret agent for Queen Elizabeth. This harassment helped split the book traders of Edinburgh into two religious factions, and such religious factionalism would emerge again in the Edinburgh trade of the 1680s.

The most prestigious and lucrative rights for religious publishing were of course those connected to the 'bible patent'. But in early modern Scotland this was not a strictly defined right as it was in England. While it was regarded as one of the duties of the royal printer to deliver printed bibles to the nation, both the government and the Church were more concerned with issues of supply and textual quality than the preservation of restrictive copyrights. The reasons may be put simply: the early modern Scottish book trade, and certainly no single royal printer, was never able to meet the demand for scripture from the population at large. This would remain the case in the modern period. Therefore, as seen in various Privy Council rulings in the 1670s and 1680s, the bible rights of the royal printer only extended to those editions and formats that he or she could keep in print. When in 1576 Thomas Bassandyne and Arbuthnot were given the licence to print Scotland's first bible, which appeared in 1579, it was for only ten years, in part due to Robert Lekpreuik's failure to produce an edition during the early years of the twenty-year bible licence granted to him in 1568, though admittedly during a time of civil war.[31] Supply was ever the key issue.

Printing the bible was not an automatic prerogative of the King's Printer. Such rights were excluded from Chepman and Myllar (1507), Robert Waldegrave (1590) and Robert Charteris (1603).[32] Thomas Finlason's gift of 1612 provided for non-exclusive rights to bibles, and these conditions were repeated in the Robert Young and Evan Tyler gift of 1641, with an emphasis that any printer must be allowed to print or import folio bibles, a format rarely printed in Scotland because of the high production costs. Andro Hart, who no doubt on account of his presbyterianism never became King's Printer, appears to have received no copyright protection for his outstanding folio Geneva bible of 1610, though it was subject to a subscription drive organised by the Church and would be much copied on the Continent.[33] Subsequently the patents granted to Andrew Anderson (1671) and Robert Freebairn (1711) do, however, allow for an exclusive right to all bibles, although no printing or import restriction was valid without the existence of a matching edition from the royal press.[34]

The regulatory framework and copyright law was put into something of a crisis in the 1670s, and bibles became a focus for this contentiousness. After developing a tradition of book trade liberalisation, book and press controls in Scotland suddenly took a lurch into new territory. The critical cause of disquiet was the extensive 41-year patent granted to the new King's Printer Andrew Anderson in May 1671. This provided unprecedented general rights and supervisory powers over the press. Anderson, his partners and assignees were not only 'his Majesties ... onlie sole and principall printer', with rights to print all bibles, liturgy and school books, but they were also 'Masters, Directors and Regulators of his Majesties office of Printing', with powers to police imports, prevent printers setting up presses who had not served apprenticeships, and they could, subject to the Privy Council, 'seclude and debarr all others [of the] freedoms and immunities' of trade.[35] Why such restrictions and why in 1671? While economic policies in Scotland tended to take on more mercantilist and Continental qualities after the Restoration, book-trade controls took on a more English flavour. Charles II was happy to strengthen the regulation in Scotland in the absence of a trade and registration vehicle such as the Stationers' Company and an official censor such as Roger L'Estrange, who had been appointed 'Surveyor of the Imprimery and Printing Press' in England in 1663. Charles's man in Scotland, the Secretary, John Maitland, Earl and Duke of Lauderdale, was happy to oblige given that Anderson paid for the gift and that Lauderdale chose to rule Scotland with a more centralising and controlling authority than any other chief minister since 1603. The existing Scottish system of regulation and copyright, where the Privy Council handled complaints on a title by title basis, was therefore at risk from an alien hybrid of regulatory powers within the Anderson gift. The liberties asserted by the Privy Council in 1614 were forgotten. However, by the time L'Estrange was dispatched to Holyrood in 1686, with the task of running James VII's press office and a futile campaign to win hearts and minds over to Catholic toleration and the repeal of the Test

Acts, the Privy Council had reasserted control in the terms of the Hart judgment of 1614.[36]

The disputes of the 1670s and 1680s proceeded with venom, violence and venality. Initially Anderson policed his rights with excessive zeal. In autumn 1671 the Glasgow workshop of the printer Robert Sanders, the elder, was raided and ransacked by Anderson and his henchmen. Sanders' tradesmen were beaten up, driven off and temporarily imprisoned for, Anderson claimed, printing without due authority. The Privy Council freed Sanders and his men and insisted the case was heard before the Lords of Council, but both the Glasgow and Edinburgh book trade were outraged. Realising that he was somewhat isolated in the trade, Anderson began to take on partners in an attempt to build up a new printers' 'society'. Over the next few years these would include the Edinburgh printers and booksellers George Swintoun, James Glen, Thomas Brown and David Trench, but there was still considerable resistance from elsewhere. In late 1671 a petition was delivered by the printers Robert Brown, James Miller, John Cairnes, John Masone, Gideon Shaw and Sanders, protesting at the Glasgow riot and demanding both compensation and an end to the Anderson monopoly. Yet in December 1671 the Privy Council had no choice but to rule in favour of Anderson, even though Sanders and other printers were to be allowed to import bibles until the King's Printer delivered up matching editions.[37] It is clear that the majority of the Privy Council believed the Anderson patent was too monopolistic.

Only a few weeks later Anderson turned his attention to Aberdeen and the burgh printer John Forbes, the younger, accusing him of the same crimes as Sanders. We shall see below that Anderson had additional darker motives for attacking Forbes, but when he did so he found himself opposed by the city of Aberdeen as well as by Forbes. In February 1672 Anderson was forced to concede that Forbes had the right to print under authority of the Aberdeen colleges, burgh magistrates and bishop. Anderson was, however, forced to make some concessions to secure the ratification of his patent by act of Parliament: in September 1672, the very month that the estates passed the act, Anderson conceded the right of all printers to produce editions of a range of Latin texts and seems to have realised that the Privy Council would not support his patent beyond reason.[38]

The subsequent events in the late 1670s and early 1680s left Sanders dreaming of the burgh protection enjoyed by Forbes, although Sanders' refusal to accept the terms of the Anderson gift show him to have been a strong-willed and determined opponent. After Anderson's death in 1676 his widow Agnes Campbell, who would become the most wealthy Scottish printer of the early modern period, outshone her husband in litigiousness.[39] In 1677 and 1680 she prosecuted Sanders before the Privy Council for printing texts that infringed her rights. Confiscation, a £2,000 fine and a short spell in prison was his fate in 1677, although in 1680 a more lenient sentence of confiscation indicated that the government was showing more exasperation with Campbell and her monopoly rights. The case brought by Campbell in June 1678, over the setting up of presses in Edinburgh by Gideon Shaw and other book traders without her permission, reveals the lengths she was prepared to go to protect her position and her strength in the Edinburgh market. Shaw may never have recovered from the case, having gone to the expense of importing skilled workers, and died in 1687 with extensive debts.[40] Matters came to a head in 1681. In July of that year Shaw and the other book traders of Edinburgh protested again over the Campbell monopoly. Two factors encouraged them to visit the issue again: firstly, Lauderdale's political influence had waned the previous year and also the Privy Council had established a new committee of trade, the nineteen-year exemption from duties for new manufactories in the 1661 Act for Erecting Manufactories being due to expire, and this carried out a detailed economic survey of Scotland between January and April 1681. The printers had a chance to press their case anew. Meanwhile, that autumn Campbell printed an edition of the acts of Parliament, not unreasonably given her royal patent. But that November she was challenged before the Privy Council by the printer David Lindsay who, with his partners George Wedderburn and John Cairnes, had acquired the right to print parliamentary acts by licence and authority of the Clerk Register, a traditional procedure for statute printing. The case and final judgment was a great setback for Campbell. The Privy Council confirmed Lindsay's right, and ordered the burning of Campbell's printed acts. Her policing prerogatives were no longer to extend to imports from England, unless specifically in competition with her own existing bible printings. Most important of all, her general rights were to be reduced to the terms of the patent given in 1641 to Evan Tyler, then royal printer. Any general responsibility for policing the trade was a dead letter. Campbell's appeal to the Lords of Session in the winter of 1682–3 failed and her weak argument for the status quo, that 'one press [was] sufficient' for official documents, was seen by the investigating committee as acting, like her old patent, 'to restrain the liberty of printing too much'.[41]

Campbell and the Anderson patent may now have been cut down to size but the question of bibles remained. Illegal bible imports were a particular problem in the Restoration period, especially those from England and Holland. Dutch-printed English-language bibles arrived in Scotland from the 1640s, the presses of Amsterdam and Leiden, so important to the Covenanters from a political and propagandist point of view, providing a bountiful harvest of scripture. From the Restoration the great Amsterdam bible presses of Stam, Schippers and Athias were especially productive in bibles for England and Scotland: for the Scottish market these were always without the 'papist' Apocrypha, and, from the 1660s, mostly the King James and not the Geneva version so popular in Scotland before the Cromwellian period.

In fact Glasgow became the centre for the illicit trade in Dutch bibles and it proved very difficult for Agnes Campbell to police the west. Nevertheless, in March 1680 she successfully prosecuted Sanders before the Privy Council for importing bibles from Holland. He was forced to pay damages and to destroy his imported stock.[42] By then, however, the trade in illegal Dutch imports was well established in Glasgow. Sanders, the elder, had already set up trade contacts with Anna Marie Stam, widow of the great Amsterdam bible printer Fredericksz Stam. Sanders was contracted by widow Stam, with 'full power, authority and command in her stead', to recover the debt of 890 guilders due to her for supplying bibles to the Glasgow merchant Thomas Davidson.[43] The Stam family, it seems, became one of the many catalysts for conflict between the royal printer and the Glasgow book trade. In 1678 Campbell took Sanders to the Court of the Dean of Guild in Edinburgh and then to the Court of Session for poaching her bible printer, a certain Jacob Stam.[44] It is hard to believe, in spite of some sporadic victories, that Campbell could have won, in commercial terms, this particular war of the widows. Policing the Glasgow trade was very difficult given the quantity of scripture and liturgy that came and went, much of it in transit to Ulster, New England and Virginia.

Bible imports from England were also a threat to the royal bible patent. Campbell regularly complained to the Privy Council over these incursions but only had one major legal success. Bible printers such as Andro Hart were more concerned with exporting bibles to England than excluding them from Scotland. But according to her bitter rival James

Watson, the younger, in 1688 Campbell 'fell tooth and nail upon the booksellers [of Edinburgh seizing] a good quantity of bibles brought from London'. In May of that year agents of Campbell seized octavo bibles at Leith which had been imported from London by the Edinburgh bookseller Alexander Ogston. Ogston was well connected to the legal profession, having received his burgess ticket free in 1680 on the recommendation of the Lord Advocate, Sir George Mackenzie of Rosehaugh, and the College of Justice. However, 'the black widow' won the day, and our source, the lawyer Sir John Lauder, was left to reflect on the meanness of her octavo, which was shown to the court to justify her entirely legal actions.[45] It is clear from such cases that illegal importing and printing were carried out by many respectable book traders and were even seen as an aspect of legitimate commerce.

If the Scottish bible trade was confused with regard to legal and illegal activity that for almanacs was chaotic. Indeed the copyright history of the seventeenth-century Scottish almanac provides an exemplar for copyright law and deliberate skulduggery. From a commercial point of view these small octavo booklets, merely sixteen pages long and typically sold for only 4*d.*, were nonetheless the most valuable literary properties in the late seventeenth century. By the 1690s these almanacs carried advertising, a reflection of their mass circulation and their character as stepping-stones to the Scottish periodical and newspaper revolution that began at the turn of the century.[46]

The earliest-known almanacs emanating from the presses of Scotland's three printing burghs were those of Aberdeen (1623), Edinburgh (1632) and Glasgow (1661).[47] These developed very much as town or burgh almanacs, both licensed and protected by the respective town councils and magistrates and able to expand circulation within their burgh markets and beyond. There are many examples of burgh protectionism, particularly in Edinburgh and Aberdeen. In October 1667 the magistrates of Aberdeen responded to a petition from the burgh printer and bookseller John Forbes, the elder (*fl.*1650–75), protesting at the activities of a chapman and street trader Alexander Gray, who had brought into Aberdeen 1,000 copies of an 'alien' almanac. This breached the market monopoly of Forbes's own edition. The council upheld Forbes's complaint and agreed to ban all such 'alien' almanacs within Aberdeen, provided that Forbes continued to sell his own at a reasonable price.[48]

The 'Aberdeen almanac' was not merely the earliest but also the most successful, appearing in large print-runs of 50,000 or more, which compares favourably with the larger print-runs of English editions. It was the printer Edward Raban (*c.*1585–1658), an Englishman of German descent and Aberdeen's first printer, who, commissioned by the Aberdeen bookseller David Melville, introduced the 'Aberdeen almanac' in the 1620s. Raban was no doubt inspired by continental models which he encountered during his travels as a soldier and during his training as a printer in Amsterdam and Leiden.[49] However, it was John Forbes, the younger (*fl.*1662–1704) who, in the 1660s and 1670s, developed the reputation of the 'Aberdeen almanac' as the most prestigious edition in Scotland. The jealousy from Edinburgh was considerable. It seems likely that Andrew Anderson, having acquired that wide-ranging royal licence in 1671, deliberately attacked the printing rights of Forbes in early 1672 with a view to strangling Forbes's most valuable asset, the 'Aberdeen almanac'. The threat of legal action by Anderson and his Edinburgh cartel had to be taken seriously by Forbes, who knew that only a few weeks before Sanders' press in Glasgow had been ransacked. Anderson argued the same case, that Forbes had printed without permission, but he failed to take account of the strong views of Aberdeen town council who were outraged at this attack on their independence and right to license within their own environs. The magistrates were prepared to contemplate a book-trade war with Edinburgh, but before Aberdeen took their case to the Privy Council, Anderson realised he had pressed matters too far, and in February 1672 wrote to the magistrates of Aberdeen conceding Forbes's right to print under licence of the town, universities and bishop of Aberdeen.[50]

Such was the success of the 'Aberdeen almanac', however, that various pirated editions were produced in Glasgow and Edinburgh. Counterfeit problems had also dogged almanac printing in England, so why not in Scotland?[51] For Scotland, deception came before illegality and in the 1660s and 1670s Robert Sanders in Glasgow printed various almanacs feigning calculation by Aberdeen mathematicians; Edinburgh editions also falsely claimed Aberdeen authority. In his almanac of 1674 Forbes declared in doggerel rhyme: 'No almanacks are from Aberdeen but where there Armes are to be seen', and it was the habit of burgh printers to add the city coat of arms as a badge of authenticity. The most infamous legal case over such counterfeiting arose in 1684, the year in which Forbes exclaimed threateningly in his latest edition: 'If Counterfit, then Hang for it!'.[52] In 1682 and 1683 Robert Sanders in Glasgow and Agnes Campbell in Edinburgh each produced counterfeit Aberdeen editions. In February 1684 Forbes, with the support of Aberdeen town council, prosecuted Sanders and Campbell, old enemies now become co-defendants, and after the case was referred to a committee the Lords ruled in favour of Forbes. He won his case in law because he was 'in use and possession of printing yeirly ane almanack as printer of the toun and coledge of Aberdein', and therefore his copyright was sustained. Indeed Aberdeen's copyright had also been breached. Sanders, while openly printing his name and Glasgow on his 1684 edition, had attempted to forge the city arms of Aberdeen which, as we have seen, always adorned the almanac and therefore his offence was viewed as especially reprehensible (see figures 1 and 2). Sanders and Campbell were warned as to their future conduct and that their counterfeits should cease, but counterfeit Aberdeen editions continued to slip into the market-place. Even the likes of John Reid who, as we have seen, like Sanders was constantly battered by Agnes Campbell's lawyers, produced his own Aberdeen edition in 1690.[53] Sanders, nevertheess, also printed a legitimate Glasgow almanac. This first appeared in 1661/2 and was compiled by the mathematician James Corse, who was paid for dedicating his almanac to Glasgow town council. No records exist of a major court case concerning copyright breaches related to the Glasgow edition, but by 1664 Corse almanacs were coming from the presses of Edinburgh as well as Glasgow.[54] The copyright position was completely chaotic: it was a classic case of every man for his or her self.

The first Edinburgh almanac, printed in 1632, came from the press of John Wreittoun and was based on an English edition written by the mathematician John Whyte.[55] Regular Edinburgh printings did not occur, surprisingly, until after the Restoration. The most successful Edinburgh almanac of the 1680s and 1690s was that compiled by the mathematician James Paterson. Paterson was prickly and disputatious and he and the mathematicians of the Aberdeen colleges conducted a bitter feud via their respective almanacs over the correct calculation of Easter, and other questions relating to the calendar and Old and New Style dating.[56] Paterson, however, was no more successful than Forbes in avoiding pirating. In late 1684 Paterson obtained a one-year licence to print his Edinburgh almanac unopposed. Confusingly, a week later burgh protection arrived as the Edinburgh magistrates gave him 'warrant to publish yearly almanacs', in effect a monopoly outlawing other Edinburgh editions as long as he

ABERDEEN'S True ALMANACK
OR NEW
Prognoſtication
For this Year, One thouſand ſix hundreth Eighty and five,
So, They who are not Honeſt, I'm ſure ſhall hardly thrive.

Moſt curiouſly calculated for all brave BRITTAIN, yea, and *Ireland* too (if you pleaſe,) without any palpable Error: (*unleſs by Criticks*) but more eſpecially for the Meridian of famous BON-ACCORD, whoſe *Elevat.* is 57d. 10m.

By an Old painful Aſtroquomer, and real well-wiſher to his Countrey.

BON-ACCORD

Inſignia Urbis abredoniae

Almighty GOD preſerve Our Gracious KING;
All's Subjects Hearts, to due Obedience bring.

Printed in ABERDEEN by JOHN FORBES, Printer to that Famous CITY & UNIVERSITY.

Fig.1. The titlepage of John Forbes's almanac *Aberdeen's True Almanack* of 1685 with the cracked printing block which was used for five decades. (*Reproduced courtesy of the Trustees of the National Library of Scotland*)

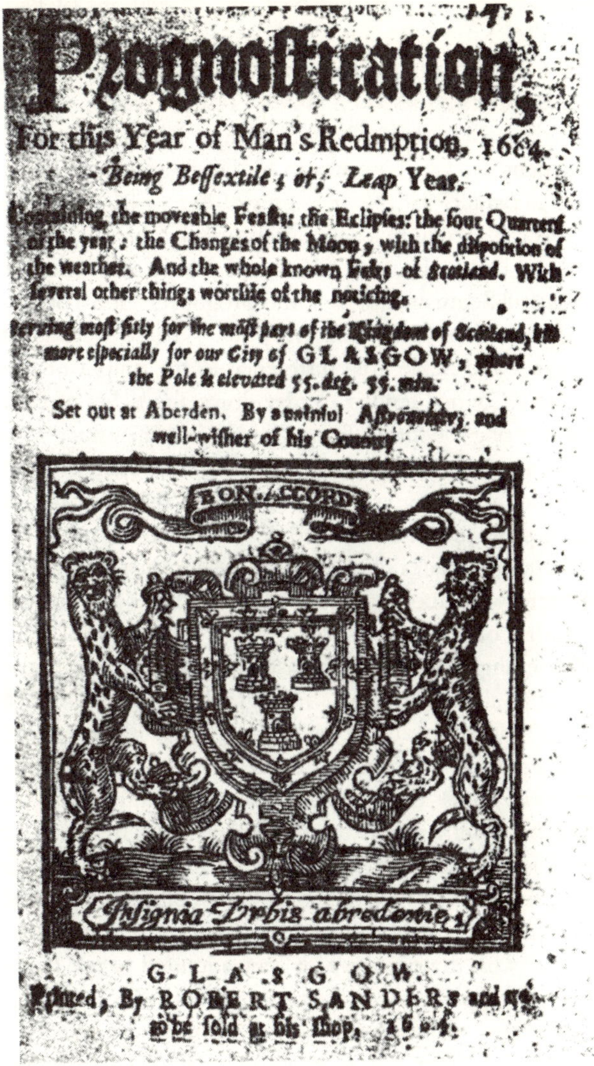

Prognostication,

For this Year of Man's Redmption, 1684.

Being Bessextile, or, Leap Year.

Containing the moveable Feasts: the Eclipses: the four Quarters of the year; the Changes of the Moon, with the disposition of the weather. And the whole known Fairs of Scotland. With several other things worthie of the noticing.

Serving most fitly for the most part of the Kingdom of Scotland, but more especially for our City of GLASGOW, where the Pole is elevated 55. deg. 55. min.

Set out at Aberden. By a painful Astronomer, and well-wisher of his Country.

G L A S G O W.

Printed, By ROBERT SANDERS and are to be sold at his shop, 1684.

Fig.2. Robert Sanders' 'counterfeit' almanac *A New Prognostication* of 1684, with the fake, undamaged coat of arms. (Reproduced from *Bibliographia Aberdonensis*, Spalding Club, ii (Aberdeen, 1929), p. 485)

published his own.[57] None of this checked the activities of Campbell, who proceeded each year to print her own pirated editions of Paterson's text from at least 1685 to 1690.

The last and most farcical element in the shambolic copyright history of Scottish almanacs arose when James VII and II came to power. In 1685 James agreed to appoint the Catholic printer James Watson, the elder, to the unprecedented post of 'printer to his family and household', a position that existed in parallel with the position of King's Printer. Watson died in 1687 and was replaced in this anomalous post by the Catholic and German engineer Peter Bruce (Breusch). Both men were given not only a monopoly to print all Scottish almanacs and prognostications, but also the right to those almanac editions already in print.[58] These were ludicrously unworkable rights and made little difference to the output of other presses. Even the Privy Council tended to play down the rights of the 'household printer' by ignoring a petition from Watson in 1687 asking for fines to be imposed against those breaching his almanac monopoly.[59] While Paterson played safe and used the presses of Watson and Bruce, Forbes and Sanders continued to print their editions and Agnes Campbell proceeded with her regular Edinburgh pirates. Even in the relatively small print market of Scotland, there were too many of these small books circulating for any effective control of copyright or licensing.

Counterfeiting and duplicity also occurred at imprint level. It is frequently difficult for modern bibliographers to establish the correct source of early printings and it was as hard for contemporaries. If a book could masquerade as a legitimate domestic printing then any breach of copyright could pass undetected. After the Restoration such tactics became common with regard to the general bible trade. In England the King's Printers Thomas Guy and Henry Hills were found in 1684 to have altered the titlepages of officially seized Dutch bibles that had been illegally imported. The printers sold these on at reduced prices when their own stock was low, with the objective, as they admitted to the House of Lords committee, of crippling the university presses.[60] In Holland counterfeit bible printing was an essential part of commercial activity. When the Oxford student William Nicolson visited the Amsterdam press of Jan Schippers' widow in 1678 he described a remarkable scene: 'They print many English Bibles of all sizes; upon the title pages they sett — London printed by R. Barker and the Assigns of John Bill…'. Bibles with counterfeit imprints for Cologne, Leipzig and Mainz were also being printed.[61]

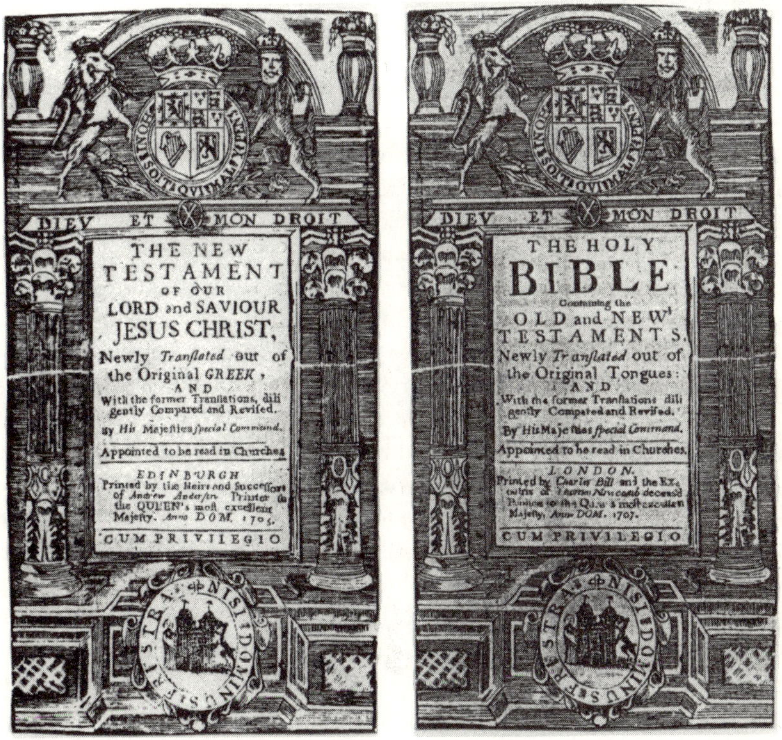

Fig.3. The titlepages of two Bibles printed by Agnes Campbell in 1707, the version on the right being a counterfeit London Bible. Reproduced from Dr John Lee's *Memorial for the Bible Societies in Scotland* (Edinburgh, 1824)

It is in this context that we must view Agnes Campbell's controversial counterfeit English bible of 1707.

After many years of protesting to the Privy Council about the damage caused to her business by illegal imports of English bibles, in 1707 Agnes Campbell printed her own 'English bible' in Edinburgh with the imprint 'London, printed by Charles Bill' (see figure 3). If Scottish book-buyers preferred bibles printed in England, she now provided them.[62] This dishonesty has caused a historiographical dispute between Campbell's biographer James Fairley, writing in the 1920s, and Dr John Lee, the nineteenth-century authority on Scottish bible printing. The printing is now lost, but Fairley claimed that Lee fabricated the whole episode to attack Campbell. In fact Lee remained neutral about 'the black widow' and had no reason to invent the story.[63] When everyone else was busy with pirates and false imprints, why should Scotland's royal printer be any different? The attraction of such a printing in the year 1707 is fairly obvious. The case does, nonetheless, capture that quality of commercial deceit and greed which characterised Scottish copyright in the early modern period.

The demise of the Scottish Privy Council came in 1708, the last copyright granted by it being Thomas Watt's nineteen-year licence for his grammar and vocabulary, granted in the same year.[64] The long history of the Council as copyright agency and book-trade court came to an end and this made it urgent that a solution was found to Scottish copyright procedures. There has been much confusion over the relationship between the trades of England and Scotland. Typical are William Jackson's comments, in his paper 'Counterfeit Printing in Jacobean Times', where he labelled Andro Hart's legitimate 1614 edition of Bacon's *Essaies* as an 'Edinburgh piracy', as though at the time Edinburgh was subject to laws from London (see figure 4).[65] Before 1707 Scottish copyright was as independent as that of France in relation to England. In a similar way, the timing of the 1710 'Statute of Anne' has also been subjected to largely English interpretations: traditionally the act is seen to have followed on from pressure exerted by the English book trade after years of confusion over copyright. However, the free market created by the Act of Union and the disappearance of the Privy Council in 1708 show that Scottish factors were very important to the timing of the 1710 act.[66] When the act came into being, for the first time neither the Scottish nor the English book trade had the legal right to print solely for their own domestic markets or to duplicate each other's publications. The Scottish book trade in

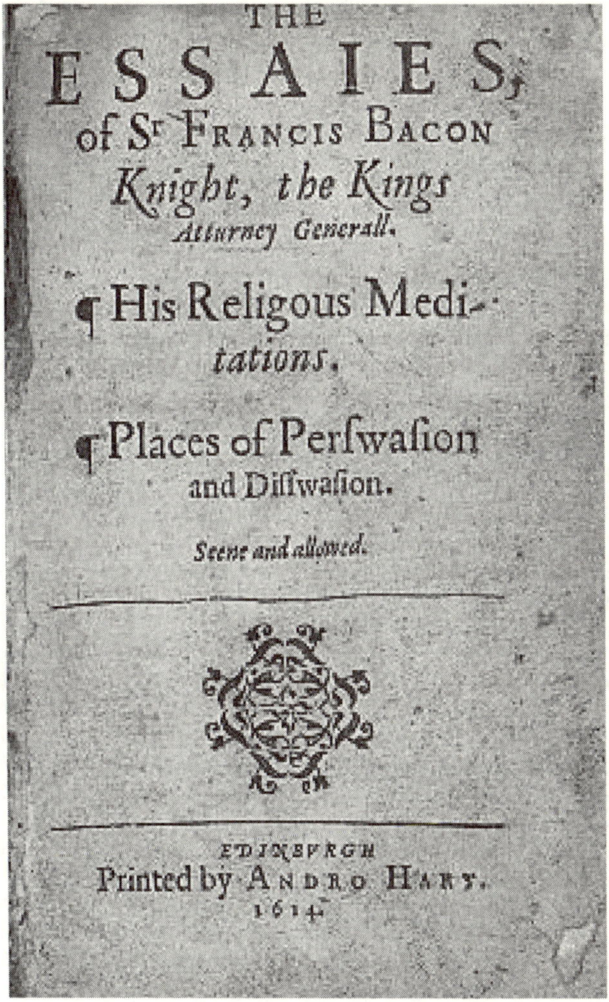

THE
ESSAIES,
of S[r] Francis Bacon
Knight, the Kings
Atturney Generall.

¶ His Religous Medi-
tations.

¶ Places of Perſwaſion
and Diſſwaſion.

Seene and allowed.

EDINBVRGH
Printed by Andro Hart.
1614.

Fig. 4. Titlepage of Andro Hart's so-called 'pirate' edition of Francis Bacon's *Essaies* (1614), an entirely legal publication for the Scottish market

particular found this arrangement unsustainable, and the journey from reprint wars to the infamous Donaldson case and House of Lords ruling in 1774 was begun. In 1710 Scottish book traders wished their own copyrights protected, but also access to those in England. Put simply, the Scottish trade 'wanted to have their cake and eat it.'

While the act of 1710 did not by any means end piracy and illegal activity, 1708 did mark something of a watershed. It brought to an end 200 years of independent copyright history, during which licences for individual books were sought after and generally respected by much of the trade and maintained by a willing, though sometimes overwhelmed, Privy Council. However, copyrights on the most popular printings, such as almanacs, simply proved unworkable. For the conscientious author protecting his literary property, such as the grammarian James Kirkwood, the system worked fairly well, but for the many printers of almanacs and importers of illegal bibles copyright crime certainly paid.

References

1. For a general survey of Scotland see Alastair J. Mann, *The Scottish Book Trade 1500 to 1720: Print Commerce and Print Control in Early Modern Scotland* (East Linton, 2000), chapter 4; Mann, 'Scottish Copyright before the Statute of 1710', *The Juridical Review* (2000), pt. 1, pp. 11–25 and Mann, 'The Book Trade and Public Policy in Early Modern Scotland' (Ph.D., Stirling, 1997), pp. 167–222. The only previous survey is W. J. Couper, 'Copyright in Scotland before 1709', *Records of the Glasgow Bibliographical Society*, v, 9 (1931), pp. 42–57; but see also Dr John Lee, *Memorial for the Bible Societies in Scotland* (Edinburgh, 1824), *passim*, and Warren McDougall, 'Copyright Litigation in the Court of Session, 1738–1749 and the Rise of the Scottish Book Trade', *Edinburgh Bibliographical Society*, v, pt. 5 (1987). The otherwise excellent John Feather, *Publishing, Piracy and Politics: An Historical Study of Copyright in Britain* (London, 1994) does not consider Scotland before the eighteenth century.
2. The phrase 'copy right' does not appear in the Company records until 1701. G. E. Briscoe Eyre and C. R. Rivington (eds) *A Transcript of the Registers of the Worshipful Company of Stationers, from 1640–1708*, 3 vols (London, 1913–14), iii, pp. 494–6.
3. J. Feather, *A History of British Book Publishing* (London, 1988), p. 21; Lyman Ray Patterson, *Copyright in Historical Perspective* (Nashville, 1968), pp. 78–113; Mark Rose, *Authors and Owners: The Invention of Copyright* (Harvard, 1993), pp. 11–12. For a revisionist view of the continuing importance of English book patents, and suggestions that they seriously challenged Stationers' Company authority, see Arnold Hunt, 'Book trade patents, 1603–1640', in A. Hunt, G. Mandelbrote and A. Shell (eds), *The Book Trade and its Customers: Historical essays for Robin Myers* (Winchester, 1997), pp. 27–54, with a useful list of over 70 patents at pp. 40–54.

4. Patterson, *Copyright*, pp. 86–7; *Registrum Secreti Sigilli Regum Scotorum: Register of the Privy Seal of Scotland* (printed series) [*RSS*], i, p. 223 no. 1546 and R. Dickson and J. P. Edmond, *Annals of Scottish Printing: from the introduction of the art in 1507 to the beginning of the seventeenth century* (1890, reprinted Amsterdam, 1975), pp. 7–8; *RSS*, ii, p. 653, no. 4335; *RSS*, v. pt. 1, pp. 143–4, no. 658.
5. Feather, *History of British Publishing*, pp. 80–3; Feather, *Publishing, Piracy and Politics*, pp. 10–36, Mann, *The Scottish Book Trade*, pp. 96–7, and Mann, 'Scottish Copyright', p. 13. In Roman law, as seen in Justinian's *Institutes*, ii.2: '*de rebus incorporalibus*', the acceptance of incorporeal rights is confirmed.
6. 21 James I c.3. See Christine MacLeod, *Inventing the Industrial Revolution: The English patent system, 1660–1800* (Cambridge, 1988), pp. 17–19; Rose, *Authors and Owners*, pp. 45–7; Patterson, *Copyright*, pp. 86–7. The fourteen-year period seems to have been chosen as twice the standard apprenticeship to allow masters a balanced period to exploit their rights before servants entered into competition.
7. Colin Clair, *A History of Printing in Britain* (London, 1965), p. 132. For an account of the general patent and monopoly controversy, see MacLeod, *Inventing the Industrial Revolution*, pp. 10–17.
8. Feather, *Publishing, Piracy and Politics*, p. 29 and p. 34.
9. C. Blagden, *The Stationers Company, 1403–1959* (London, 1960), pp. 138–45; Mann, *The Scottish Book Trade*, p. 117. For more recent reflections and the extensive historiography of the Stationers' Company, see: Robin Myers and Michael Harris (eds), *The Stationers' Company and the Book Trade, 1550–1990* (Winchester, 1997); Robin Myers, *The Stationers' Company Archive: an account of the records, 1554–1984* (Winchester, 1990), pp. xv–xvi; Robin Myers (ed.), *The Stationers' Company: a history of the later years, 1800–2000* (Chichester, 2001), pp. 247–8.
10. *Registers of the Privy Council (Scotland)* [*RPC*], series i, 13, pp. 219–22, pp. 299–302 and p. 240; T. Thomson and C. Innes (eds), *The Acts of the Parliaments of Scotland*, 12 vols (Edinburgh, 1844–75) [*APS*], v, p. 263. The monopolies abolished in Scotland in 1641 included those for tobacco, leather, pearling and armoury.
11. For the establishing of these burgh presses see Mann, *The Scottish Book Trade*, pp. 7–12.
12. St Andrews, the oldest Scottish university, was briefly the home of a press in the 1540s, 1570s and 1620s but not in any continuous fashion. It developed a relationship with the college/university printer in Edinburgh who produced most of its academic works and theses.
13. J. Stuart, (ed.), *Extracts from the Records of the Burgh of Aberdeen* (1872), i [*ABR*], pp. 245–6; Aberdeen Charter Room, Manuscript Records of Aberdeen Council, Council Registers [ACR], lv, ff. 66–7 and J. P. Edmond, *The Aberdeen Printers, 1620 to 1736*, 4 vols (Aberdeen, 1884), iv, p. xiv; J. D. Marwick, M. Wood and H. Armet (eds), *Extracts from the Records of the Burgh of Edinburgh*, 13 vols (Edinburgh, 1869–1967) [*EBR*], (1869–1967) [*EBR*], xiii, p. 173 (17 August 1709); Couper, 'Copyright before 1709', p. 46.
14. *APS*, viii, pp. 206–7; *RPC*, iii, pp. 12, 460–1; National Archives of Scotland [NAS], Privy Seal Registers, PS3/4, 248; *RPC*, iii, 13, p. xx; NAS. Registrum magni sigilli [RMS], Register of the Great Seal of Scotland manuscript registers (paper register) C3/15 no. 388; NAS. Court of Session Papers, Productions and Processes CS29/ box 436.1 (Mackenzie). For a full account of the legal battle see Mann, 'Book Commerce,

Litigation and the Art of Monopoly: The case of Agnes Campbell, Royal Printer, 1676–1712', *Scottish Economic and Social History*, vol. 18, pt. 2 (1998), pp. 140–1.

15. For Hart in general see Mann, *The Scottish Book Trade, passim*; Mann, *New DNB* entry for Hart, and W. Cowan, 'Ando Hart and his Press', *Edinburgh Bibliographical Society Papers*, i, no. 12 (1896), pp. 1–14.
16. *RPC*, series i, 10, pp. 827–8 and p. 252. For text see also Mann, *The Scottish Book Trade*, p. iii.
17. For details on licensing procedures see Mann, *The Scottish Book Trade*, pp. 139–41.
18. *RSS*, i, p. 223, no. 1546. For an outline of sanctions see Mann, *The Scottish Book Trade*, pp. 108–9.
19. NAS. Manuscript Registers of the Privy Council, PC2/24, 319v. Couper provides some details on fines: see Couper, 'Copyright before 1709', p. 56.
20. NAS. PS1/100, 305; *RPC*, iii, 5, pp. 141–2; pp. 526–8. For Alexander and psalms see Mann, *The Scottish Book Trade*, pp. 39–40, p. 100, p. 107 and p. 109.
21. Mann, *The Scottish Book Trade*, pp. 129–33.
22. *RPC*, iii, 7, pp. 3–4; ibid, pp. 3l–2; *RPC*, iii, 8, pp. 250–1; Sir John Lauder of Fountainhall, *Historical Notices of Scottish Affairs*, 2 vols (Edinburgh, 1848), ii, pp. 464–5.
23. NAS. Court of Session Papers, Productions and Processes CS157 –66/2 (1687) and CS96/ 3–6 for inventory books for Hislop; CS138/5219 (November 1699); CS158/445 (April 1705) and W. J. Couper, 'Robert Sanders The Elder', *Records of the Glasgow Bibliographical Society*, iii (1915), pp. 46–9 for Sanders; CS29/ box 436.1 (papers from 1713, 1715–16 before House of Lords appeal 1718) for Watson. For details of the Watson case see Mann, 'Agnes Campbell', pp. 140–3.
24. Mann, *The Scottish Book Trade*, p. 154.
25. *RPC*, iii, 4, p. 292; *RPC*, iii, 5, p. 211 and p. 268; NAS. PC2/26, 47v.
26. A. W. Pollard, 'Some notes on the history of copyright in England, 1662–1774', *The Library*, 4th series, iii (1922), p. 99 and Feather, *Publishing, Piracy and Politics*, p. 27.
27. For text of council ruling see Dickson and Edmond, *Annals of Scottish Printing*, pp. 84–5; Mann, *The Scottish Book Trade*, pp. 129–30.
28. NAS. PS1/87, 67; PS1/87, 227; *RPC*, i, 11, pp. 643–4 and *RPC*, i, 12, p. 77.
29. *RPC*, i, 11, p. 626; Mann, *The Scottish Book Trade*, p. 45.
30. *RPC*, i, 12, pp. 15–16; *ibid.*, note 66; David Calderwood, *The History of the Kirk of Scotland*, 8 vols (Edinburgh, 1842–9), vii, pp. 382–3; *RPC*, i, 12, pp. 249–50; *ibid.*, p. 309 and p. 328. For summary of 1619 see Mann, The *Scottish Book Trade*, p. 171. For 1596 see Mann, *The Scottish Book Trade*, pp. 25–6, and for a summary of the Edinburgh presbyterian book trade community, and role of women in sustaining it, see Alastair J. Mann 'Embroidery to Enterprise: the Role of Women in the Book Trade of Early Modern Scotland' in E. Ewan and M. Meikle (eds), *Women in Scotland, c.1100–c.1750* (East Linton, 1999), pp. 141–3.
31. *RSS*, vii, p. 94, no. 642; NAS. PS1/43, 103r; *RSS*, vi, p. 53, no. 230. For the Bassandyne and Arbuthnot Geneva Bible see Mann, *The Scottish Book Trade, passim.*
32. Waldegrave: NAS. PS1/61, 58; Lee, *Memorial*, appendix viii; Charteris: NAS. PS1/74, 143v and Lee, *Memorial*, appendix xiv.
33. Finlason: NAS. PS1/ 82, 55v–45v and *RPC*, i, 9, pp. 451–2; Lee, *Memorial*, pp. 160–3. Lee's is still the best analysis of bible printing in the period.

34. Freebairn: NAS. RMS (paper register) C3/15 no. 388.
35. *APS*, viii, pp. 206–7; Lee, *Memorial*, appendix xxix, pp. 56–61.
36. Feather, *History of Book Publishing*, pp. 52–5; J. Walker, 'The Censorship of the press during the reign of Charles II', *History*, 25 (1950), pp. 219–38; *APS*, xi, pp. 138–9.
37. *RPC*, iii, 3, pp. 422–6; J. MacLehose, *The Glasgow University Press 1638–1931* (Glasgow, 1931), p. 83.
38. ACR, lv, 262–3; Edmond, *Aberdeen Printers*, iv, p. xlvi.
39. For Campbell in general see Mann, 'Agnes Campbell', pp. 132–56.
40. *RPC*, iii, 5, pp. 141–2; *RPC*, iii, 6, pp. 418–19 and *RPC*, iii, 5, pp. 479–80.
41. Lauder, *Historical Notices*, i, p. 311; *RPC*, iii, 7, 257; NAS. RMS, C3/10. no. 343; for the appeal which was concluded in January 1683, see Sir John Lauder of Fountainhall, *The Decisions of the Lords of Council and Session from June 6th 1678 to July 30th 1712*, 2 vols (Edinburgh, 1759–61), i, p. 205 and Lauder, *Historical Notices*, i, p. 393.
42. *RPC*, iii, 4, pp. 418–19.
43. Gemeentearchief Amsterdam, Notarial Archive [GAA NA] 4779. 101–2. Mann, 'Agnes Campbell', pp. 149–50.
44. NAS, Hay of Haystoun papers GD34/665 (1678).
45. James Watson, *The History of the Art of Printing* (1713), preface, p. 16; *EBR*, x, p. 392; Lauder, *Decisions*, i, p. 496 and Lauder, *Historical Notices*, ii, p. 866.
46. The only comprehensive account of almanac printing is William R. McDonald, 'Scottish Seventeenth-Century Almanacs', *The Bibliotheck*, IV, pt. 1.8 (1966), pp. 257–322, but for summary material see Mann, *The Scottish Book Trade*, pp. 15–16, pp. 103–4 and Mann, 'The Case of Agnes Campbell', pp. 143–5.
47. For a comprehensive listing see McDonald, 'Scottish Almanacs', pp. 297–322.
48. ACR, lv, 58–61; *ABR*, ii, pp. 245–6; Edmond, *Aberdeen Printers*, iv, p. xlv.; L. B. Taylor (ed.), *Aberdeen Council Letters, 1552–1681*, 6 vols (Oxford, 1942–61), iv, pp. 321–2.
49. For Raban's career see Alastair J. Mann, 'The Press and Military Conflict in Early Modern Scotland', in S. Murdoch and A. Mackillop (eds), *Fighting for Identity: Scottish Military Experience c.1550–1900* (Leiden, 2002), pp. 266–7.
50. *RPC*, iii, 3, p. 424; ACR, lv, 362–3; Edmond, *Aberdeen Printers*, iv, p. xlvi.
51. Feather, *Publishing, Piracy and Politics*, p. 45.
52. For quotations see *A New Prognostication* (Aberdeen, 1674) (Aldis no. 2024) and *Bon-Accords Ephemeris, or New Prognostication* (Aberdeen, 1684) (Aldis no. 2446).
53. *RPC*, iii, 8, 384; Edmond, *Aberdeen Printers*, iv, pp. li–lii; Lauder, *Decisions*, i, p. 273 and p. 276; McDonald, 'Scottish Almanacs', pp. 269–76.
54. J. D. Marwick and R. Renwick (eds), *Extracts from the Records of the Burgh of Glasgow* (Glasgow, 1876–1906), ii, p. 469.
55. McDonald, 'Scottish Almanacs', p. 259 and p. 298.
56. McDonald, 'Scottish Almanacs', pp. 276–9.
57. *RPC*, iii, 10, p. 16; *EBR*, xi, p. 128.
58. Lee, *Memorial*, p. 146; *RPC*, iii, 12, pp. 460–1; Lauder, *Decisions*, i, p. 424; NAS, PS3/4,248 and *RPC*, iii, 13, p. xx.
59. *RPC*, iii, 13, pp. 120–2.
60. Historical Manuscripts Commission, 17. House of Lords, I, 1678–88 (London, 1887), no. 409, p. 274. Affidavit dated 5 July 1684.

61 J. W. Stoye, *English Travellers Abroad, 1604–1667* (London, 1952), pp. 256–7; P. G. Hoftijzer, *Engelse boekverkopers bij de beurs: De geschiedenis van de Amsterdamse boekhandels Bruyning en Swart* (Amsterdam, 1987), p. 110; Mann, 'Agnes Campbell', pp. 150–1.

62. Mann, 'Women in the Book Trade', p. 144, and plate in Lee, *Memorial*.

63. John Fairley, *Agnes Campbell, Lady Roseburn: Relect of Andrew Anderson: A Contribution to the History of Printing in Scotland* (Aberdeen, 1925), pp. 23–6 and Lee, *Memorial*, pp. 160–3.

64. Lee, *Memorial*, p. 157.

65. William Jackson, 'Counterfeit Printing in Jacobean Times', *The Library*, 4th series, xv (1934), p. 367.

66. For a discussion of this timing see Mann, *The Scottish Book Trade*, pp. 122–4.

Offensive Behaviour in the English Book Trade, 1641–1700

MAUREEN BELL

THE SUBSTANCE OF this paper arises from a year largely taken up with making ready for publication a work of reference begun in the 1980s by the late D. F. McKenzie.[1] His insistence on the close and meticulous reading of documentary evidence for book trade activity is well known, not least from his Sandars Lectures on 'The London Book Trade in the Later Seventeenth Century' and his articles on the London book trade in the years 1644 and 1668, recently reprinted in *Making Meaning: 'Printers of the Mind' and other essays*, edited by Peter McDonald and Michael Suarez.[2] Convinced of the need to read the evidence of the physical object — the book — alongside the surviving historical evidence of its contexts of production as supplied by short-title catalogues, Stationers' Company records and other historical documents, Don McKenzie conceived of *A Chronology and Calendar of Documents relating to the London Book Trade, 1641–1700*, which would bring together edited abstracts of documents from the sources he had himself so fruitfully mined, so as to provide a preliminary narrative of the trade in the latter half of the seventeenth century.[3] In 1995, having drafted much of the first third of the work (1641–60), he asked me to take responsibility for its completion; and now that all the entries are in place, it seems an auspicious time to give some of these materials a public airing.

What follows, therefore, relies almost totally on the abstracts which will form the published *Chronology and Calendar*, and while these can, and indeed should, be supplemented by reference to other primary and secondary sources, I hope to be able here to give a flavour of the kind of documentary evidence it contains, the kind of questions the interfiling of records from many sources suggests, and the extent to which the *Chronology and Calendar* can provide a starting point for a detailed discussion of the trade in the later part of the seventeenth century.[4] This cornucopia of material of course contains references to 'offensive' behaviour on many levels: behaviour which culminated in the trials and executions of printers and authors; the kinds of offence which led frequently to the imprisonment and occasionally to the prosecution of stationers and their wives; the Stationers' Company's own legal actions against those who offended against its prerogatives, rules and bye-laws. To take one small example of the latter, the Stationers' Company's difficulties with the behaviour of its unruly Beadle, Randall Taylor, would make a study in itself. Taylor was, it seems, frequently up to no good. He was suspected of dealing in seditious books[5] and implicated with Samuel Mearne in the reselling of Dyer's sermons, which they had previously seized as seditious.[6] Complaints of his 'disrespectfull carriage & behaviour' (involving threats and swearing at the Master and Wardens) were so frequent that in 1682 the Court lost patience with him, drawing up rules for the better direction of the Beadle, to which Taylor submitted.[7] It is surprising that Taylor kept his position as Beadle for so long, given his appalling behaviour,[8] yet ten years later he was still Beadle, though apparently no more zealous than before in his pursuit of his duties. On 4 September 1693, reminding booksellers and printers of their duty to provide three copies of every newly-printed book for the King's library and the two universities, the Court warned him that he would have his rent doubled or would lose his tenement rented from the Company if he failed to 'use his utmost endeavour to procure three Bookes of a sort of all such Bookes as he hath of late published and have not already been brought to the Master'.[9] How, then, to begin to represent adequately such a range and variety of 'offensive' behaviour?

Not surprisingly, what is considered 'offensive' changes over time and relates to specific social, political, religious and cultural circumstances: in the historical record, 'offensive' is inevitably defined by the one who complains of the offence and therefore depends on his or her particular context. The problem of definition is, however, not easily solved by looking to seventeenth-century discussions of trade regulation. In 1644 John Milton, in his *Areopagitica*, famously ridiculed pre-publication censorship on many grounds, alive to the problems of changes in specific historical and political circumstances which rendered censorship an unstable concept. The term 'offensive' is not, however, one which he used in *Areopagitica* in relation to books, and the word 'unoffensive' occurs only once in his polemic. The term 'offensive' was used in seventeenth-century discussions of legislation and one instance in particular points to the difficulty of the term for Milton's contemporaries and successors. On 17 April 1695 the Commons were considering yet again the renewal of the Licensing Act. In listing their reasons for disagreeing with the Lords' amendment to the *Act for continuing . . . several laws* the Commons included the following:

15. Because that Act [i.e. the Licensing Act] prohibits printing and importing not only heretical, seditious, and schismatical Books, but all offensive Books; and doth not determine what shall be adjudged offensive Books: So that, without Doubt, if the late King *James* had continued in the Throne till this time, Books against Popery would* not have been deemed offensive Books.[10]

Any detailed consideration of what was deemed offensive at any time between 1641 and 1700 must avoid generalization: if contemporaries were well aware of the fluctuations in what 'offensive' might mean when applied narrowly to books, so must we be. Application of the term more broadly, to the *behaviour* of those in the book trade — printers, booksellers, bookbinders, mercuries, hawkers, chapmen and indeed authors — requires even more circumspection. Inevitably, the category of the 'offensive' will encompass a range of behaviour characterized legally, socially, politically, religiously and personally, and signalled in the historical record by words as various as 'treasonable', 'seditious', 'scandalous', 'blasphemous', 'unlicensed', 'dangerous', 'popish', 'heretical', 'abominable', 'libellous' and simply 'illegal'. The *Chronology and Calendar*, considered as a massive database containing thousands of such incidents, might eventually enable us to map the occurrence and variation over time of these epithets. For the time being, however, I am using a catch-all term, 'offensive', for which I can only apologise and — in my defence — offer an obligingly circular illustration of contemporary usage cited by the *OED* (definition 5: 'Having the quality of transgressing or committing offence; of the nature of a transgression') from 1650:

Some things are forbidden because they are justly offensive; and some things are onely therefore offensive because they are forbidden.

(Hall, *Cases Consc.* 1650, 219)

Another, more particular, dimension of the slipperiness of historical contexts is added by my reliance here on the documents collected for the *Chronology and Calendar* as the primary evidence for this discussion. The multiple viewpoints offered by the documents certainly add a richness to the narrative, but at the same time they report 'offensive' printing and publishing from radically different standpoints: sometimes conflicting, sometimes coinciding and sometimes deliberately obfuscated. First, there is the narrative provided by the public record of those in political authority, notably the Houses of Commons and Lords, the King in Council and the Protector in Council. The public record of debate and decision as it appears in the *Journals* of the Houses of Commons and Lords is supplemented by the parliamentary papers recorded in the reports of the Historical Manuscripts Commission and in the *Calendar of State Papers, Domestic Series*, where we find in addition the administrative papers, notes, warrants and correspondence of the Secretaries of State. The manuscript Court Books of the Stationers' Company, on the other hand, provide a different angle on the workings of the trade and its internal regulation, to which we can add the record of the surviving printed output of the period as recorded in Wing and *ESTC* (only very selectively represented in the *Chronology and Calendar*). Add to these a host of more random, often private, documents — letters, memoranda, manuscript newsletters, family correspondence — culled from the many HMC volumes and from the *Calendar of State Papers*, all of which report, comment on and enhance with detail the events and personalities occurring in the public record, and the complexity of the *Chronology and Calendar* as narrative thickens.

In approaching this mass of material with 'offensiveness' in mind, and in order to present a flavour of the possibilities such a gathering of documentary evidence offers, I have adopted two methods. The first approaches the documents systematically but broadly, by taking a sample survey of 'offensive' themes across the period; the second selects one specific document in order to demonstrate in detail how its contextualization amongst the documents reported in the *Chronology and Calendar* can shed light on the less visible workings of the trade.

Sample survey

Using 1648, 1658, 1668, 1678, 1688 and 1698 as sample years an outline of some of the issues — and of change over time — can be attempted, though the selection of particular years risks distorting the fuller reading which the whole 60 years' worth of documents can provide. What kinds of publication were pursued as 'offensive' in these years? In every single year it is quickly apparent that the 'offensive' behaviour which preoccupied the political authorities (monarch, parliament, Secretaries of State) was, for the most part, and not surprisingly, far removed from the preoccupations of the trade itself as they are recorded in the Court Books of the Stationers' Company. Occasionally the interests of the two groups overlap: in February 1648, for example, the Stationers' Company was ordered by the

House of Lords to assist in the pursuit of the authors, publishers and printers of *The Parliament's ten commandments* and *Ecce the New Testament*[11] and later that year a Commons Committee for the Suppressing of Pamphlets was to consult with the Company about effective means of suppression.[12] But while Parliament concerned itself with the pursuit of 'dangerous' books, unlicensed pamphlets, the publications of 'delinquents and malignants', newsbooks, printed petitions and the 'scandalous' activities of ballad singers, playhouses and mercury women, the Court of the Stationers' Company concerned itself almost entirely with offences against itself and its members: Stationer sues Stationer;[13] mortgages are argued over;[14] and damages are awarded when one Stationer pirates another's copy.[15]

1648 was a year of confused authority, with the Lords, Commons, the army and on occasion the Prince of Wales all attempting to impose their authority on what was being printed. In 1658, by comparison, the record of high-level government concern with the punishment of offences in printing is much thinner, the settled authority of Protector in Council having at least reduced the confusion of multiple authorities of the previous decade. The authors Stubbs, Heylyn, Saunderson and Harrington were all pursued for their publications; the Stationers' Company was reminded of its legal obligations by the Protector[16] and directed to comply with the order to burn Heylyn's books.[17] Again, however, the Company's preoccupation, at least as it is recorded in the Court book, is with offences against its own regulations: in February, for example, hearing a dispute over copy with Mrs Alsop; investigating the seizure of bibles; hearing a plea for holiday pay by journeymen; and pursuing illegal dealing in the Company's Stock books.[18]

The first Restoration year of the sample, 1668, sees Roger L'Estrange, now Surveyor of the Press, much exercised by the offensive behaviour of the opposition press, and consequently the record of pursuits is particularly full. Several Stationers and their wives and widows were arrested (Darby, Gaines, Elizabeth Calvert, Anna Brewster, Joan Darby),[19] authors pursued (William Penn, John Wilson)[20] and books complained of (*Vox & lacrimae anglorum*; *The poor-whores petition*; *Nehushtan*; *The sandy foundation shaken*; *Queries about Ireland*). In March libels from Rotterdam were sought in London, Yarmouth, Hull and Scotland;[21] in London secret presses in Blue Anchor Alley and in Southwark were pursued;[22] and L'Estrange was attempting concerted control over the trade. His survey of printing presses in July identified a number of 'supernumerary' printers whom the Company was to prosecute and a crack-down on hawkers later in the year produced a list of 'The Hawkers desired to stand'.[23] The Stationers' Company seemed to be fully, if forcibly, engaged in the process: on 20 April the Company was ordered by the Secretary of State to assist in searches[24] and the royal bookbinder Samuel Mearne seized Elizabeth Calvert's press.[25] The Stationers Norton, Mearne and Roycroft were rewarded by promotion within the Company to the Court of Assistants and the Company was told by the King that it 'would be held accountable henceforth for the scandalous abuses committed by the press'.[26] The Company was clearly being enlisted by the political authorities as never before in the fight against sedition. Stationers were forbidden to use hawkers and told to make frequent searches;[27] the Company in turn leant on press makers and founders to be accountable,[28] and even pursued other Companies which — presumably for their own business dealings — owned a press.[29] While the Court Books still record the usual offensive behaviour (disputes over copies; the long-running legal action over the law book patent) there was, it seems, a new and bracing engagement with the government, largely driven by L'Estrange.

The picture of activity a decade later, in 1678, is remarkably similar to that in 1668. L'Estrange was still attempting to drive the Company into compliance with his efforts at control and supernumerary printers were still a cause for concern. Parallels with 1668 are striking and familiar names occur in the pursuit of offensive printing: Brewster, Marvell, Harrington. The slide into the Popish Plot brought printers and sellers of Catholic books under intense scrutiny, notably Matthew Turner and Nathaniel Thompson. A secret press was discovered run by the Quaker Andrew Sowle;[30] another illegal press was seized at Mortlake;[31] and other printers in Southwark and (possibly) Moorfields were under suspicion.[32]

The year 1688 provides perhaps the best demonstration of the instability of the category 'offensive'. Whereas in 1678 the mounting anxiety of the Popish Plot had demonized Turner and Thompson as dangerous purveyors of popish books, by 1688 the previously outlawed Catholic books were approved by a Catholic monarch and their printers, booksellers and authors had sought and received patronage and protection from James II.[33] The threatened invasion by William of Orange disordered the unsettled category 'offensive' yet again, and the point at which Williamite propaganda changed from being 'offensive' and seditious to acceptable and legal is difficult to pin down. The struggle for control of printed propaganda is visible in the records towards the end of the year. The audience for such printing was itself confused and uncertain as to which way the political struggle would go. On 4 November 1688, for example, Ralph Spencer, a merchant of Leeds, was given 'a sealed bundle' by William Milner, merchant of Leeds, 'in which he found a printed pamphlet of 28 pages in large folio entitled *A memorial from the English Protestants for their Highnesses the Prince and Princess of Orange.* He immediately took the pamphlet to Thomas Potter, Justice of the Peace, presumably afraid of being accused of receiving seditious literature.[34] As the possibility of a change in the monarchy became more likely, the stationer Henry Hills, a beneficiary of James's patronage, attracted hostility from his neighbours although James tried to protect him. On 13 November:

> The King, hearing that the house of Mr. Hills, his printer in Blackfriars, has been attempted three times by the rabble, above 1,000 appearing there the previous night and both breaking his windows and threatening more mischief, desires that he order a sufficient guard to be placed about his house this night, to be continued while the rabble continue their insolencies towards him.[35]

By 18 December L'Estrange himself was in Newgate prison.[36] By the end of the year James had fled and the game was up for Hills, who likewise escaped abroad.[37]

The last year of the sample, 1698, provides little excitement by comparison with 1688. The Houses of Lords and Commons became increasingly irritated by printing which infringed their privileges; apart from Stamp Duty, legislation affecting the press was concentrated on the licensing of hawkers and pedlars[38] and on the suppression of blasphemy and profaneness. One name associated with the offensive behaviour of the opposition in 1668 and 1678 recurs: in November a warrant was issued to search for a seditious pamphlet printed at the house of one Darby in Bartholomew Lane near Smithfield, to seize the printed copies and the original, and to apprehend Darby himself.[39]

A sample survey of this kind, reported here only in outline, serves to confirm and to illustrate the view that the *Chronology and Calendar* offers in fact not one but multiple narratives intertwined. As far as 'offensive' behaviour is concerned, the focus of the legal and political authorities of the nation only occasionally and unevenly coincided with the preoccupation of the Stationers' Company as trade institution. The latter was predominantly concerned with policing infringements of its own rules concerning, for example, apprenticeship, copy ownership and the monopoly rights of the English Stock. When co-opted by the state as an instrument of control, as in the 1660s and 1670s under pressure from L'Estrange, the Company apparently responded as required; but resolutions were often not acted upon, or were followed through only when the Company's interest coincided with that of the state (as, for example, with the pursuit of traders in books belonging to other companies; or in pursuing hawkers and stallholders, and the 'foreign' sellers of books). On occasion the Company's apparent compliance was totally undercut by the activities of its own members (the selling on of seized 'offensive' stock, such as imported bibles; Mearne and Taylor's complicity in 1673 in selling Dyer's sermons, earlier seized by Mearne from Elizabeth Calvert's secret press[40]). And apparent compliance often seems to have petered out. One example, of the Company's approach to the problem of supernumerary printers, will suffice to illustrate the half-heartedness of the Company's apparent compliance with L'Estrange's demands.

L'Estrange's survey of presses, undertaken in July 1668, identified Darby, Winter and Rawlins as 'supernumerary printers' and noted that the three men were to be indicted at the next sessions. The following month it was reported that indictments had been preferred against three illegal printers, presumably these.[41] Yet three years later — in 1671 — the supernumerary printers were still not suppressed, the Court now resolving (perhaps after more pressure[42]) as follows:

> All Supernumerary, and Illegal Printing houses, to be Supprest, vnles the Master, doe Enter into Bond, as the Printers are to doe, at the deducement.[43]

Having recorded this resolution, the Court Books offer no evidence of further action, and the fact that two years later, in 1673, pressure was still being applied suggests that none had been taken. The Company's Court was visited on 23 May 1673 by L'Estrange in person, who produced a letter from Lord Arlington 'Concerning the Compleateing of the By Lawes, and suppressing of Illegall Printers', whereupon a committee was appointed 'to Attende the Lord Arlington in giueing him an account concerning the supernumerary Printers'.[44] A list of printing houses taken in 1675 reports that John Winter's press, along with the presses of Peter Lillicrap and Edward Oakes, had been 'bought in' by the Company since 1672.[45] But at the end of the list, the first two names reported as 'Printers set up since the Act was in force' are those of John Darby and William

Rawlins — two of the three supernumerary printers first identified and pursued in L'Estrange's survey of 1668 — plus eight more. Despite their 'supernumerary' status Darby and Rawlins clearly remained active printers throughout this period, Darby continuing to print 'offensive' literature until the end of the century; both were called to the livery.[46] It is hardly surprising, therefore, that L'Estrange continued to doubt the Company's good faith in complying with his attempts to purge illegal presses.

Catharine Knight

My second attempt to mine the materials of the *Chronology and Calendar* for 'offensive' behaviour takes a specific incident from *CSPD* whose circumstantial detail is intriguing. Years ago, when collecting information on the activities of women in the book trade, I noted down an example of the recorded interrogation of a woman who stitched pamphlets. Catharine Knight was arrested on a warrant issued on 9 November 1675[47] which ordered that her house be searched for the pamphlet *A letter from a person of quality*.[48] Her examination before Sir Joseph Williamson, Secretary of State, was taken the following day. The detail of her account justifies quoting the abstract from *CSPD* in full:

Examination of Catharine Knight, of the parish of St Giles', widow, taken before Secretary Williamson. The woman who was in her chamber, when the messenger came, and slipped away, lives about Smithfield, but she refuses to tell her name. She had some of the same books, viz., a quartern, from her before, and the money received for them was on the table when the messenger came. The said woman was to have this quartern also now seized with her. She received 32*s*. for the quartern she sold before. She had 150 copies in all of the said book, and this unknown woman had the greatest part of them. She disposed of no copies but to this woman. This woman was with her last night and bought a quartern for which she paid 32*s*. this morning. Being asked again if she disposed of any copies to any but the said woman, she answered she sold 25 or 50 to a certain fat woman who keeps a bookselling shop at the foot of the stone stairs going up to the Court of Requests, and that she and the other woman were the only persons to whom she disposed of any. The fat woman had them at 18*d*. a piece, and paid her 36*s*. in the whole. She carried the copies to the fat woman yesterday sennight, and delivered them to the maid, the mistress being in the shop, in the afternoon. The maid fetched 36*s* and then had the books. She went to the shop and showed one of the books to the mistress and asked if she would buy any, telling her they were 18*d*. a piece. The mistress answered she would tell her maid to pay for them, on which the maid went with the examinate through the Hall in New Palace Yard, where she paid her 36*s*.

> for a quartern she had. She came by the knowledge of this fat woman by the unknown woman, who told her she believed she would have some of them. Asked where she had any of the said copies, she said they were left for her altogether on Saturday sennight at the house where she was taken, in the shop wrapped up in a cloth. Nobody was in the shop but a little boy, the party that brought them laying them down and saying they were for the examinate. The cloth they were lapped up in was a piece of striped stuff. They were in sheets, and were stitched up by herself alone. No person has ever been since to inquire after them or ask money for them. She knows not from whom or whence they came or who left them. Returning home about 10 that morning the little boy told her something was left for her. She was nowhere but at one Bayley's, where she formerly lodged. She never dealt in the dispersing of any books whatever before, and does not know any printer or bookseller. She never acquainted her landlord or anyone else in the house with anything of this matter. The unknown woman, besides what she had last night and was to have had this morning, had about 12 before at 16*d.* a piece. Her landlord is Robert Champ, who keeps a potter's shop at the *Coach and Horses* in St. Giles'. Saturday sennight the unknown woman had some of those books from her the first time. She has known her for several years, but refuses to say on what occasion she first knew her. Meeting her the said Saturday, the examinate told her she had some books to sell, asking if she would have any, and there, going into an alehouse she does not remember, the examinate went home and fetched a parcel of the books, selling them for 16*d.* a piece.[49]

This account of Catharine Knight's examination takes us into the murky and usually invisible world of those who were at the sharp end of L'Estrange's investigations and it provides considerable detail about the chains of distribution which so frustrated his attempts at control. Mrs Knight's claim that 'She had never dealt in the dispersing of any books whatever before, and did not know any printer or bookseller' is presumably disingenuous. But, given the nature of the chain of distribution, it is entirely possible that she never came into contact with a printer or even a bookseller: her copies arrived, apparently anonymously, wrapped in a striped cloth. That she knew what to do with them, however, suggests at least some prior acquaintance with, or instruction in, the process of folding and stitching. She also knew which women would take the copies off her hands. The woman from Smithfield, whom she refused to name and who 'slipped away', was apparently her primary customer, paying 16*d.* per copy; the fat woman with a bookshop at the foot of the stairs (later revealed as a Mrs Breach), to whom she sold fewer copies, is charged a slightly higher price of 18*d.* per copy. The reason for the difference in price is not clear.

Perhaps Mrs Breach, as a later buyer, was charged more because the pamphlet had become much sought after; or perhaps, as friend and primary customer taking most copies, the 'unknown woman' was given a preferential rate. The prices and payments confirm that copies were sold in batches of 25 ['a quartern'] and that for every 25 copies bought the buyer benefited from a slight discount, paying for only 24. Mrs Knight's information accounts for up to 112 of her 150 copies having been sold on: 62 to the anonymous woman from 'about Smithfield' and 25 or 50 to the 'fat woman'.

The inviting detail of this document remained in my notes as an intriguing but frustratingly isolated instance of the practicalities of the distribution of stitched pamphlets. When placed within the run of documents collected for the *Chronology and Calendar*, however, Mrs Knight's evidence takes on a more precise context and the identities of some of her unnamed contacts become clear. On Monday 8 November, the day before the warrant for searching her house was issued, complaint was made to the House of Lords concerning a 'dangerous Book, printed, intituled *A Letter from a Person of Quality to his Friend in the Country*'. The book was ordered to be burnt the following Wednesday (10 November) at the Royal Exchange and in the Old Palace Yard, Westminster and a committee was established 'to enquire out the Author, Publisher, and printer of it'.[50] A warrant was issued to L'Estrange to search and seize all copies and to search for the author, printer or publisher.[51] On the following day (9 November) the book was declared 'a lying, scandalous and seditious Book' by the House of Lords and a Mrs Breach was examined by the Lords' committee, having been caught red-handed selling the book. It seems likely that the warrant issued for the pursuit of Catharine Knight could have arisen from the questioning of Mrs Breach:

> *Mrs. Breach*, whose shop at the stair-foot in Westminster Hall was searched, confessed to having sold a book with this title [i.e. *A letter from a person of quality*] to Mr. Patricius Roberts. It cost her 2*s.* 6*d.*, but she knew not the party she bought it of. Her servant said she saw the book in her mistress' hands, but knew not who brought it to the shop, nor to whom it was sold. She knew not the hawking woman who carried books about.[52]

Mrs Breach was presumably the fat woman who kept a bookshop 'at the foot of the stone stairs going up to the Court of Requests' referred to by Mrs Knight as her second customer. Plomer identifies her with the Mrs Breach who appears in one imprint from 1649, *The controversie concerning liberty of conscience* by John Cotton.[53] Interestingly, Mrs Breach claims here to have paid 2*s.* 6*d.* for the pamphlet, which is presumably less than she sold it for to Roberts; but considerably more than the 18*d.* (1*s.* 6*d.*) per copy Mrs Knight said she was charged. Already the price has jumped by a shilling.

By the next day, 10 November, the bookseller Starkey was being sought by the House of Lords committee concerned and members of the Stationers' Company were required to do their duty by searching for seditious books:

> Ordered ... That the Lords Committees appointed to consider what Brand and Judgement by this House shall be set and given upon a Printed Book, intituled, *A Letter from a Person of Quality to his Friend in the Country*, and to enquire out the Author, Publisher, and printer of it, have hereby Power given them, to send for Persons, Books, and Writings; and in particular Mr. *Starkey*, the Bookseller; and that their Lordships have likewise Power to require the Master and Wardens of the Company of Stationers to do their Duties enjoined by the Statute of 14° *Car'l.* 2^{di}, concerning searching for seditious Books.[54]

There is no record of the Company's compliance in either the *Journal of the House of Lords* or in the Court Books of the Stationers' Company, but documents described by the Historical Manuscripts Commission indicate that the Stationers found two distributors, Mary White and Mrs Jackson, as they reported on 11 November:

> The Master and Wardens of the Stationers' Company, Mr. Collins, and Mr. Mearne, the King's Printer, being called in, said they had found the dispersers: one Mary White, at a coffee-house behind the Exchange, had bought three dozen copies, and six were found upon her. They supposed Mrs. Knight furnished her with them; she sold a large number to Mrs. Jackson, of Charterhouse Lane. The books were wet yesterday; they were too well printed for a private press. The Committee then commanded the Stationers to use their utmost diligence in search. Ordered to report, That the Committee finding the discovery of the author of this book to be a matter of difficulty, do offer to the House whether the House will not think fit to desire His Majesty to issue out a Proclamation promising indemnity to the printer or disperser of the book, who shall first discover the author thereof.[55]

Mrs Jackson of Charterhouse Lane was presumably the woman who 'lived about Smithfield', who had narrowly escaped the Messengers of the Press when they visited Catharine Knight's chamber and who had suggested that Mrs Knight offer copies to Mrs Breach.[56] The speed of distribution is attested by the remark about the sheets being wet the day before. While the evidence points to printing at an established rather than a private press, no pursuit of an individual printer is suggested. In the absence of other evidence an appeal by proclamation, offering indemnity to anyone discovering the author, was the Lords' committee's only suggestion for further action.

The regulation of printing was much on the minds of MPs that week. Thursday 11 November also saw the first reading in the Commons of a Bill for continuing the Licensing Act. Private letters written to Sir Ralph Verney on the same day report the Lords' burning of 'a desperate letter, alias libel, extant about the Test voted seditious' [i.e. *A letter from a person of quality*] and that it was 'first sold for 12*d*., and now valued at 20*s*.'[57] Meanwhile, the Lords' committee concerned about *A letter from a person of quality* was receiving L'Estrange's latest 'Propositions concerning Libels, &c.' in which he turned his attention to the problem of manuscript libels:

Mr. L'Estrange's Propositions concerning Libels, &c. Libels should include Manuscripts, which are more mischievous than prints; for they are commonly so bitter and dangerous that not one in forty ever comes to press, though, by the help of transcripts, they are well nigh as public. For the suppression of prints, a general Warrant from the King in Council, such as he had formerly, would suffice him. With regard to Libels in writing, he remarks that certain stationers are supposed to be the chief and professed dealers in them. When they come to be detected, the common pretence is, 'They were left in my shop,' or 'sent in a letter, I know not by whom,' which is generally a shift. In the former case, the stationers should be ordered to enter a Hall and swear to have nothing to do with Libels; and, secondly, any person receiving a Libel, and not giving notice thereof to a Justice within a certain time, should suffer as an abettor of it; and, on failing to produce the person of whom he had it, he should suffer as the author of it.[58]

L'Estrange's startling proposition that any person in receipt of a libel be punishable *as the author* indicates his increasing desperation in the face of witnesses whose silence prevented him from tracing the chain of distribution.

On 12 November Sir Robert Vyner reported to Williamson on his examination of Mrs White, the woman found by the Stationers' Company to have been dispersing *A letter from a person of quality* at a coffee house behind the Exchange:

He had lately examined Mrs. White about selling the ill pamphlet; in his opinion she was a poor innocent, weak creature, that to get a penny knew not what she did. She had promised to stay the party that brought them, but they had probably taken alarm and did not appear. He requested that mercy be shown towards her, supposing that Williamson had others, more considerable, of whom he could make examples.[59]

Interestingly, Vyner's appeal for mercy towards Mrs White as 'a poor innocent, weak creature' suggests a reluctance to prosecute poor women hawkers which itself no doubt contributed to L'Estrange's increasing sense of frustration.[60] The *lack* of evidence against 'others, more considerable of whom he could make examples' was precisely L'Estrange's problem. Mary White was brought before the Lords' committee the next day, 13 November, by the Master and Wardens of the Stationers' Company. In the face of her professed ignorance, and having summarised the evidence, the Lords' committee gave up:

the Master and Wardens of the Stationers' Company brought with them Mary White. She said she knew not the woman that brought them to her; she had about 3 doz. at 1*s*. apiece. *Mr. Starkey*, the bookseller said he knew nothing about the book. He was asked whether he delivered a bundle of them to Mrs. Breach, who told him that the bishops would persecute him. *Widow Knight* said 150 copies were left at her house; she had sold them all except 30, which Mr. Secretary had. No further proceedings.[61]

That, it would seem, ended the matter and no further investigation is recorded.

What, then, can we conclude from this reading of Catharine Knight's evidence from *CSPD* in the larger context of six days in November 1675 as represented by the *Chronology and Calendar*? First, we now have considerable circumstantial detail about the distribution of offensive pamphlets; the speed with which they were taken from press to stitcher and from stitcher to hawker and bookseller; and the inflationary effect of public condemnation, in this case burning, on the profits to be made from libels. Particularly notable is the role of women in this branch of the trade: fetching and carrying, stitching and distributing, making payments and selling on by hawking around coffee houses and through legitimate book stalls, like Mrs Breach's at the foot of the stairs in Westminster Hall. The investigation netted only those small fry who were closest to the point of sale to the customer and failed completely to find any culpable printer, publisher or author. The desperation of L'Estrange's suggestion that the receiver of a libel be punished as the author of it takes on particular force in such a context. The Stationers' Company apparently played only a small part in the drama and only three Stationers are individually named in the documents. Collins and Mearne (whose zeal in pursuit of his own interest is better attested than his zeal in pursuit of his legal duties) produced Mary White, the hawker, and offered a supposed — but not proved — connection between White and Mrs Knight and Mrs Jackson. John Starkey was the only Stationer named as a suspect, but although he eventually appeared before the House of Lords' committee, his denial of any knowledge of the books was apparently accepted at face value and was not further pursued, presumably because the women distributors insisted on their ignorance of stationers and, consequently, there was no evidence to substantiate suspicions of his involvement.[62] Any hope of uncovering the author was clearly unrealistic. In fact, Locke had left for the Continent shortly after the Lords' judgement on the book was given on 9 November.[63]

Above all, it is clear that when it came to investigations such as this (and comparison can be made, for example, with the 'pyramid selling' of pamphlets organized by Joan Darby and Anna Brewster in 1668[64]), the women who dealt with distribution were, paradoxically, both easy to arrest and difficult to link with the 'real' culprits: authors, printers and booksellers. Particularly telling is Vyner's remark about Mary White, the hawker: 'a poor innocent, weak creature, that to get a penny knew not what she did'. Vyner's assessment might well have been accurate, and the legal pursuit of such a woman would have been fruitless. But examination of other incidents from the Restoration period involving women who were apprehended for dispersing seditious literature has suggested that this perception of their ignorance and innocence was one which women used frequently to their advantage to evade prosecution.[65] Promises from Stationers that the women would be 'saved harmless' can only have served to bolster their silence in the face of questions.[66]

Particularly striking in this single example of an investigation into the circulation of an 'offensive' pamphlet is the social range of those concerned in it. In the space of five days in November 1675 the pursuit touches social levels from poor hawker to King, with the House of Lords, Privy Councillors, Secretaries of State, members of the Stationers' Company, the Surveyor of the Press, Messengers of the Press, gentry in the country, and the customer Patricius Roberts all in some way interested. Most importantly, while shedding light on the distribution and pursuit of libels in general and *A letter from a person of quality* in particular, the dependence of authors and Stationers on those outside the Company and most vulnerable to detection — the distributors, stitchers and hawkers — is brought, for a moment, sharply into focus.

Two suggestions have been offered here as to how the vast mass of evidence collected in the *Chronology and Calendar* might be approached, in order to deepen our understanding of 'offensive' behaviour in the book trade of the period from 1641 to 1700. In making possible the systematic investigation of events and themes across the 60-year period (by sampling, for example, individual years in more detail than has been possible here; or by mapping specific topics such as book burnings, trials of Stationers, arrests of hawkers), it will enable us to test some assumptions about the activities of Stationers and authorities alike. The intention is not that the *Chronology and Calendar* will offer the user a substitute for primary research,[67] but that it will, in McKenzie's words, 'serve as a preliminary narrative to a history of the trade in the Wing period as well as a source for references to anyone whose book-related activities surfaced in the documents.'[68] By acting as index to a concentration of evidence and detail from multiple sources, as demonstrated in the single small example of Catharine Knight, its many narrative strands will alert readers to the ways in which the trade in 'offensive' books was of concern to individuals from every level of society and depended for its success on agents far beyond the ranks of the Stationers' Company.

References

1. I am indebted in particular to Dr Peter Hinds and Dr Andrew Cook for their encouragement and helpful suggestions in response to an earlier draft of this paper; to the Postgraduate Research Seminar of the English Department, University of Birmingham, for lively discussion of some of this material; and to participants in the 25th annual book trade history conference for their penetrating questions and welcome advice.
2. D. F. McKenzie, 'The London Book Trade in 1668', *WORDS: Wai-te-ata Studies in Literature* 4 (1974) pp. 75–92; 'The London Book Trade in 1644', in *Bibliographia: Lectures 1975–1988 by Recipients of the Marc Fitch Prize for Bibliography*, ed. John Hordern (Oxford: Leopard's Head Press, 1992), pp. 131–52. Both are reprinted (in chronological order of writing) in *Making Meaning: 'Printers of the Mind' and other essays*, ed. P. D. McDonald and M. F. Suarez, S.J. (Amherst: University of Massachusetts Press, 2002), pp. 109–25 and pp. 126–43.
3. Sources trawled comprise printed sources (*Calendar of State Papers, Domestic Series* [hereafter *CSPD*]; *Journals of the House of Commons* [*CJ*]; *Journals of the House of Lords* [*LJ*]; *Reports of the Historical Manuscripts Commission* [*HMC*]; contemporary pamphlets) and the manuscript Court Books of the Stationers' Company [SC].

4. A small-scale study to test the extent to which the *Chronology and Calendar* might illuminate the trade of pedlars and hawkers was published as M. Bell, 'Sturdy rogues and vagabonds: Restoration control of pedlars and hawkers', in *The Mighty Engine: the printing press and its impact*, ed. P. Isaac and B. McKay (Winchester and New Castle, Delaware: St Paul's Bibliographies/Oak Knoll Press, 2000), pp. 89–96. That the *Chronology and Calendar* is intended as a *starting point* for research should be stressed: recourse to the original documents, especially those in the Public Record Office, is always to be advised.
5. *CSPD* Chas II, Entry Book 28, f. 94. Throughout the *Chronology and Calendar*, references from *CSPD* give volume and piece number rather than page, to facilitate consultation of original documents in the Public Record Office.
6. *HMC* ix (2) 77–8 g^5; *CSPD* Chas II, v. 366, p. 263.
7. SC E f. 153v. His particular offences in 1682 included 'appearing in the Court Room without his hat and without summons, and ... dining with the Assistants and with the Livery': C. Blagden, *The Stationers' Company: a history, 1403–1959* (London: George Allen & Unwin, 1960) p. 161.
8. He was, perhaps, protected by his relationship with Mearne. The frequent complaints of his foul language and threats by the Court to discipline him, found in the Court Books, are not comprehensively documented in the *Chronology and Calendar.*
9. SC F f. 191.
10. *CJ*, xi. 305–6. The 'not' is clearly an error; the asterisk refers to a footnote in the *CJ* text which reads '*Sic Orig.*'.
11. *LJ* x. 14; *LJ* x. 64.
12. *CJ* v. 695.
13. 21 January 1648, SC C f. 250.
14. SC C f. 252v.
15. SC C f. 253–253v.
16. *CSPD* Council v. I.78, pp. 709–11, no number.
17. *Respondet Petrus*; SC D f. 33.
18. SC D f. 27–8.
19. *CSPD* Chas II, Ent. Book 28, f. 12; *CSPD* Chas II, v. 88, n. 68 (wrongly calendared in *CSPD* as ?1663); *CSPD* Chas II, Ent. Book 30, f. 28.
20. *HMC* xii (7) 60–1, n. 1023; *CSPD* Chas II, v. 248, n. 46.
21. *CSPD* Chas II, v. 236, n. 107 (Rotterdam, 13/23 March).
22. For the suspicions of a press in Blue Anchor Alley, see *CSPD* Chas. II, v. 236, n. 178; v. 237, n. 140; v. 239, n. 5. For the Southwark press, see *CSPD* Chas. II, v. 239, n. 93; v. 248, n. 88; and SC D f. 139v.
23. *CSPD* Chas II, v. 243, n. 181; *CSPD* Chas II, v. 251, n. 196.
24. *CSPD* Chas II, Ent. Book 30, f. 29.
25. *CSPD* Chas II, v. 239, n. 28; SC D f. 139v; *CSPD* Chas II, Ent. Book 30, f. 32.
26. *CSPD* Chas II, Ent. Book 31, f. 8; SC D f. 140.
27. SC D f. 143v.
28. SC D f. 146.
29. A written answer from the Pinmakers confirming that they had no press was demanded, SC D f. 146v.

30. *CSPD* Chas II, v. 403, n. 59; *CSPD* Chas II, Entry Book 334, p. 497.
31. SC D f. 310v/ SC E f. 56; SC D f. 312/ SC E f. 57.
32. *CSPD* Chas II, v. 403, n. 125A; *CSPD* Chas II, v. 403, n. 52.
33. See, for example, the warrant of privileged books prepared for Turner on 15 August 1687, *CSPD* Jas II, 44/337, pp. 339–41.
34. *HMC* vii. 415.
35. *CSPD* Jas II, 44/97, p. 15. As Robin Myers has pointed out to me, Hills's trade dealings had made him many enemies, for whom his catholic sympathies no doubt proved an opportune excuse for revenge.
36. *HMC* xiv (4) 211–12.
37. *CSPD* Jas II, 44/338, p. 159.
38. For an argument that legislation controlling hawkers and pedlars was in part a response to the distribution of 'seditious' pamphlets, see Bell, 'Sturdy rogues and vagabonds: Restoration control of pedlars and hawkers'.
39. The reference is either to John Darby, still alive at this date, or possibly to his son of the same name. CSPD W&M, 44/349, p. 95.
40. The incident of Dyer's sermons is described in John Hetet, 'The Wardens' Accounts of the Stationers' Company, 1663–79', in *Economics of the British Book Trade 1605–1939*, ed. R. Myers and M. Harris (Cambridge: Chadwyck-Healey, 1985), pp. 32–59, esp. pp. 51–2.
41. 3 August, *CSPD* Chas II, v. 244, n. 77.
42. *CSPD* Chas II, v. 281A, n. 260, dated ?1670.
43. 3 August 1671, SC D f. 187.
44. 23 May 1673, SC D f. 215v.
45. 29 March 1675, *CSPD* Chas II, v. 369, n. 97. All three reported as deceased.
46. More than twenty years later, in 1698, a warrant was issued for searching Darby's house and for his arrest for a seditious pamphlet (November 1698, *CSPD* W&M, 44/349, p. 95).
47. CSPD Home Office, Warrant Book 1, p. 89.
48. Usually attributed to either Shaftesbury or Locke; or possibly a collaboration between the two. See K. H. D. Haley, *The First Earl of Shaftesbury* (Oxford: Clarendon Press, 1968) pp. 391–3 for a discussion of the possibility of collaboration.
49. *CSPD* Chas II, v. 374, n. 261. A copy of the examination, read before the Lords' Committee on 11 November, is annexed at *HMC* ix (2) 66. I am grateful to Peter Hinds for checking the *CSPD* abstract against the PRO original and confirming that nothing of substance has been omitted or altered. A warrant for the arrest of Robert Champ, keeper of a potter's shop, and of his wife and 'a little boy usually in the shop' was issued on 10 November (*CSPD* Chas II, Home Office, Warrant Book 1, p. 90). I have found no record of their examination.
50. *LJ* xiii. 13.
51. *CSPD* Home Office, Warrant Book 1, p. 89.
52. *HMC* ix (2) 66 (Lords Com. Book).
53. Henry R. Plomer, *A Dictionary of the Booksellers and Printers who were at work … from 1641 to 1667* (London: Bibliographical Society, 1907), p. 31; Wing C6421.
54. *LJ* xiii. 17.

55. *HMC* ix (2) 66 (Lords Com. Book).
56. For the proximity of Smithfield and Charterhouse see *The A to Z of Restoration London*, with introductory notes by Ralph Hyde and index compiled by John Fisher and Roger Cline (London: London Topographical Society, 1992), sheet 14.
57. 11 November, *HMC* vii. 466–7 and 493.
58. *HMC* ix (2) 66 (Lords Com. Book, Annexed).
59. *CSPD* Chas II, v. 374, n. 281.
60. On the cultural and legal inhibitions which made the prosecution of women in the book trade difficult, see M. Bell, 'Elizabeth Calvert and the "Confederates" ', *Publishing History*, 32 (1992), pp. 5–49.
61. *HMC* ix (2) 66 (Lords Com. Book).
62. Starkey had been arrested in 1673 on a warrant from Lord Arlington and was refused bail on 5 December: *CSPD* Chas. II, v. 388, n. 48.
63. Haley, *The First Earl of Shaftesbury*, p. 392.
64. See Bell, 'Elizabeth Calvert and the "Confederates" '.
65. *Ibid.* and see M. Bell, 'Women and the Opposition Press after the Restoration', in *Writing and Radicalism*, ed. J. Lucas (London: Longman, 1996), pp. 39–60.
66. Bell, 'Elizabeth Calvert and the "Confederates" '.
67. Its reliance, for example, on printed sources such as *CSPD* and *HMC*, whose abstracting practices are erratic and sometimes unreliable, means that the *Chronology and Calendar* can be no substitute for a full reading of the original documents.
68. D. F. McKenzie, 'Prefatory Note' in 'A Chronology and Calendar of Documents relating to the London Book Trade 1641–1700, vol. I 1641–1660', bound typescript (1989) deposited with the British Library, Bodleian Library and Cambridge University Library.

Crimes of Conscience: the last will and testament of John Dunton

HELEN BERRY

THIS CHAPTER HIGHLIGHTS the role of the late-Stuart publisher and bookseller John Dunton in documenting sharp practice in the English and Irish book trades, which he witnessed first-hand in his business dealings, and to which he himself contributed. One document in particular — Dunton's will — reveals in detail certain controversial episodes in his life; in this document, Dunton retrospectively scrutinized his own conduct and the treatment that he had received from others. The will is thus an important source for the biographical details of Dunton's life, but, beyond this, it provides the modern reader with insights into the often fraught relationships between late-Stuart authors, publishers and booksellers. This chapter also examines one particular episode of skulduggery that Dunton exposed in print in *The Dublin Scuffle* (1699), in which he anatomizes his ill-treatment at the hands of the Dublin bookseller Patrick Campbell.

Dunton's chief interest to posterity is as an innovator in the book trade. An editor and publisher, as well as bookseller, he was the first to apply the name 'conger' to the wholesaling associations which he observed developing in the book trade at this time, although he remained on the fringes of this activity.[1] He was also the author of numerous political and satirical pamphlets, and pioneered a new type of periodical in question-and-answer format, the *Athenian Mercury* (later developed in the *British Apollo*).[2] Another of Dunton's achievements is his rambling autobiography, *The Life and Errors of John Dunton, Late Citizen of London* (1705), which provides a unique resource for historians of the book trade in late-Stuart London, with its thumbnail biographical sketches of the men and women engaged in the trade who were known personally to the author.

A brief synopsis of Dunton's biography will serve as a useful reminder (even for those to whom this reasonably well-known bookseller is no stranger) of the details of his life and career. Born in Huntingdonshire in 1659, he was the son of the Revd John Dunton, who later became rector of Aston Clinton in Buckinghamshire.[3] He did not receive a university education, and confounded the family tradition by taking up an apprenticeship in 1674 with the Presbyterian bookseller Thomas Parkhurst. It was this period of his life about which Dunton was most regretful in later life — a time when drinking, falling in love, and organizing feasts with fellow Whig apprentices was his only concern. He married Elizabeth Annesley in 1682, and set up shop at the sign of the Black Raven in the Poultry. The 1680s were turbulent years for dissenters, and Dunton's close association with his Presbyterian in-laws led him into difficulty (his father-in-law was Dr Samuel Annesley, the ejected minister of St Giles Cripplegate, whose congregation included Daniel Defoe). He stood as security for the debts of his sister-in-law Bithiah Bishop, Susannah Wesley's sister, and was forced to leave the country when her creditors demanded repayment. Thus began a series of 'rambles' in continental Europe and the New World. In 1685 he tried to restore his fortune by setting off to Boston to reclaim £500 which was owed to him there, taking with him his apprentice, Samuel Palmer, and a cargo of books. Dunton's venture was a success (owing largely to the diligence of Palmer): his books were bought by the young men of Harvard; he met Cotton and Increase Mather; and he returned to England in 1686 with a history of the Salem witch trials (which later became a bestseller) and a copy of the Bible in Algonquin, the first translation into a native American language.

In 1687 Dunton was off rambling again, this time in the Low Countries, travelling as far as Cologne and Mainz before his return in 1688. All this time, Elizabeth ran his warehouse while he was away, managing the business to some profit. On his return, Dunton enjoyed his most successful years. He started to publish Whig propaganda, with *The Bloody Assizes* (1689), and his *Voyage Round the World* (1691), an account of the travels of 'Don Kainophilus', which was later said to have influenced Laurence Sterne's most famous creation, *Tristram Shandy*. Also in 1691, Dunton started to publish the *Athenian Mercury*, his 'question project' where coffee-house readers were invited to send their questions on any subject to the 'Athenian Society' (in reality, only Dunton, Richard Sault and Samuel Wesley). The project ran successfully for nearly six years. In 1692, Dunton was made free of the Stationers' Company, and his career was riding high. He was associated briefly with the Reformation of Manners campaign, printing *Proposals for a National Reformation of Manners* (1694), but also the somewhat questionable *Night-Walker; Or, Evening Rambles in*

Search after Lewd Women (1696). Then, in 1697, Elizabeth died, and Dunton's fortunes took a turn for the worse.

Throughout his career, the bookseller had vexed close friends with his tendency to publish what they considered to be private confidences, alienating first Samuel Wesley, with whom he had collaborated closely in compiling the *Athenian Mercury*, and then his friend the hymn-writer Isaac Watts, who instructed Dunton not to write to him any more, since, he reasoned, 'there's no writing to a Man that prints every Thing'.[4] Dunton lacked discretion in failing to moderate the subject of his printed works to take into account the sensibilities of family and friends: this was not sharp practice as such, but a boorish want of tact. Of this he appears to have been largely oblivious, even as he fell deeper into debt and destitution from the late 1690s.

Following a disastrous second marriage to Sarah Nichols in 1697, Dunton used the press to issue public denunciations of his new mother-in-law, Mrs Jane Nichols of St Albans, when she refused to pay off his debts. Shortly afterwards, he attempted to offset his losses by going to Ireland, a disastrous trip that harmed both his pocket and his reputation, and was the subject of *The Dublin Scuffle* (1699). Worn down by these failures, he announced that he was retiring from business for ever, 'But as to Printing much on my own Risque, I've down [*sic*] with it,' he wrote to his second wife Sarah, only half-seriously, warning her in the light of their personal difficulties that he *would* consider printing 'a short Essay upon *New Marriage*'.[5]

In 1705, Dunton published his retrospective *Life and Errors,* after which the quality of his published output started to decline. He produced several spin-offs from his Athenian project, and numerous political pamphlets, latterly professing himself a loyal subject to the Hanoverian princes. He successfully petitioned George I for a token of recognition for services rendered, which he duly received in the form of a gold medal, but one gets the impression that by this stage his fortunes had begun seriously to decline, separated from his second wife, living in a series of lodgings and spending some time in the Fleet Prison for debt. Stephen Parks found that it was during Dunton's incarceration in June 1711 that he made his will, perhaps in fear that he would never leave the debtors' prison alive, an intimation of mortality that was possibly exacerbated by news of the burial in the same month of his former master, Thomas Parkhurst.[6] Upon his release from prison, Dunton published one more notable pamphlet, *Neck or Nothing* (1713), a reply to Sir Robert Walpole's interpretation of parliamentary history.[7] He died in reduced circumstances on 24 November 1732.

Estimating the size of Dunton's estate at the time he made his will, and at the time of his death, is problematic. In his will, he mentions his claim upon some valuable fixed assets, notably property in the form of his share of the Dunton family's claim upon various lands and property in Buckinghamshire, over which he seems to have lost control well before his death. In 1708, Dunton had estimated that his personal estate was worth £4,000, including his expected inheritance of farmland at Chesham, with an additional £6,000 owed to him in rents from tenants, and loans from relatives.[8] However, by 1711 he was unable to pay a debt of £110 owed to Thomas Darrack, the printer of *Athenianism* and the *Athenian News: Or, Dunton's Oracle*, and this resulted in his incarceration. It is noteworthy that he bequeathed in his will whatever 'Lands, Woods, or Houses', of an unspecified value, had descended to him in Little Missenden, Chesham and other Buckinghamshire parishes, to his executrix, Maria Jones and her heirs, rather than to his blood kin on his father's side, from whom he stated he was more or less estranged. In any case, by this time the fixed assets that he had inherited were not at his own disposal: Dunton also confessed that he had long since mortgaged his 'Several Estates in Land' to John Hall, a Norwich merchant, as security for a 'bargain of Woods he bought of me' and a loan of money.[9] The proposed disposal of his fixed assets in his will was therefore more of a statement of intent: his blood relatives were not to receive his lands, were he ever in a position to buy them back.

The disposal of movable goods was another matter, and there is new archival evidence that provides details of what was found in Dunton's lodgings and on his person at the time of his death. It was unusual, though not unprecedented, that no probate inventory was compiled following the bookseller's death in 1732. The reason for the lack of a probate inventory is not given (even though a second executor, Richard Nowland, had been appointed to replace Maria Jones, who predeceased Dunton). Instead, a 'Declaration instead of an Inventory of all and Singular the Goods Chattells and Credits of John Dunton' was compiled, which listed Dunton's possessions (Fig. 1 and Appendix). The Declaration may not have been comprehensive: one notable omission is his considerable collection of books, which were auctioned separately (see below). This

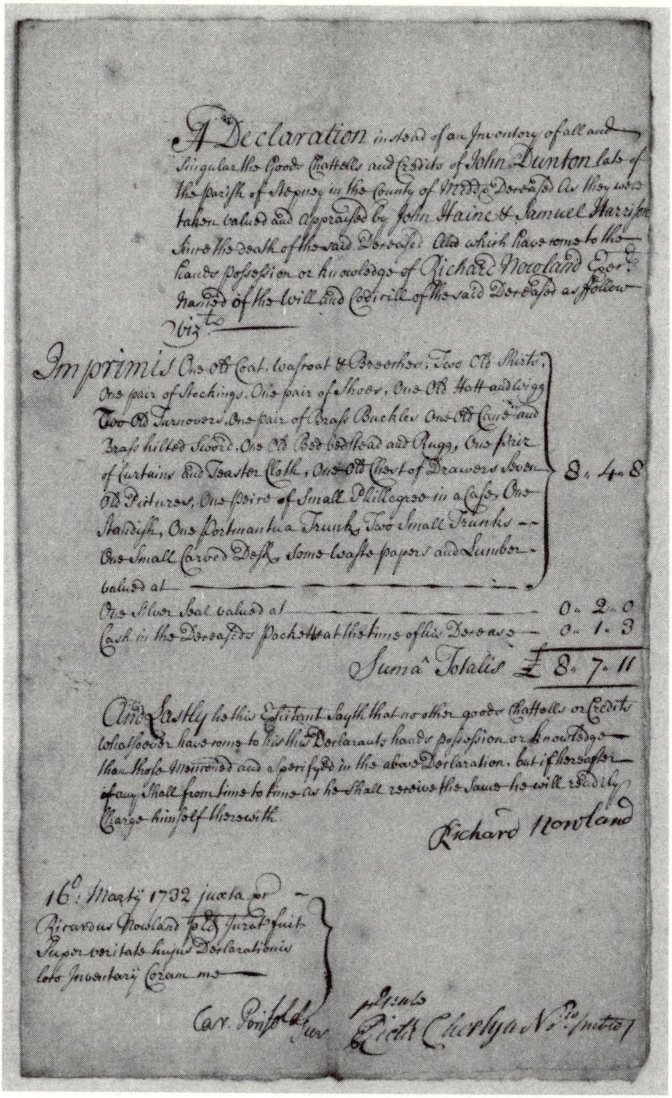
A Declaration instead of an Inventory of all and Singular the Goods Chattells and Credits of John Dunton late of the parish of Stepney in the County of Midd[x] Deceased As they were taken valued and appraised by John Haine & Samuel Harrison Since the death of the said Deceased And which have come to the hands possession or knowledge of Richard Nowland Exor named of the will and Codicill of the said Deceased as follow viz[t]

Imprimis One Old Coat, Wastcoat & Breeches, Two Old Shirts, One pair of Stockings, One pair of Shoes, One Old Hatt and Wigg, Two Old Turnovers, One pair of Brass Buckles, One Old Cane and Brass hilted Sword, One Old Bed bedstead and Rugg, One pair of Curtains and Tester Cloth, One Old Chest of Drawers, Seven Old Pictures, One paire of Small Phillegree in a Case, One Standish, One Portmantua Trunk, Two Small Trunks — One Small Carved Desk, Some waste papers and Lumber valued at — 8. 4. 8

One Silver Seal valued at — 0. 2. 0

Cash in the Deceaseds Pockett at the time of his Decease — 0. 1. 3

Suma Totalis £ 8. 7. 11

And Lastly he this Exhibitant Sayth that no other goods Chattells or Credits whatsoever have come to his this Declarants hands possession or knowledge than those Mentioned and specifyed in the above Declaration, but if hereafter if any Shall from time to time As he Shall receive the Same he will readily Charge himself therewith.

Richard Nowland

16° Martij 1732 juxta pr Ricardus Nowland pred[ictus] Jurat[us] fuit Super veritate hujus Declarationis loco Inventarij Coram me

Cav. Ponsfold Sur

Presente Rich[ar]d Cherlyn No[ta]rio Pub[lic]o

Fig. 1. A Declaration of John Dunton's goods at the time of his death, dated 16 March 1732/3. Reproduced courtesy of The National Archives (PROB 31/114/216)

document allows us to establish for the first time that Dunton's ready cash and movable goods in his lodgings at the time of his death (minus his books) came to only £8.7*s*.11*d*., including the sum of 1*s*.3*d*. that was found 'in the Deceaseds pocketts at the time of his Decease'. What happened to his fixed assets (mortgaged as they were) is less certain, but it is doubtful, given his lack of publishing output in the last two decades of his life, whether he was able to raise sufficient funds to pay off his mortgage to Hall before his death.

Given the problems of assessing his exact financial position in relation to his debts, Dunton's will is less revealing as an accurate account of the value of his estate in 1711 (let alone at the time of his death in 1732), than as a personal record of his attempt to set his affairs in order in anticipation of his death. An unusual feature of Dunton's will is that he wrote it himself, rather than summoning a public notary (see Fig. 2).[10] The original sixteen-page document (written on both sides of eight, badly-worn half-folio sheets) was signed on 21 June 1711, and has many extraordinary features — not least its length and complexity.[11] It is approximately ten to fifteen times longer than other wills by middling-sort testators proved in the Prerogative Court of Canterbury at this time.[12] There are two short codicils — the first dated 10 September 1729, the second witnessed on 22 December 1729, appointing Dunton's landlord Richard Nowland, a weaver of the parish of St Dunstan, Stepney, his executor following the death of his original executrix, his friend Maria Jones.[13] When Dunton died in November 1732, his second executor was still living, but there is a marginal note at the foot of the will, dated 27 June 1744, indicating that at some time during the intervening years the new executor Richard Nowland had also died, and that the will had not yet been administered by this late stage (the deaths of Jones and Nowland were no doubt the main contributory factors to the delay in administering the will). Finally, twelve years after Dunton's death, the administration of his will was completed by Thomas Darrack, who was presumably the same creditor who had initiated Dunton's imprisonment in 1711.

Some aspects of Dunton's will conform to normal features of a legal document produced at this time — in a short preamble, the testator leaves his soul to Almighty God, before embarking upon a detailed account of his beneficiaries and intended legacies. Very quickly, however, Dunton departed from formulaic wording and began to resort to his usual mode of authorship, opening up a stream of consciousness about his life and career

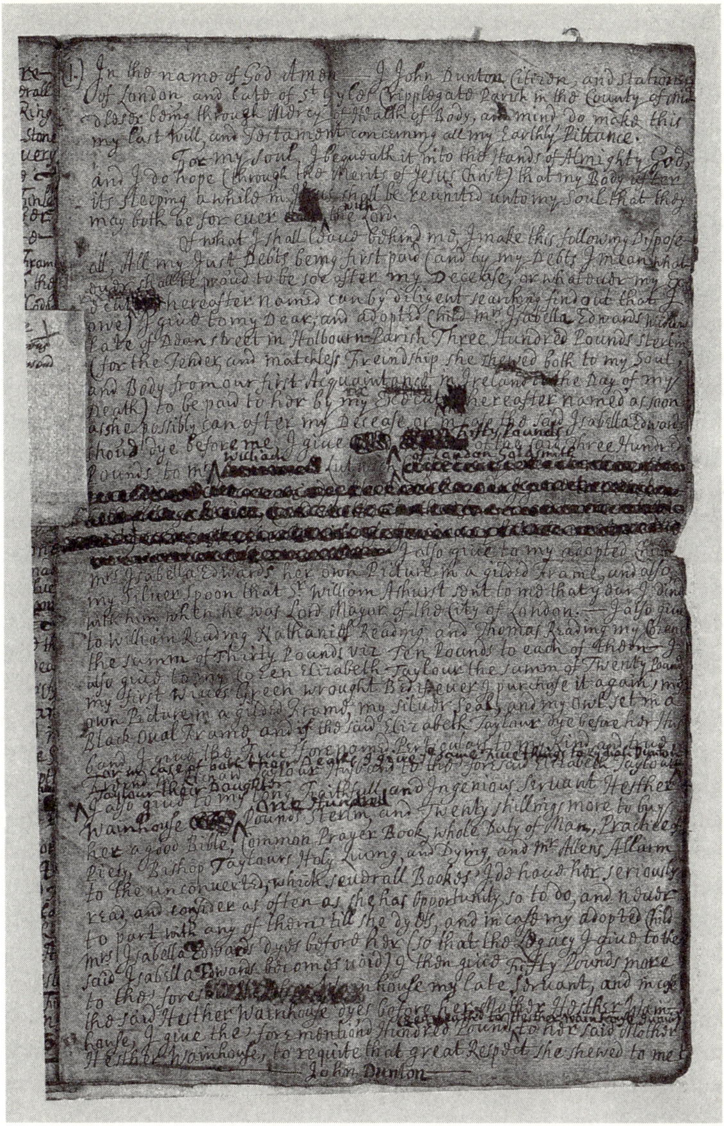

(1.) In the name of God Amen — I John Dunton Citizen, and Stationer of London and late of St Gyles Cripplegate Parish in the County of Middlesex being through Mercy of Health of Body, and mind do make this my last Will, and Testament concerning all my Earthly Pittance.

For my Soul, I bequeath it into the Hands of Almighty God, and I do hope (through the Merits of Jesus Christ) that my Body after its sleeping a while in [illegible] shall be reunited unto my Soul that they may both be for ever with the Lord.

Of what I shall leave behind me, I make this following Dispose-all, All my Just Debts being first paid (and by my Debts I mean what ever shall be proved to be soe after my Decease, or what ever my Ex[illegible] hereafter named can by diligent searching find out that I owe) I give to my Dear, and adopted Child Mrs Isabella Edwards Widow late of Dean street in Holbourn Parish Three Hundred Pounds Sterling (for the Tender, and matchless Freindship she shewed both to my Soul, and Body from our first Acquaintance in Ireland to the Day of my Death) to be paid to her by my Executor hereafter named as soon as she possibly can after my Decease, or in case the said Isabella Edwards should dye before me I give [illegible] Fifty Pounds of the said Three Hundred Pounds to Mr William [illegible] of London Goldsmith [illegible]

[illegible]

I also give to my adopted Child Mrs Isabella Edwards her own Picture in a gilded Frame, and also my Silver Spoon that Sr William Ashurst sent to me that day I dined with him when he was Lord Mayor of the City of London. — I also give to William Reading Nathaniel Reading and Thomas Reading my [illegible] the summ of Thirty Pounds viz Ten Pounds to each of them — I also give to my Cozen Elizabeth Taylour the summ of Twenty Pounds my first Wives Green wrought Bed [illegible], my own Picture in a gilded Frame, my Silver Seal, and my Owl set in a Black Oval Frame, and if the said Elizabeth Taylour dye before her Hus[band] I give the Fore-named Particulars [illegible] Taylour their Daughter. I also give to my Loving Faithfull and Ingenious Servant Hesther Wainhouse One Hundred Pounds Sterling, and Twenty shillings more to buy her a good Bible, Common Prayer Book, whole Duty of Man, Practice of Piety, Bishop Taylours Holy Living, and Dying, and Mr Allens Allarm to the unconverted, which severall Books, I do hope she'll seriously read, and consider as often as she has Opportunity so to do, and never to part with any of them till she dyes, and in case my adopted Child Mrs Isabella Edwards dyes before her (so that the Legacy I give to the said Isabella Edwards becomes void) I then give Fifty Pounds more to the foresaid Hesther Wainhouse my late Servant, and in case the said Hesther Wainhouse dyes before her Mother Hesther Wainhouse, I give the fore mentiond Hundred Pounds to her said Mother Hesther Wainhouse, to requite that great Respect she shewed to me

John Dunton

Fig. 2. The first page of John Dunton's original will, dated 21 June 1711 and written in his own hand. Reproduced courtesy of The National Archives (PROB 10/1786/f. 1)

that echoes his earlier autobiography. In his will, he weaves a narrative of his life and reflects upon his attitude towards death, revealed in the lengthy instructions he gives for his funeral arrangements, including the details of a receipt in his possession for the purchase of a substantial elm coffin 'with a Double Lidd Covered with Cloth set of[f] with black Nails'. There are also instructions for his funeral sermon, which was to have been preached by Samuel Burgess, whom he exhorted to set 'my whole Life Conversation and Writings in a true light the World may see (notwithstanding ... my many great Sins, and Infirmities) my Sincere Respect to all good Men of whatsoever perswasion.'[14] Cousins, distant relatives and servants receive bequests of between 20 shillings and £100. Significantly, Dunton left the main portion of his movable assets, not to blood kin, but to Isabella Edwards, whom he calls his 'adopted daughter'. Isabella was to have received £300, her picture in a gilt frame, and a silver spoon.[15] He also left five pounds to Mrs Elizabeth Slash, a pastry cook in Highgate, whom he calls his 'adopted Mother', having lost his own mother, Lydia, at a young age. One can see how, as this document unfolded, Dunton was prompted to rewind his life history, to remember schoolfriends and people who had done him small services and 'kindnesses' throughout his life. The author goes back at length over his travels, illnesses, working career, and personal struggles. He names, for example, no fewer than 35 people who were each to receive ten shillings for a mourning ring — including his second wife Sarah, for whom this was to be her only legacy. In each section of his will, the conjuring of a name brings back a recollection; usually brief and scant in detail, but occasionally prompting entire pages of digression. What emerges from this extraordinary document are the two greatest regrets which remained with Dunton in middle age: the first was his remarriage, which appears to have been undertaken solely for financial motives; the second, an episode which had troubled him for many years, was his treatment of his former master, Thomas Parkhurst.

Dunton's feelings about his second marriage are expressed in his will through repetitive requests to be buried, not with Sarah, but alongside his first wife, Elizabeth, to whom he gave the pet name of Iris. He composed the following epitaph for their joint tombstone, which he recited in his will:

I'm come to bed, having lost my Pen, and Sight,
To Sleep with Iris in her Cell this Night,
And leaving all for her, will never take
Another Farewell 'till our Ashes wake.[16]

Sadly, there is no evidence that his final wish to be buried next to his first wife in the nonconformist burial ground at Bunhill Fields was ever carried out.

Dunton used his will to give instructions on the settlement of unresolved issues that troubled his conscience, both large and small. For example, among various small debts was his obligation to the widow and children of Caleb Leader, a former member of his father-in-law's congregation, to whom he bequeathed five pounds for the widow, and five pounds for Leader's child or children, 'if the said Caleb Leader ever lent me any Books which I did not return to him'.[17] He also instructed his executrix to ensure that a 'Manuscript Book of Essayes, and that other Manuscript concerning the Materialls of a Ship' be returned to one Peirce Fineux, 'a Gentleman living in Canterbury', with instructions to 'forgive' him the 'considerable Summ of Money he owes me'.[18] It is here that we come to Dunton's account of an outstanding debt of greater magnitude — his account of his dealings with Thomas Parkhurst. Based upon the evidence of this document, it appears that Dunton cheated his master while he was an apprentice, and that the material debts he owed him were never repaid. A quotation from this section of the will conveys a sense of the anxiety which Parkhurst's former apprentice felt over this subject:

Further it is my Will that my Executrix pay to Mr Thomas Parkhurst (the Master with whom I serv'd my Seven Years Apprenticeship) the Sum of Fifty Pounds Sterlin which Fifty I wou'd have her pay to him (or in case of his death to his Heirs or Executors) out of the first Moneys [s]he shall receive either for my Land or Personall Estate ... on the Account of certain Losses which the said Thomas Parkhurst received by me (during the whole Time of my Apprenticeship with him) at various Times (I know not how many times, or what were the Exact Losses he received by me) I never cou'd Satisfye my Self what they were, or probably they had bin long since discharg'd, for I gave my First Wife Elizabeth Dunton positive Orders to do it, when I went to Boston in New-England, but she thinking the Losses Mr Thomas Parkhurst Sustained by me not so considerable as I did deferr'd doing of it so when I came home again I thought it necessary to leave them as a Debt upon my Estate....[19]

And on it goes, in similar vein, for another two pages. The exact nature of these debts, as Stephen Parks has argued, rests upon Dunton's admission in his will that he was guilty of 'Over-rating my Fathers Library', that is, persuading Parkhurst to buy his father's library for an inflated price, which was then sold in an auction organized by Parkhurst on 29 November 1680.[20] Whether he concealed defects in the books belonging to his father, or kept the most valuable books for himself is unknown: Dunton mentions only the cost to Parkhurst, which he estimated in his will at about £40. He raised the sum to be repaid to Parkhurst's family to £50, 'Obliged in conscience to see them [i.e. his debts] paid and consequently the very Interest money due for them wou'd amount to something considerable from the first time these debts were contracted to this time' (a span of nearly four decades). Such was Dunton's bad conscience over the matter, that he continued to specify in detail the means of repayment: 'I ... desire my Executrix to be very Exact in finding out the time when I first went and was first bound Apprentice to Mr Thomas Parkhurst that so neither Mr Thomas Parkhurst (or in case of his death that his Heirs or Executors) may receive no manner of Loss or Dammage as to the length of time for which I have been his Debtor, for the Several unknown Sums (and Interest for them).'[21] He describes the time of his apprenticeship to Parkhurst as 'the best of my Life', although 'I was mistaken and mislead by Temptations in my Apprenticeship'. Dunton reflects at length upon this episode and his guilt, in a manner that assumes the didactic tones of someone addressing a wider audience than his immediate heirs (which is perhaps an indication that he may have thought that his will would be published one day):

> reflecting upon these unknown Debts to Mr Thomas Parkhurst, I wou'd therefore advise all Persons (but more especially Apprentices) to receive the Holy Sacrament of the Lords Supper very young for I verily think had I received it whilst I liv'd under my Reverend Fathers Roofe it wou'd have been a Guard against my contracting these unknown Debts to Mr. Thomas Parkhurst which have bin the greatest Burthen of my life....[22]

Having now laid the blame upon his father, as well as his first wife, for not preventing or mitigating his crime, Dunton goes on to say that the guilt he felt over this matter prevented him from taking communion for many years (even though his adopted daughter Isabella Edwards pressed him to do so), a serious step for an avowedly religious man, by which Dunton entered into a form of self-imposed social ostracism as punishment for his sins.[23] Finally, he urged his executrix not to acquaint anyone of this repayment. He also, intriguingly, adds 'this request I make [so] that

Fig. 3. The last page of Dunton's original will, showing his signature and those of the witnesses. Reproduced courtesy of The National Archives (PROB 10/1786/f. 16)

Religion (which is a Reall and Serious thing) may never be evil spoken of on the Account of any youthfull Slips, or mistakes of mine.'[24] Perhaps he had in mind here the moral debt of a young Anglican to an upright Presbyterian, who, had he known of his apprentice's errors, might have thought it confirmation of the corrupting influence of established religion.

At the heart of Dunton's life, then, was the knowledge that he had jeopardized his reputation even before he began his career as a bookseller, owing to his unscrupulous conduct towards his former master, whom he greatly respected. Worse than the possibility of these crimes being discovered, perhaps, was Dunton's own sense of guilt. It is this part of his history which should inform our interpretation of all Dunton's subsequent attempts to bolster his own credit through his published works and private correspondence. As a bookseller, it took considerable effort to maintain a reputation for creditworthiness and honest dealing, and what appear to us to have been trivial slights, to the contemporary man of business could have been a serious threat to his livelihood.[25] In his printed works and private papers, Dunton revealed his own concern to preserve his reputation as an honest trader, even posthumously. A bibliophile and bookseller all his life, Dunton devoted some thought and care to the disposal of his books in his will (perhaps mindful of his own duplicity in disposing of his father's library), for he expressed particular concern that they should be disposed of honestly:

> I also give to my Kind and worthy Freind [*sic*] Mr Daniel Waghorn of Noble Street, near Old Street Ten pounds.... I also give to the forementioned Daniell Waghorn my whole Library of Bookes both Bound and Sticht that are now to be found in that Closet which he made for me [obscured word], provided he promises to my Executrix, hereafter named never to sell any Book, or Pamphlet out of the said Library without first examining whether it be Perfect or not (I having a great many Bound and Sticht Books Imperfect) that so no person may be wrong'd that purchases any of them.[26]

Waghorn, it seems, was not expected to keep the books or sell them for his own profit, but to act as their custodian. Further on in the will, Dunton gives his brother-in-law, John Sudbury, a watchmaker, his 'Library of Books before bequeathed to Mr Daniel Waghorn provided upon Mr Daniel Waghorns delivering the said Library of Books to him my Brother Sudbury will pay to him down in ready Money Ten pounds'.[27] We do know from a contemporary sale catalogue that Dunton's library was sold on 23 April 1733, though the amalgamation of his books with another library makes it difficult to establish the provenance and exact value of the books he owned, or whether the books constituted his personal library, stock in trade, or a combination of the two.[28]

It is here, in the context of Dunton's introspective musings on his own sharp practice, that we turn to consider one particular episode which reveals much about his obsession with maintaining an honest reputation: Dunton's experiences in Ireland, as described in his own words in *The Dublin Scuffle* (1699). This sequence of events also illustrates the rivalries between English and Irish publishers and booksellers in a period of intensifying competition in the expanding early modern book trade. The background was Dunton's fortunate experience of New England during the 1680s, when he was warmly received in Boston. This trip encouraged Dunton to believe, mistakenly, that he could repeat the experiment over a decade later in Ireland. In 1698, the year after Elizabeth's death and his hasty remarriage, when his new mother-in-law proved reluctant to settle his debts, Dunton's plan was to generate an alternative source of income by exporting a 'General Collection' of miscellaneous books to Dublin. He intended to hold a series of auctions at Dick's Coffee-House in Skinner Row, with sale catalogues distributed at the coffee-houses in Limerick, Cork, Kilkenny, Clonmel, Wexford and Galway.[29] Dublin, however, was not Boston, and many of his rivals in the book trade were less than welcoming.

In the early decades of the seventeenth century, Irish booksellers had relied upon the import of foreign printed material via general merchants, since there was a tight restriction upon printers in Ireland. Only one printer was at work in Dublin at any one time between 1551, when the first book was printed in Ireland, and 1680.[30] However, in 1680, the monopoly of the King's Printer over domestically-printed items was broken by the Dublin bookseller Joseph Ray, and by the 1690s the city had developed a tightly-knit community of printers as well as booksellers.[31] These now began to resist the incursion of London booksellers on their patch. Known for their independence, and for producing pirated copies of books sold in London, the Dublin booksellers concentrated mainly upon expanding Irish markets. By 1700, there were at least six printers operating in the city, and perhaps as many as seventeen stationers (to judge from the names appearing in guild records and in the imprints of Dublin-printed books).[32] In terms of international competition, as James Raven has argued, the

Dublin booksellers 'had more to fear from London booksellers than London booksellers had to fear from them'.[33]

Auctions, as Giles Mandelbrote has observed elsewhere, had always generated controversy as a method of selling books.[34] What irked the Dublin book trade was the way in which Dunton's arrival personally brought competition to their doorstep. Dunton's *bête noir*, Patrick Campbell, was a Freeman of the Dublin Guild of Cutlers, Painter-Stainers and Stationers, and had a bookshop at the sign of the Blue Bible in Skinner Row, near to Dick's Coffee-House.[35] Campbell was a Scots Presbyterian, and courted controversy with his publications on religion and politics. The publisher of over twenty books and pamphlets before 1701, in 1688 he was listed with those rebels who had fled from Ireland before 5 November, and narrowly missed being condemned as a traitor. In 1698, the year of his 'Dublin Scuffle' with Dunton, Campbell attached the wrong titlepage to one of his publications, selling as 'Cockers Arithm[etic]' copies of what was in fact another mathematical treatise, 'Hodders Arithmetick', and thereby deceiving his customers by accident (as he claimed) or design.[36] Later, in 1710, Campbell was brought before the grand jury in Dublin for selling London copies of 'the St. Germain Letter found at Douay, and Queries to new Hereditary Right-Men'.[37] Whether Campbell was really the unscrupulous bully that Dunton made him out to be is debatable, but he was clearly someone who possessed the ability to weather adversity, which was a necessary part of being a bookseller at this time.

The precise details of their rift are as follows. In *The Dublin Scuffle*, Dunton described in epistolary style how he appointed his friend Richard Wilde to organize and conduct three book auctions on his behalf in Dublin, starting on 7 July 1698. The timing of this was significant: as Michael Harris has shown, there was a seasonal pattern to the London book auctions, with a scaling down of activities in June and July, and a complete hiatus in August and September.[38] Dunton probably took advantage of this summer sabbatical in the timing of his Dublin venture. Upon arrival in Ireland, however, he decided to take the waters at Wexford rather than conduct the planned Dublin auctions himself. Dunton no doubt thought his business was in good hands: Wilde was a bookseller, auctioneer and printer, a Londoner based in Dublin who also had close connections with the publishing houses of Skinner Row. (Later, Wilde was remembered in Dunton's will as 'the Chief Manager of all the Auctions I made at Dublin', with a legacy of 'Five pounds as an Acknowledgement of the extraordinary Services he did me in procuring books for me in London and Selling of them for me in Ireland').[39]

Another figure in the Dublin episode was Dunton's erstwhile friend George Larkin, who acted as both agent, proof-reader and general factotum. A letter from Larkin to Dunton written in 1703 survives among the Rawlinson manuscripts in the Bodleian Library, and gives an idea of their working relationship. In that year, Larkin was engaged in correcting the proofs of Dunton's *Athenian Oracle,* and the two were evidently on intimate terms: Larkin expressed sympathy that his employer was afflicted with piles and the stone, and engaged in a playful mock-heroic exchange of news, referring to his own wife Mrs Larkin as 'the Marchioness'.[40] Larkin predeceased Dunton, but the bookseller showed his gratitude by bequeathing to his son, George Larkin junior, ten pounds in honour of the man 'whose Memory, and Children will be ever Dear to me upon the Account Civil'.[41]

The course of these auctions in Dublin (the third and last of which took place on 7 November 1698) sheds much light on the range of dubious practices in which booksellers engaged at this time. Dunton assured the gentlemen scholars of Ireland that, had he been allowed to proceed as planned, honesty would have characterized his auction, the implication being that this was not usually the case. If a gentleman had come to buy a pennyworth of books from him, so Dunton said, he would have ensured that the price would not have been artificially raised by '*Underhand Bidding*'; nor would he have allowed his '*scarce and valuable*' books to be removed from the sale in advance, so 'that all might have *equal Treatment*'.[42] But all did not go according to plan. Dunton secured an agreement in Dublin whereby he was to have had the back room at Dick's Coffee-House for as long as his sale lasted. In the event, the auction did not take place, if Dunton is to be believed, owing to the bully-boy tactics of Patrick Campbell, who intervened to prevent the sale going ahead at Dick's by offering the proprietor double what Dunton had given him to secure the premises. Here, Dunton railed at both the unscrupulousness of Campbell ('Pressing *Dick* to the Bargain by those moving Arguments *of a double Price*') and the disloyalty of the coffee-house proprietor, who 'finding that 'twas the Law of *Auctions*, that he who bids most is the Buyer ... lets the Room to *Patrick*, at the Time when 'twas actually mine, without being so fair as to cry *Ten Shillings Once ... Ten Shillings Twice*.'[43] To compound Dunton's problems, having been evicted from Dick's Coffee-House, he attempted to move the sale to Pat's Coffee-House, near St Michael's Church in Dublin High Street, but was again thwarted when, in the presence of Wilde and Larkin, Campbell apparently threatened to have the printer of Dunton's sale catalogues arrested.[44]

Dunton relished making (quite literally) a drama out of this crisis in a book-length account of these incidents. There is no doubt that he had long capitalized on the popularity of print controversies to make money, and saw this as an opportunity both to right the alleged wrongs received at Campbell's hands, and to generate some profit for himself. He spared no detail with regard to the favourable treatment he had received from printers, stationers and binders eager to serve him in Dublin (thereby drawing attention to his own credit and reputation), and marshalled the support of the Bishop of Clogher and six witnesses who provided written testament to his honesty.[45] Dunton also ridiculed Campbell by satirizing his Scottish accent (at one point, Dunton says ''Tis true, Gentlemen, he [Campbell] calls himself the *een Mon of Coonshence*; but I am afraid to tell you, what *Persuasion* he is of, seeing he has so very little either of *Justice or Humanity*').[46] He repeatedly referred in jest to Campbell as the 'Mon of Coonshence' and, in publishing his account of their enmity first, hoped to make a pre-emptive strike.

In the event, Campbell's only defender in print was Richard Pue, the proprietor of Dick's Coffee-House himself, who was also a bookseller and newspaper proprietor.[47] Pue issued an advertisement in the *Flying Post* which was reprinted at Dublin on 7 November 1698, describing Dunton's accusations as 'False and Malicious', and Campbell as 'Cautious and well informed'.[48] Dunton, in turn called Pue a 'Witty and Ingenious Man, [who] *makes the best Coffee in* Dublin' (implying that he was more accomplished as a *barrista* than as a bookseller). Dunton heightened the controversy by reprinting this advertisement in the *Dublin Scuffle* and presenting it to his readers as though they were the judges in this case, inviting them to infer Campbell's guilt from his deployment of a lackey (with the observation '*Conscience makes Cowards of us all*').[49] There is a sense of Dunton's protesting too much his own innocence and importance in the conduct of his business in Ireland ('all that I've said yet,' he claims 25 pages into his diatribe, 'is but *self defence*.') Yet his frequent appeals to conscience suggest that this was the only recourse of a bookseller whose trade depended upon fair play, more than the law. Addressing the printer of his auction bills,

Dunton predicted that Campbell would get his come-uppance 'when he casts up his Accounts, either with *his own Conscience* (if it be his Custom to keep a fair Reckoning there) or when he comes to count his Gains by his *Envious Auction*, which fastens the brand of foul Guilt upon him…'. The cause of all this skulduggery was clear to Dunton: 'it seems *Patrick* has a Mind to be the *sole bookseller* and *Auctioneer* in *Dublin*, at what Rate soever.'[50]

The disrespect which Dunton was apparently shown by Campbell does much to explain the extraordinary outpouring which this episode prompted. Another of Dunton's enemies in Ireland had been one Turner, who put it about that the London bookseller had borrowed 40 shillings from him when he came to Dublin, and not repaid him. Dunton rejected the allegation that he was indebted to Turner, claiming he 'could never creep to any Thing' since he had been 'born to a good Estate in Land, and had made it treble by a late Marriage; that I had brought a venture of Books to *Dublin* (of near *Ten Tun*) which could not yield less than 1500*l*.' and that, should he need the odd £100 to pay customs charges, 'I could have it at a Words speaking.'[51] This confident statement about having been born into a landed family and made a good marriage (to Sarah Nichols) may indeed have been an accurate reflection of Dunton's public optimism in 1699. However, the figure which Dunton set upon the value of the books he took to Dublin was certainly an exaggeration: it has been estimated that between 1693 and 1697, an average of ten tons of books were imported into Ireland from England each year, at a total value of £1,000 *per annum*.[52] Dunton reflected upon Campbell in the *Dublin Scuffle*, 'I bless God, my Name and Reputation stands [*sic*] much above him, but he Labours … to bespatter me all he can.'[53] The author seems to assume that the reader will be entertained by his own bluff and *brio*, and will despise Turner and Campbell for their pettiness, but Dunton betrays an underlying sensitivity here to wider questions of credit, rivalry and status in the book trade. Only the very rich could display such bravado about credit: for the rest, loss of reputation led straight to the Fleet Prison. Dunton's career nose-dived following his return from Ireland for a variety of personal and professional reasons. The next twelve years brought a disastrous change of fortune, notwithstanding the success in the interim of his *Athenian Oracle* in 1703–4, which was reprinted in 1706 and 1708, and various other 'Athenian' projects.[54] Perhaps his debts were just too great, and his disappointment in being slighted by his rich mother-in-law, Jane Nichols, insurmountable. Whatever the case, by 1711, Dunton could not raise £100 to avoid the Fleet Prison, was estranged from his second wife, and had mortgaged his land. Although he thrived upon risk in his career, and remained an innovator to the end, he failed to make a profitable living as an author or bookseller. Ultimately, his greatest failing was perhaps that he had no sense of when to publish and when to maintain a judicious silence.

Dunton's authorial voice in *The Dublin Scuffle* is echoed in the preoccupations of his last will and testament, which displays a similar self-scrutiny, and indeed insecurity on the author's part concerning the matter of his status and reputation as a member of the book trade. Even as he wrote his will, the prolific author of scurrilous pamphlets and 'one thousand projects' could not miss the final opportunity to set the record straight; he even set out the details of the advertisement announcing his death and the settlement of his 'Promises, Contracts and Debts', to be published in the *London Gazette* and the *Postman* 'as those two Papers goe into more hands than the other News-Papers'. Although Dunton ultimately failed to maintain his good name, the written record that he left is an intriguing insight into the struggle of one man to balance the demands of the book trade with the dictates of his own conscience.

References

*My thanks to the Editors of this volume for their scholarly advice, to Jeremy Boulton for the benefit of his knowledge of early modern wills and probate inventories, and to Christine Ferdinand for her encouragement.

1. Stephen Parks, *John Dunton and the English Book Trade. A Study of His Career with a Checklist of His Publications* (New York, 1976), p. 207.
2. For a recent summary of the extensive historiography of Dunton and his publications, see the present author's *Gender, Society and Print Culture in Late-Stuart England. The Cultural World of the Athenian Mercury* (Aldershot, 2003), pp. 25–8.
3. The main source for Dunton's biography is his *Life and Errors of John Dunton, Late Citizen of London* (London, 1705). The life history presented here is taken from the *New Dictionary of National Biography* entry on John Dunton by the present author.
4. Bodleian Library, Oxford, Rawlinson MS D72/66/f. 119.
5. Rawlinson MS D72/17/f. 32, John Dunton to his wife Sarah (n.d.).
6. Parks, *John Dunton*, p. 166. Thomas Parkhurst was about 80 years old at the time of his death, and was buried on 9 June 1711: see Guildhall Library MS 4439. Whether news of Parkhurst's death had reached Dunton in the Fleet Prison is questionable: in his will, Dunton bequeathed money to Parkhurst as though he were still alive, e.g. 'I referr it wholely to Mr Thomas Parkhurst (or in case of his Death to his Heirs, or Executors)'. PRO/PROB 10/1786/f. 10. I am grateful to Giles Mandelbrote for alerting me to the timing of Parkhurst's death and its likely impact upon Dunton.

7. Parks, *John Dunton*, p. 186.
8. *Ibid.*, p. 161.
9. PRO/PROB 10/1786/f. 9.
10. Nigel Goose and Nesta Evans observe that the majority of early modern wills were *not* written by lawyers, although testators who used the Prerogative Court of Canterbury, which had jurisdiction over Dunton's will, were more likely to use them. The most usual scribes were parish clergy or other literate professional men: townspeople were especially likely to use scriveners or public notaries. Only 'very occasionally' were they written by the testator himself. Nigel Goose and Nesta Evans, 'Wills as an historical source' in Tom Arkell, Nesta Evans and Nigel Goose (eds), *When Death Do Us Part. Understanding and Interpreting the Probate Records of Early Modern England* (Oxford, 2000), p. 49.
11. The original will in Dunton's own hand, from which the quotations for the current study are taken, is held in the National Archives: PRO/PROB 10/1786. A copy of the will is available on-line via the National Archives website: www.nationalarchives.gov.uk, PROB 11/657.
12. This assertion is made by comparison with neighbouring documents with the same accession number in the PCC archive and in discussion with Jeremy Boulton, to whom I am grateful for his advice *pers. com.*
13. PRO/PROB 10/1786/f. 1.
14. PRO/PROB 10/1786/f. 15.
15. PRO/PROB 10/1786/f. 1.
16. PRO/PROB 10/1786/f. 16.
17. PRO/PROB 10/1786/f. 3.
18. PRO/PROB 10/1786/f. 6.
19. PRO/PROB 10/1786/ff. 9–10.
20. Parks, *John Dunton*, p. 12.
21. PRO/PROB 10/1786/f. 11.
22. PRO/PROB 10/1786/ff. 11–12.
23. In addition to being deprived of spiritual comfort, the non-communicant forfeited his symbolic place in the adult community: see Eamon Duffy, *The Stripping of the Altars. Traditional Religion in England, c.1400–c.1580* (New Haven and London, 1992), p. 94.
24. PRO/PROB 10/1786/ff. 11–12.
25. See Craig Muldrew, *The Economy of Obligation. The Culture of Credit and Social Relations in Early Modern England* (London, 1998), *passim.*
26. PRO/PROB 10/1786/f. 2.
27. PRO/PROB 10/1786/ff. 2–3.
28. Stephen Parks (ed.), *Sale Catalogues of Libraries of Eminent Persons, Vol. 5, Poets and Men of Letters* (London, 1972), pp. 1–44.
29. John Dunton, *The Dublin Scuffle: Being a Challenge Sent by John Dunton, Citizen of London, to Patrick Campbel* [sic], *Bookseller in Dublin. Together with the Small Skirmishes of Bills and Advertisements* (London, 1699), p. 5.
30. M. Pollard, *Dublin's Trade in Books, 1550–1800* (Oxford, 1989), p. 2.
31. *Ibid.*, pp. 6–7.
32. *Ibid.*, p. 11.

33. James Raven, 'The Book Trades', in Isabel Rivers (ed.), *Books and their Readers in Eighteenth-Century England: New Essays* (London and New York, 2nd edn, 2003), p. 19.
34. Giles Mandelbrote, 'The Organization of Book Auctions in Late Seventeenth-Century London', in Robin Myers, Michael Harris and Giles Mandelbrote (eds), *Under the Hammer: Book Auctions Since the Seventeenth Century* (New Castle, Delaware and London, 2001), p. 15 and *passim*.
35. M. Pollard, *A Dictionary of Members of the Dublin Book Trade, 1550–1800* (London, 2000), p. 82.
36. *Ibid.*, p. 83.
37. *Ibid.*
38. Michael Harris, 'Newspaper Advertising for Book Auctions before 1700', in Myers, Harris and Mandelbrote (eds), *Under the Hammer*, p. 10.
39. PRO/PROB 10/1786/f. 3.
40. Rawlinson MS D72/18/ff. 65–6, George Larkin to John Dunton (15 April 1703).
41. PRO/PROB 10/1786/f. 3.
42. Dunton, *Dublin Scuffle*, p. 6.
43. *Ibid.*, p. 20.
44. *Ibid.*, pp. 17–18.
45. *Ibid.*, pp. 46–7, 52.
46. *Ibid.*, pp. 21, 23, 26–7.
47. Pollard, *Members of the Dublin Book Trade*, p. 473.
48. *Flying Post* (7 November 1698) — as printed in *Dublin Scuffle*, pp. 42–3. None of the London editions of *The Flying Post; or, Post Master* printed between July and December 1698 contains a reference to Pue's advertisement — more evidence of skulduggery?
49. Pollard, *Members of the Dublin Book Trade*, p. 473; *Dublin Scuffle*, p. 29.
50. *Dublin Scuffle*, p. 36.
51. *Ibid.*, pp. 21–2.
52. Pollard, *Dublin's Trade in Books*, p. 40.
53. *Dublin Scuffle*, p. 23.
54. Berry, *Gender, Society and Print Culture*, pp. 24–5.

Appendix

John Dunton's Possessions
[Source: PRO/PROB 31/114/216, dated 16 March 1732/3]

A Declaration instead of an Inventory of all and Singular the Goods Chattells and Credits of John Dunton late of the parish of Stepney in the County of Middx Deceased As they were taken valued and appraised by John Haine and Samuel Harrison Since the death of the said Deceased And which have come to the hands possession or knowledge of Richard Nowland Exec[uto]r named of the Will and Codicill of the said Deceased as ffollow viz –

Imprimis One old Coat, Wascoat and Breeches; Two Old Shirts, One pair of Stockings, One pair of Shoes, One Old Hatt and Wigg, Two Old Turnovers, One pair of Brass Buckles One Old Cane and Brass hilted Sword, One Old Bed bedstead and Rugg, One Pair of Curtains and Teaster Cloth, One Old Chest of Drawers Seven Old Pictures, One peice of Small Phillegree in a Case, One Standish, One Portmantua Trunk Two Small Trunks – One Small Carved Desk Some Waste papers and Lumber valued at —	8. 4. 8
One Silver Seal valued at —	0. 2. 0
Cash in the Deceaseds Pocketts at the time of his Decease	0. 1. 3
Sumâ Totalis	8. 7.11

And Lastly he this Exhi[bi]tant Sayth that no other goods Chattells or Credits whatsoever have come to his this Declarants hands possession or knowledge than those Mentioned and Specifyed in the above Declaration, but if hereafter if any shall from time to time as he shall receive the same he will readily Charge himself therewith.

Richard Nowland

The History of the False Raised Band

NICHOLAS PICKWOAD

IT MAY SEEM a little perverse to take one small, apparently innocuous and certainly commonplace feature typically associated with bindings of the nineteenth and twentieth centuries and devote a whole article to it. I have, however, long been interested in it as an indicator of the ways in which people have regarded the appearance of their books, something which, until relatively recent years, has rarely been recorded; even now most of the evidence relates to collectors rather than the general reader of books.[1] If one were able to ask a variety of people through the era of the hand press what image came to mind when they heard the word 'book', one might get some surprising answers, depending on when they lived, where they lived and, of course, their income. For some, a book might be no more than a cheap romance in a simple parchment or paper binding; for a child in school, perhaps a binding of tanned sheepskin with raised bands; for the better off, in northern Europe at least, polished calf and gold tooling; for someone living in a mediterranean country, full parchment. In most cases, we can only speculate as to how different bindings might relate to different types of book, or, indeed, the extent to which their owners would recognise different types of book. For the church-goer, however, we have a sort of archive of the way in which the book, The Book, has been depicted in ecclesiastical art over many centuries. It represents an image which would have been recognised by the public at large, and it is a remarkably conservative image. The Bible, right up to the nineteenth century, if not beyond, almost always appears in a late medieval guise, with thick boards (suggesting wooden boards), clasps on the foredge, and above all, raised bands on the spine.[2] This must, I suspect, be partly why the image of the book with raised bands survived long beyond its structural origins; it is an image which influenced the design and appearance of books of all sorts from the second half of the fifteenth century until very recently — if not until today.

From the last quarter of the eighteenth century, in northern Europe at least, most books which have been sewn at all have been sewn on recessed

Fig. 1. Detail of a Franklin Library advertisement of 1986

supports, which would normally result in a smooth spine without raised bands.[3] Yet in this period, books sewn in this manner and mostly bound in leather have repeatedly been given false raised bands. Why did this vestige of medieval structure prove so attractive that it was faked on countless thousands of books? The phenomenon is still with us. Even in recent years, the advertisements put out by the companies selling special 'high quality' editions of famous works in special bindings have boasted of the raised bands which make their bindings so special. The image of the Senior Consulting Editor of Doubleday tenderly stroking the spine of one such book and sighing 'The raised spine is a giveaway. That's quality binding' plays on the long-held belief that 'real' books should have raised bands (Fig. 1). The fact that such a claim can be made at all shows us that there is at least a semi-conscious feeling that you *can* tell the quality of a book by its binding, and that raised bands are well established as beacons of a quality that is often, in fact, conspicuously lacking.

The false raised band has sometimes aroused strong feelings, particularly from binders who have a particular interest in the quality of book structures and to whom a false band is simply anathema, a denial of all that makes them craftsmen. This principled objection manifested itself precociously, as we shall see, in Roger Payne in the late eighteenth century, just at the time when the British trade in general abandoned sewing on raised supports, which created raised bands on the spine of a book, in favour of recessed supports. It was a central tenet of the Arts and Crafts-inspired binders from Cobden Sanderson onwards. In my own training by Roger Powell, himself a pupil of Douglas Cockerell, who in turn had learned to bind from Cobden Sanderson, it was simply unthinkable to use false raised bands. Such binders were, of course, working in reaction to what they saw as the abandonment by the trade of structural features that were part and parcel of the 'well-made' book. The raised band was one of the issues over which the craft and the trade engaged in a battle for the soul of bookbinding, and it does indeed raise fundamental questions about form and function, about craft and trade practices, about sharp practices and honest ornamentation and about the changing æsthetic of the book through the centuries. It may be small, but it offers a potent interpretative tool in understanding books and their buyers, and it has a surprisingly long history.

Before going further, I shall offer some definitions. The word *band* is used to describe the raised ridges made across the spines of books, originally by the sewing supports to which the gatherings are sewn to create readable bookblocks. In some bindings, there may also be smaller raised bands, either kettle-bands, formed over the kettle-stitches (the stations at head and tail of the gatherings at which the sewing thread changes from one gathering to the next, picking up the thread from the previous gathering), or between the sewing supports, in which position they are usually called half-bands. I will be exploring the origins and history of both in what follows.

Where they are actually created by the sewing supports or kettle-stitches, these are defined as genuine bands or genuine half- or kettle-bands. Where they are not formed by the genuine structural components of a book, they should be described as false bands, and it is often necessary to look at them very carefully to sort out which is which. False bands are most often created by laying lengths of material, usually cord or leather or more recently narrow strips of card, across the spine and moulding the covering material (leather, parchment or textile) over them, to give the spine the appearance of having been sewn on raised supports. This is often done when the book is sewn on recessed supports which would otherwise leave a smooth spine.

So far as I am aware, nobody knows exactly when and where false raised bands were first used. J. A. Szirmai records them on a German binding of 1442, bound by the Carthusians of Buxheim,[4] but because I study mostly printed books, the earliest examples that I have found date from the second half of the fifteenth century, although these have also been German. Szirmai implies, though it is not clearly stated, that the false bands on the Buxheim binding are single bands placed between genuine double supports, and this combination must surely be associated with a number of German bindings which were originally sewn on a mixture of genuine single and double supports, resulting in bands of different size on the spine.[5] A fine example on a manuscript dated 1457 survives in the Herzog August Bibliothek in Wolfenbüttel.[6] This is a distinctively German habit, probably found mostly in southern Germany and used in at least the last quarter of the fifteenth century and into the beginning of the next. It suggests to me a rather adventurous and occasionally precocious approach to the construction of bookbindings, which may have been encouraged by the expansion of the production of printed books at the end of the century. This period also saw the introduction of the stuck-on endband and other features, such as the selective lacing of the sewing supports into the boards, which we normally associate with much later periods. Occasionally it would appear that these German binders were consciously flouting the conventions of their day, which might explain a south German binding, on an edition of 1497, sewn on four double supports with only one single support, placed in the centre of the spine (Fig. 2).[7] I know of no entirely convincing explanation for the use of this combination of single and double bands, but it seems to fit in with a rather sculptural, plastic conception of the book which is also found in the sometimes elaborate shaping of wooden boards on German books, which may in its turn be connected with the storage of books separately on flat or sloping shelves. In such circumstances, the elaborate three-dimensional quality of these bindings would show to greater effect.

Support for an æsthetic explanation is found in the appearance in the 1470s of the first examples of false bands which I have personally observed. A Strasburg edition, printed not later than 1473, retains a

Fig. 2. Binding covered in alum-tawed pigksin, sewn on four double supports with a single, genuine, half-band between supports 2 and 3. Iamblichus, trans. M. Ficino, *De Mysteriis Aegyptorum, Chaldæorum, Assyriorum*, Venice: Aldus Manutius, 1497 (University of Kentucky, PA 4220.A4. D40)

contemporary German binding sewn on five double supports (plus two *Kapitalbünde*, to which I shall return below) and has six false half-bands, one placed between each sewn support (Fig. 3).[8] What seems clear to me is that the use of false bands in this position is very early evidence (from the 1440s at least) of an important phenomenon — a desire on the part of the binder to reproduce at lower cost the particular appearance of a binding which derives from an expensive structural tradition — though whether to accommodate his client or to deceive him we shall probably never know. I doubt this phenomenon was common at this early date, but I have seen other examples from later in the fifteenth century, such as an edition of 1485, bound by the Tübingen binder Johannes Meigfogl and sewn on double white alum-tawed supports, with false bands placed between them.[9] The exposed insides of the boards of this binding allow one to see quite clearly that the half-bands are not laced into the boards and that they are not sewn around.

The *Kapitalbund* is another especially German phenomenon and is the name given to the single sewing supports found at the head and tail of the spines of some mostly south-German bindings of around 1500, the other sewing supports being either double or, frequently, paired single supports.[10] They were sewn as part of the main sewing structure of the book but serve a double function, as both support and endband, and are always laced into the boards. They are another example of this apparently German habit of structural experimentation, though here with a definable structural logic (Fig. 4). They are often associated with paired single supports, yet another example of German binders experimenting with the visual impact of novel structures, and they create a very characteristic appearance which must have been appreciated by early owners. It was presumably for this reason that before the end of the fifteenth century they appear as false bands. In the Special Collections of the University of California, Los Angeles, there is a Venice edition of 1499 in a German binding with lengths of twisted alum-tawed skin stretched across the spine at head and tail (in the position of *Kapitalbünde*), but clearly not included in the sewing of the textblock (Fig. 5).[11] Another German binding, also on a Venetian edition, this time of 1488, has false *Kapitalbünde* made from cord (Fig. 6).[12]

It is sometimes hard to know whether to call these false bands or false endbands, especially as they sometimes appear to serve some practical function in allowing the covering skin to be turned over them, as on a

Fig. 3. A binding covered in alum-tawed pigskin, sewn on seven double supports with *Kapitalbünde* and false half-bands. Gallus, Abbas Cisterciensis, *Malogranatum*, Strasburg: Heinrich Eggestein, before 1473 (Herzog August Bibliothek, E 163.2° Helmst)

Fig. 4. A German binding, dated 1520, sewn on two double supports with *Kapitalbünde* at head and tail. Gabriello Barletta, *Fructuosissimi atq[ue] amenissimi Sermones*, Paris: J. Parvus, 1518 (Herzog August Bibliothek, E 89.8° Helmst)

Fig. 5. (above) False *Kapitalbund* of twisted alum-tawed skin. Plautus, *Viginti Comœdiæ cum interpret. Petri Vallae et Bern. Saraceni*, Venice: Simon Bevilaqua, 1499 (UCLA Special Collections)

Fig. 6. False *Kapitalbund* of cord. Propertius, *Elegiae*, Venice: Andreas de Paltasichis, 1488 (Herzog August Bibliothek, Qu H 10)

Strasburg edition of 1489.[13] As so often happens when looking at the structural components of historical bindings, a field in which contemporary documentation appears not to exist, we are left to interpret what we see and guess at the thought processes that created what we find. I think, however, that the application of structurally useless bands to the spine of the book (as in the UCLA example) must have been a response to some sort of demand or expectation on the part of the customer. That demand or expectation — if not simply æsthetic in its origin — must have signified some factor of recognition that is now lost to us. Sometimes false bands raise questions to which we are unlikely to find answers.

The false *Kapitalbund* is easily, perhaps at first inextricably, confused with another type of false band apparently first found in German-speaking Europe, the false kettle-band. It is indeed often difficult if not impossible to distinguish one from the other, though the structural elements that they imitate are quite distinct. A basic distinction is simply one of size, as the *Kapitalbund* is likely to be much more substantial than a kettle-band. There is a German binding on a mid fifteenth-century book of hours which has a false band created by a length of alum-tawed skin glued to the spine lining, with the covering skin then moulded over it.[14] It lies over the area where the kettle-stitches should be (but not necessarily directly over them), and somewhat further away from the head and tail than *Kapitalbünde* are usually found. If this is truly an imitation of a kettle-band which, by the end of the century, is a common feature on many northern European bindings, it is the earliest I know and was created by what was to become a conventional technique. Another example, on a Venetian bible of 1480, has false bands whipped with white thread at the head and blue thread at the tail to the tie-downs of the endbands.[15] This rather insecure, and apparently highly unusual, attachment was presumably all that was needed to hold them in place until the book was covered. From the very end of the next century, thin single false bands are found glued at the head and tail of another German binding, on a Frankfurt edition of 1597.[16] With the ends of the cord from which it is made frayed and pasted to the outside of the boards (another typically German technique), this is nothing more than a decorative add-on to an otherwise perfectly conventional binding (Fig. 7).

German binders continued throughout the sixteenth century to use the false half-band, and examples are not hard to find, appearing under covers of tanned and tawed skin (Fig. 8),[17] and even expensive silk textiles. It would appear, however, that they are almost always associated with

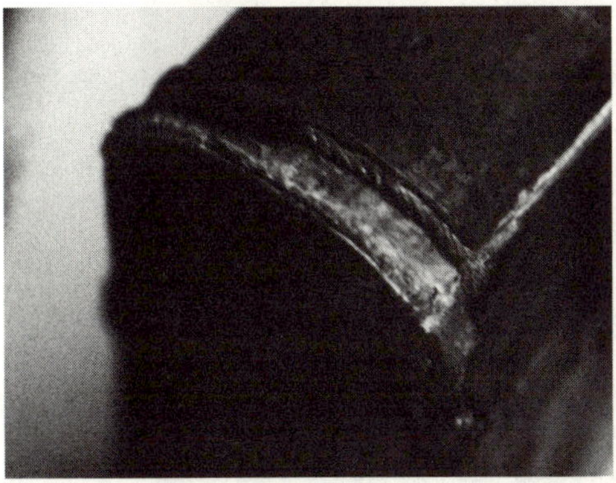

Fig. 7. (left) A false band created by a length of cord glued across the spine at head and tail. Duarte Lopez, *Regnum Congo*, Frankfurt: Johann Saur, 1597 (Herzog August Bibliothek, 184 Hist.2°)

Fig. 8. A binding in alum-tawed skin sewn on four double supports with false half-bands and kettle-bands. Cyriacus Spangenberg, *Adels Spiegel*, Schmalkalden: Michel Schmück, 1591 (Herzog August Bibliothek, T 958.2° Helmst)

Fig. 9. False half-bands on a binding covered in black silk, showing a panel stamp of the baptism of Christ on the front board and the date 1568. Martin Luther, *Das XVII. Capitel S. Johannis, von dem Gebete Christi*, Magdeburg: Andreas Gehne, 1568 (Herzog August Bibliothek, 990.75 Theol)

tooled or otherwise decorated bindings, including one in black silk with the boards decorated with panels, blocked in *Zwischengold*, of the baptism of Christ and David and Bathsheba, dated 1568 (Fig. 9).[18] I have seen a rather different type of false band on an edition of 1589, in which the book is sewn on only two double-cord supports with a third somewhat larger false double-cord support in the centre.[19] This would appear to be an attempt to make an otherwise perfectly conventional and comparatively inexpensive structure and binding (a quarter binding with parchment manuscript on the sides) look more expensive, a phenomenon I shall return to below. However, the oversize false band rather spoils the effect, if that was what was intended, and it may be that the intention was no more than decorative (Fig. 10).

The use of false *half*-bands was not confined to Germany, and the mid sixteenth-century Italian examples are generally better known, though the presence of many earlier German examples would suggest that the Italian binders may have borrowed the idea from north of the Alps. There are numerous examples to be found, from a number of the major centres of binding. The German student, Nikolaus von Ebeleben, who studied in Bologna from 1543 to 1549, when the Italian fashion for half-bands was at its height, had a number of books bound with half-bands and then took them back to Germany.[20] The practice proved very popular for some 40 years, and a damaged example on a Venetian edition of 1553 (Fig. 11) shows the most common way in which these false bands were formed.[21] In this example the binder has made the false bands — both kettle- and half-bands — out of lengths of twisted tanned leather, which were glued to the spine before covering. In some examples I have seen, where the half-bands are very thin, they were formed by simply nipping up the damp leather during covering, without any material underneath. This technique is found on a 1541 Venetian edition of the *Decameron* in a contemporary Venetian binding, now in Swaffham Parish Library (Fig. 12).[22] The style even reached Crete, then a possession of the Venetian Republic, where a Greek psalter was written in 1544 and where presumably it was bound in an unusual hybrid of eastern and western techniques.[23]

Despite the adoption by French binders in the 1530s of many Italian fashions in bookbinding, it seems they did not adopt the use of half-bands with any enthusiasm: an example on a binding executed in the 1540s for Jean Grolier and attributed to the Cupid's Bow Binder is the only one known to me.[24] In this binding, the half-bands were formed by lengths of

Fig. 10. (left) A false double band between two genuine double supports. Gregor Bersmann, *Poematiorum libri duo*, Servestae: Bonaventura Faber, 1589 (Herzog August Bibliothek, P 1418.8° Helmst)

Fig. 11. A length of twisted tanned leather used to create a false kettle-band, visible below the endband tie-downs. Domenico Manzoni, *La brieve risolutione di arithmetica*, Venice, 1553 (University of Wisconsin at Madison, CA 2648)

Fig. 12. False bands created out of nipped-up leather. Giovanni Boccaccio, *Il Decamerone*, Venice: Francesco Bendoni & Napheo Pasini [Ad instantia di Curtio Navò & Fratelli], 1541 (Swaffham Parish Library, SWD 4/1 [98], on deposit in Norwich Cathedral Library)

cord which were not only glued across the spine, but were also laced into the boards (unlike any of the Italian or German examples known to me). They are, however, most certainly not sewn around, and the unusual technique may in fact be an indicator of just how rarely half-bands are found in French binding of this period.

Much more typically French is use of kettle-bands at head and tail without half-bands between the sewing supports, and examples survive in large numbers.[25] Gold-tooled hatching is often found on the higher-quality versions for the rest of the century, but blind- or untooled examples are equally common on less expensive bindings. The kettle-band was not restricted to French bindings, and is found right across northern Europe, as an Antwerp example of 1525 published by E. P. Goldschmidt shows,[26] with examples to be found from at least the late fifteenth century onwards. The question to ask always is whether the kettle-band is genuine, for in many cases it will be found not to be.

Just as with the German half-bands from the late fifteenth century, the binders who made false kettle-bands were taking what began as an accentuation of a structural feature for decorative effect and turning it into pure decoration. Whether you regard this as deception or ornament is largely a matter of interpretation and your perception of craft integrity, but I believe that the loss of function which false kettle-bands as well as half-bands represent marks a decisive shift in the design of bindings, opening the door to ever-weaker structures dressed up as something they are not. It is perhaps relevant to quote Herbert Horne in *The Binding of Books* of 1894, expressing a central creed of the Arts and Crafts movement:

> Fine ornament should always be suggested by that, which it is to decorate: ornament which masks or falsifies construction, diverges from the nature of fine art, according to the degree, and manner, in which this is done.[27]

It may be a heavy load to place on such a humble artefact as a kettle-band, but it is instructive to note which binders falsify such features and which do not. I think you will find that, not surprisingly, the higher-quality binders of all ages follow Horne's injunction, and the lesser craftsmen (or those under more financial pressure) do not. The latter imitate, presumably in response to a perceived demand from their clients, what are seen to be the traditional features of good bookbinding, or simply imitate work from the more expensive end of the market. In this respect, the history of the false band follows that of the endband very closely.

Fig. 13. Kettle-bands represented by nothing more than a band of gold-tooling. Louis Gollert, *Les Memoires Historiques de la République Sequanoise*, Dole 1592 (Grolier Club Library, New York)

By the end of the sixteenth century, even in high-quality work of the sort executed for Jacques Auguste de Thou on an edition of 1592 (Fig. 13),[28] the kettle-band has been reduced to nothing more than a decorative flourish in gold-tooling, with not even a false band underneath it. Such tooling survives well into the seventeenth century in both French and French-inspired bindings. It appears, for instance, on a Dutch binding on a Paris edition of 1658, by which time the genuine raised kettle-band was scarcely even a distant memory.[29]

We now leave what might be called the age of (relative) innocence of the false raised band and come to something altogether darker, where decoration seems to cross the divide into deception. The first type of deception I want to consider is the use of false bands to create the impression that a book is sewn on more supports than is in fact the case, by glueing false bands across the spine which are of exactly the same size as the genuine supports to which the book is sewn. The earliest example I know of this phenomenon is found on a contemporary French binding on a Paris edition of 1535, where the book is actually sewn on three supports (bands 1, 3 and 5 on the spine) and bands 2 and 4 are false.[30] It is of course possible that the original owner of this book bought it sewn on three supports, laced into boards and left uncovered, which was certainly an option open to book-purchasers at that date. The owner might then have asked a binder to add extra bands before it was covered to make it match other books in his or her collection. That, at least, is the charitable interpretation. The uncharitable interpretation, and the one I am more inclined to believe, is that the binder sewed the book on three supports rather than on five because it was considerably quicker to do so, and he could therefore pocket the difference in cost. Whatever the truth, the fact remains that five supports were clearly deemed to be more desirable in terms of appearance than three, and adjusting the appearance of the book to make it look as if it was sewn on five supports was thought worthwhile. This implies a clientele which appreciated that a greater number of supports suggested better quality and durability (as it should), and was presumably prepared to pay for it.

The same phenomenon is found on English books by the beginning of the seventeenth century, and can be seen on an Antwerp-printed bible of 1608 in a contemporary English binding, from the Stoke by Nayland Parish Library.[31] It survives into the eighteenth century, as an inexpensive quarter sheepskin binding in Chester Cathedral Library bears witness (Fig. 14).[32] Bernard Middleton records that he has occasionally seen 'three genuine raised bands and two false ones', but it seems not to have been a widespread practice — at least so far as has been observed and recorded.[33] In the last quarter of the eighteenth century and the beginning of the nineteenth, the practice of marking up books for sewing on five supports and then omitting the central support (sewing 'wide in the middle')[34] resulted in some bindings being given a false band where the missing support would have been, though the structure is more typically associated with the cheapest publishers' bindings in paper, where the structure lent itself to sewing 3-on for greater economy.

The use of false bands on books sewn on recessed supports, where all the bands are false, is, I regret to say, a largely English phenomenon, and one that I wrote about many years ago in the Roger Powell festschrift,[35] but since then I have seen many more examples and can now reinforce my

Fig. 14. A binding in quarter tanned sheepskin and marbled paper, sewn on three single cords with two additional false bands. Nicholas Brady, *A sermon preach'd before the Queen at the chappel royal at St. James's*, London: printed by D.L. for John Chantry, 1706/7 (Chester Cathedral Library)

original argument. The fashionable use of recessed sewing supports from the mid-sixteenth century to create bindings with smooth spines survived in England until the mid-seventeenth century, but fell out of fashion quite rapidly after that. (Howard Nixon's catalogue of Restoration bindings has only one binding in it with a smooth spine, out of 125 bindings with raised bands — I do not include the backless binding by Richard Balley — and that one is dated 1658).[36] The disappearance of the smooth spine from the fashionable scene is matched by its appearance on bindings at the opposite end of the market, bound in calfskin and, more usually, sheepskin. These have survived in large numbers, which suggests that they were produced in even larger numbers, taking full advantage of the saving in time that comes from sewing on recessed supports with the thread simply passing behind the supports and not being taken around them[37] — something apparently recognised by English binders long before their continental counterparts

— and these inexpensive bindings with smooth spines continued to be made until the early years of the eighteenth century.[38]

The result appears to have been an association, at least in the English book-buyer's mind, between the smooth spine and cheap books, and a reaction in favour of raised bands. This seems to have created a demand that was satisfied in some instances by adding false bands to structures with recessed supports. I now have records of over 30 of these bindings on books printed in the 1670s and 1680s, and almost every library containing sizeable collections of books of this period yields one or two more examples. This appears to me to be evidence of a widespread practice, though I have not been able to identify a particular workshop that was doing it, nor indeed to identify multiple examples from the same workshop — which tends to reinforce the argument that the practice was a common one. The discovery of two copies of the same text — *The Memoires of Sir James Melvil* of 1683[39] — in bindings each with six false bands over recessed cords, but clearly with covers from different workshops, offers nothing more as yet than a coincidence; but it might suggest a trade in sewn textblocks (sewn on recessed supports) akin to the trade in textblocks folded, beaten and sawn-in ready for sewing which is indicated by one London edition of 1668.[40] Could it be that a bookseller/bookbinder (the two being often one and the same) might add false bands to a textblock bought from the London booktrade already sewn on recessed supports, to satisfy the pretensions of a customer for a 'proper' binding without going to the trouble of resewing it? We are unlikely ever to find evidence of this process, but what is perfectly clear from these bindings is that the raised band was a desirable commodity with an identifiable market of which advantage could be taken.

I am happy to be able to say that the practice is not restricted to the British Isles (I know, incidentally, of one presentation copy of a Dublin edition in an Irish library bound in this way),[41] as a French example on a Leiden edition of 1628 bears witness.[42] Could it be that we copied French practice (Fig. 15)? I know as yet of only one other example of this practice in France, and that, somewhat untypically, on a set of mid-seventeenth-century bindings in gold-tooled red tanned goatskin — which suggests a more thorough-going level of cheating than I have encountered elsewhere.[43]

Except of course when it comes to the ultimate binding deception, which was to sell the customer books which were simply glued together

Fig. 15. A French binding of the second quarter of the seventeenth century, showing a false band exposed by damage towards the head of the spine. George Buchanan, *Poemata quæ extant. Editio Postrema*, Leiden: Ex officina Elzeviriana, 1628 (author's collection)

and then given false raised bands to make them look as if they were conventionally sewn. I have seen no more than five examples, two of which at least came from the same English workshop, but they can have survived by accident only, as they must have collapsed very quickly, and many other examples are likely to have been lost.[44]

Early in the eighteenth century, false bands seem to have gone out of use completely, until they returned in the last quarter of the century, following the re-introduction of sewing on recessed supports at the top end of the market in the 1760s. John Mathewman, the binder who worked for Thomas Hollis, was one of the first English binders to revive this technique at this period.[45] He is known to have bound two copies of the same edition of 1720, one with genuine raised supports and the other with recessed supports and a smooth spine, which raises the intriguing question as to why they were sewn differently.[46] The same crimson goatskin was used on both and although different emblematic tools were used on the covers, the tooling layout is identical. Matthewman disappeared in 1769, pursued by his creditors, but the use of recessed supports continued and gradually displaced raised supports almost entirely, probably because of the greater speeed at which it allowed books to be sewn. This encouraged binders such as Christian Kalthoeber to explore once again the use of false bands, but here the impetus was entirely decorative, and I do not think that there was any intention to deceive (Fig. 16). Kalthoeber's use of paired single bands is also interesting, harking back to German bindings of the late fifteenth century. An immediate antecedent is to be found in a group of bindings from the same as yet unidentified workshop of the 1750s, which used genuine paired single supports to good decorative effect.[47] Whatever the source of the design, such false bands became a very common feature of late-eighteenth- and early nineteenth-century bindings, to the extent that Roger Payne sometimes felt moved when writing out his invoices to make highly critical remarks of the practice. In the bill for his binding of *The Vale Royall of Chester* for Sir Peter Leycester, he states very firmly that it is 'Sew'd in the very best Manner on six bands on the outside (the Bands are not saw'd in and there is not any false bands)'.[48] His protests went unheeded, however, as the false band had by then become a permanent feature of the binding trade and by the beginning of the next century had effectively displaced the genuine raised support for almost all commercial bindings in boards except, ironically, the cheapest school-books in tanned sheepskin.

Fig. 16. A binding with paired single false bands by Christian Kalthoeber. *Book of Common Prayer* and *Holy Bible*, Cambridge: Thomas Buck and Roger Daniel, 1637 (Saltram Park, The National Trust)

The introduction of the hollow back at the same period, to allow books printed on the heavier papers then fashionable to open without destroying the tooling on the spine, freed the false raised band from any need even to reflect what might be called structural reality and thus confirmed its status as a decorative feature only. As a consequence, the first quarter of the nineteenth century saw a remarkable efflorescence of quite extraordinary three-dimensional treatments of book spines, in which modest raised bands turned into large excrescences entirely devoid of any

Fig. 17. Extra wide false bands. Isaac Walton, *The Compleat Angler*, London: Thomas Gosden, 1828 (Saltram Park, The National Trust)

reference to function. The quite literal separation of the bands from the spine allowed them to take on different shapes on the same spine, and, in the case of bindings by Thomas Gosden, to take leave of reality altogether. In one binding on Gosden's favourite text, Walton's *Compleat Angler*, it is hard to determine what is raised panel and what is recessed panel (Fig. 17).[49] As Louis Sébastien Lenormand wrote in his bookbinding manual of 1827, on a hollow back 'you can have at the same time wide or narrow bands, thin or fat ones, and even form a variety of projections or recesses on the spine',[50] and it is certainly true that it is on continental bindings that you are more likely to find the uneven spacing of false bands, and even bands forming diagonals, chevrons and curves. This is the high point — or the nadir if you prefer — of the false raised band, and certainly in Britain for the rest of the nineteenth and the first half of the twentieth century there is a return to a largely dull uniformity where the bands, almost always five in number on octavos and upwards, are placed in stolidly conventional positions, laid down by a rigidly commercial tradition that rarely admitted of variation.

In our own time, the false band, or hub as it is known in the United States,[51] has become, in an ironic twist of fate, or rather economics, a badge of quality of which much is made in the advertisements for 'finely bound' editions of classic texts (Fig. 18). I treasure the claim in one such advertisement that these 'hubs' are made by Swiss craftsmen ('yes,' the blurb reveals excitedly, 'there are a few left'), presumably 'hubbing' for all they are worth in order to create the thousands of 'unique' bindings on offer. They are, as we have seen, working in a long tradition that for over 500 years has played on the book-buyer's belief that you *can* tell the quality of a book by its cover.

Fig. 18. Detail of a Franklin Library advertisement of 1976

References

1. I have discussed this subject in 'The Development of the Concept of Artefactual Conservation' in *La conservation, une science en évolution: bilans et perspectives. Actes des troisièmes journées internationales d'études de l'ARSAG*, Paris, 1997.
2. A woodcut factotum initial used by Thomas Gent of York shows just such a binding with raised bands, thick boards, and clasps presumably intended to represent a bible. *Eutropius's Compendious History of Rome: Together, with an English Translation. by John Clarke*, 2nd edn, York: Printed by Thomas Gent, 1728, p. 166.

3. I use the word 'smooth' to describe spines without raised bands, and the word 'flat' to describe spines that have not been rounded.
4. J. A. Szirmai, *The Archaeology of Medieval Bookbinding*, Aldershot: Ashgate, 1999, p. 187.
5. Szirmai, pp. 186–7.
6. Dag-Ernst Petersen, *Mittelalterliche Bucheinbände der Herzog August Bibliothek*, Wolfenbüttel 1975, p. ii, abb. IV. The book shown is Herzog August Bibliothek (hereafter HAB) Cod. Guelf. 75. 9. Aug. 2°, dating from 1457.
7. Iamblichus, trans. M. Ficino, *De Mysteriis Aegyptorum, Chaldæorum, Assyriorum*, Venice: Aldus Manutius, 1497 (University of Kentucky, PA 4220.A4. D40).
8. Gallus, Abbas Cisterciensis, *Malogranatum*, Strasburg: Heinrich Eggestein, before 1473 (HAB, E 163.2° Helmst). In 1517 this book was in the possession of the Benedictine monastery of S. Blasius in Northeim, near Göttingen.
9. Niccolò de' Tudeschis, *Lectura super quinque libros decretalium*, Basel: Michel Wenssler, 1477 (Harvard University, Houghton Library, Inc 7482).
10. I use this term to describe pairs of single sewing supports placed close to each other on the spine but sewn separately. The sewing thread between them can be taken either inside or outside the gatherings.
11. Plautus, *Viginti Comœdiæ cum interpret. Petri Vallae et Bern. Saracen*, Venice: Simon Bevilaqua, 1499 (UCLA Special Collections).
12. Propertius, *Elegiae*, Venice: Andreas de Paltasichis, 1488 (HAB, Qu H 10).
13. Angelus de Clavasio, *Summa Angelica de casibus conscientie*, Strasburg: Martin Flach, 1489 (HAB, L 821.2° Helmst).
14. Philadelphia Free Library, Lewis E. 151.
15. Biblia, Venice: Franciscus Renner de Heilbronn, 1480 (HAB, Bibel-S. 4° 125).
16. Duarte Lopez, *Regnum Congo, hoc est, Warhaffte und Eigentliche Beschreibung deß Königreichs Congo in Africa, und deren angrentzenden Länder / Erstlich durch Eduart Lopez in Portugalesischer Spraach gestellt, jetzo aber in unser Teutsche Spraach transferieret und übersetzt durch Augustinum Cassiodorum; auch mit Figuren gezieret und an den Tag geben durch Hans Dietherich und Hans Israel von Bry*, Frankfurt: Johann Saur, 1597 (HAB, 184 Hist. 2°).
17. Cyriacus Spangenberg, *Adels Spiegel: Historischer ausfürlicher Bericht: Was Adel sey und heisse, Woher er komme, Wie mancherley er sey, Vnd was denselben ziere vnd erhalte, auch hingegen verstelle vnd schwäche … / … auffs fleissigste beschrieben Durch M. Cyriacum Spangenberg*, Schmalkalden: Gedruckt zu bey Michel Schmück, 1591 (HAB, T 958.2° Helmst).
18. Martin Luther, *Das XVII. Capitel S. Johannis, von dem Gebete Christi*, Magdeburg: Andreas Gehne, 1568 (HAB, 990.75 Theol). This copy was in the collection of Herzog Julius of Braunschweig und Lüneburg. I am grateful to Katharina Mähler for supplying me with the information about this book.
19. Gregor Bersmann, *Poematiorum libri duo*, Servestae: Bonaventura Faber, 1589 (HAB, P 1418 Helmst 8°).
20. Mirjam Foot, *The Henry Davis Gift: A Collection of Bookbindings*, vol. 1, London: The British Library, 1978, pp. 300–5.
21. Domenico Manzoni, *La brieve risolutione di arithmetica*, Venice, 1553 (University of Wisconsin at Madison, CA 2648).
22. Giovanni Boccaccio, *Il Decamerone di Messer Giovanni Boccaccio nvovamente stampato et ricorretto per Messer Lodovico Dolce con la dichiaratione di tvtti vocaboli, detti, prouerbij, figure, &*

modi di dire incogniti & difficili, che sono in esso Libro, Venice: Francesco Bendoni & Napheo Pasini [Ad instantia di Curtio Navò & Fratelli], 1541 (Swaffham Parish Library, SWD 4/1 [98]).

23. *Psalter and Odes*, written in Crete by the scribe Ioannes Nathanael in 1544 (MS Greek 117, St Catherine's Monastery, Mount Sinai).
24. Michele Marullo Tarcaniota, *Epigrammatum libri IV. Hymnorum Naturalium libri IV*, Florence: Societas Colubris (Compagnia del Drago), 1497. Described by Bernard Breslauer in *Vision of a Collector: The Lessing J. Rosenwald Collection in the Library of Congress*, Washington: Library of Congress, 1991, pp. 339–41.
25. A good example can be seen on a binding by Claude de Piques on a copy of Justinian, *Quinquaginta librorum Digestorum sive Pandectarum juris Caesarei*, Paris: Charles Guillard, 1540, illustrated in the Esmerian sale catalogue (*Bibliothèque Raphäel Esmerian, Première Partie*, Paris: Georges Blaizot and Claude Guérin, 1972, vol. 1, item 78).
26. E. P. Goldschmidt, *Gothic & Renaissance Bookbindings exemplified and illustrated from the author's collection*, 2 vols, London: Ernest Benn, 1928, item 119 (vol. 1, pp. 217–18 and vol. 2, plate XLVII).
27. Herbert P. Horne, *The Binding of Books*, London 1894, pp. 19–20.
28. Louis Gollert, *Les Memoires Historiques de la République Sequanoise*, Dole 1592 (Grolier Club Library, New York).
29. Jean le Féron, *Histoire des Connestables, Chanceliers…*, etc., Paris: Imprimerie Royale, 1658 (Patrick Sourget catalogue xv, item 64).
30. I referred to and illustrated this book in my article 'The interpretation of bookbinding structure: an examination of the sixteenth-century bindings in the Ramey Collection in the Pierpont Morgan Library', *The Library*, 6th series, xvii.3, September 1995, pp. 218–20.
31. Nicholas Pickwoad, 'Cutting Corners: Some Deceptive Practices in Seventeenth Century English Bookbinding', in *Roger Powell the Compleat Bookbinder*, ed. John Sharpe, Turnhout: Brepols, 1996, p. 272.
32. Nicholas Brady, *A sermon preach'd before the Queen at the chappel royal at St. James's*, London: printed by D.L. for John Chantry, 1706/7 (Chester Cathedral Library).
33. Bernard Middleton, *The History of English Craft Binding Technique*, London: Holland Press, 1978, p. 18.
34. [George Cowie], *The Bookbinder's Manual*, London: Cowie and Strange, 1828, p. 12.
35. Nicholas Pickwoad, 'Cutting Corners', pp. 272–9.
36. Howard Nixon, *English Restoration Bindings: Samuel Mearne and his Contemporaries*, London: British Library, 1974.
37. This technique allows the thread to be tensioned at the end of the gathering and not at each support, and it is this that speeds up the process.
38. Graham Pollard, 'Changes in the Style of Bookbinding, 1550–1830', *The Library*, 5th series, xi, June 1956, p. 86. The Derry Diocesan Library has several books of the first decade of the eighteenth century with smooth spines.
39. George Scott ed., *The Memoires of Sir James Melvil of Hal-Hill*, London: printed by E.H. for Robert Boulter, 1683. One copy is in the library of Dunham Massey Hall (National Trust) and the other belongs to the author.

40. George Bishop, *A looking-glass for the times being a tract concerning the original and rise of truth and the original and rise of antichrist*, London 1668 (Houghton Library *fEC65.B5416.668L). This copy is illustrated in Nicholas Pickwoad, 'Caveat Legator', in Bernard Middleton, *The Restoration of Leather Bindings*, 3rd edn, New Castle, Delaware, & London: Oak Knoll Press & The British Library, 1998, p. 275. Since writing this, I have been able to acquire another example, on a copy of Henry Foulis, *The History of the Wicked Plots and Conspiracies of our Pretended Saints*, Oxford: printed by Henry Hall for Ric. Davis, 1674.
41. John Stearne, *De obstinatione*, Dublin: excudit Benjamin Tooke... et prostant venales apud Joseph Wilde, 1672 (Derry Diocesan Library J. 3. a. 17).
42. George Buchanan, *Poemata quæ extant. Editio Postrema*, Leiden: Ex officina Elzeviriana, 1628 (author's collection).
43. Seen on a multi-volume set in the library of the Villa i Tatti, Florence (Harvard University).
44. Nicholas Pickwoad, 'Cutting Corners', pp. 275–7.
45. W. H. Bond, *Thomas Hollis of Lincoln's Inn. A Whig and his Books*, Cambridge: Cambridge University Press, 1990, p. 39.
46. John Tolland, *Pantheisticon. Sive formula celebrandæ Sodalitatis Socraticæ, in tres particulas divisa; ... Præmittitur de antiquis & novis eruditorum sodalitatibus, ... diatriba. Subjicitur de duplici pantheistarum philosophia sequendâ*, Cosmopoli [London?], 1720 (both copies, with different settings of the titlepage, are in the York Minster Library, VII. M. 32).
47. An example of one of these bindings with paired single supports is found on a copy of Conyers Middleton, *The History of the Life of M. T. Cicero*, 2 vols., London, 1741 (Wimpole Hall, National Trust).
48. [Lord Rothschild], *Two Bindings by Roger Payne*, Cambridge: privately printed for Lord Rothschild, 1947, p. 8.
49. Isaac Walton, *The Compleat Angler*, London: Thomas Gosden, 1828 (Saltram Park, National Trust).
50. Louis Sébastien Lenormand, *Nouveau Manuel Complet de Relieur, dans toutes ses parties*, Paris: Librarie Encyclopédique de Roret, 1840, p. 97.
51. The term 'hubs' is more correctly used only of the oversized bands of laminated board or leather found on North American account-book bindings. See John F. Pleger, *Bookbinding and its Auxiliary Branches (in four parts) ... Part Three*, Chicago: The Inland Printer Company, 1914, pp. 134–41.

Guglielmo Libri

ANTHONY HOBSON

GUGLIELMO LIBRI[1] AND Thomas J. Wise are the two most famous crooks in book-collecting history. Their activities were most shocking not because their depredations were so vast, although they were, but because both men were themselves so eminent and respected. Wise was a President of the Bibliographical Society, an Honorary Fellow of Worcester College, Oxford, a member of the Roxburghe Club and the recipient of an honorary degree from Oxford University. Libri was Professor of the Collège de France, a member of the Institut and of the French historical manuscripts commission. Even after each had been unmasked, there were many who were reluctant to believe in their guilt. Charles Des Graz, then Director in charge of Sotheby's book department, wrote to Mrs Wise on 1 October 1934, three months after the publication of Carter and Pollard's *Enquiry*, deploring the attack on her husband and describing him as 'the pioneer of modern scientific bibliography, the patron and pattern of almost every great modern collector [and] ... the rock upon which the edifice of present day book-collecting is based'. In her reply Mrs Wise wrote of the 'very large number of letters expressing sympathy with, and confidence in, my husband which have reached us'. Such a reversal of reputations often takes time. We are reminded that it was nearly 70 years after the death of Feliks Dzerzhinsky, the founder of the Cheka, before his statue outside the Lubianka Prison in Moscow was toppled from its pedestal.

Count Guglielmo Bruto Icilio Timoleone Libri-Carrucci dalla Sommaia was born into a family of the Tuscan nobility in 1802. His father was a republican enthusiast, subject to fits of insanity, and an embezzler, eventually sentenced in France to imprisonment for life. He and Guglielmo's mother were legally separated when the child was five years old.

Guglielmo acquired fluent French at school, and studied Greek, Latin, English, history and philosophy. At the University of Pisa, where he matriculated at the age of 14, he read Natural Sciences and showed evidence of precocious brilliance, writing papers on 'a new electrometer' and the theory of parallels. After obtaining his doctorate he published a paper on the theory of numbers which attracted the attention of Charles Babbage. At the age of 21 he was appointed Professor of Mathematical Physics at Pisa.

He obtained leave of absence from Pisa after a year, and never returned to teach there, though he retained the title and the salary for life. Instead he travelled to Paris where he made the acquaintance of Alexander von Humboldt, the mathematician Laplace and, most important for later events, the Liberal historian and journalist Guizot. On his return to Italy, he published more papers on mathematics, but became interested in an entirely original subject, the history of science. He also started to collect and deal in books. Meanwhile the first suspicious episode had occurred. He had been appointed librarian of the Accademia dei Georgofili in Florence. He resigned suddenly and without explanation after one year. His successor checked the holdings and found that 300 books were missing. Nothing could be proved and the affair fizzled out.

In 1830 he was again in Paris and participated in the July Revolution, brandishing a gun and disarming a general. In Florence at the end of the same year he took a leading part in a conspiracy to force the Grand-Duke to grant a constitution. The plot was discovered and he was sentenced to exile. He chose to settle in France and with the help of his French friends was granted French nationality in 1833. It is a telling indication of his undoubted gifts and his growing reputation as a scientist that in the same year he was elected to the Académie des Sciences. Further prestigious appointments followed. He began to teach at the Collège de France. He was appointed professor at the Sorbonne, lecturing on the calculus of probability, and inspector of the Paris Collèges. Between 1838 and 1841 he published his most famous work, the *Histoire des sciences mathématiques en Italie* in four volumes.

Meanwhile he was indulging his taste for collecting fine books of all kinds: collecting, but also speculating and selling. Purchases at auctions were financed by loans from the Neapolitan consul. The leading Paris bookseller, Joseph Techener, was a major supplier, but he also bought on a large scale in London, from Payne and Foss, and from Rodd. His collection eventually included 40,000 printed books and over 1,800 manuscripts. We shall see how many of the latter were acquired. In 1836 he had been appointed to the Committee of Historical Monuments, whose task was to publish a collection of unpublished documents on the history of France.

Fig. 1. Guglielmo Libri. Lithograph by A. N. Noël

This gave him authority to visit libraries in order to inspect their holdings. Rarely has the sheepfold been thrown open more freely to the wolf.

Most French provincial libraries at this time were underfunded and in a more or less disorganized condition. Many had failed to integrate the vast revolutionary accessions of manuscripts from suppressed religious houses. Libri arranged for their unpublished catalogues to be sent to him in Paris before arriving in person. His arrival may at first have aroused feelings of alarm, as he made his appearance dressed like a Sicilian bandit in a huge cloak and carrying a stiletto, allegedly for personal protection. His knowledge and his reputation however reassured librarians. He was given exceptional facilities, allowed to work on the shelves, to remain after hours, even to bring food into the stacks. At Auxerre he was closely invigilated and nothing was taken. Other libraries were less fortunate. Lyons, Orléans and Tours were the ones that suffered most.

Lyons had been a brilliant centre of learning in the time of Charlemagne under a series of distinguished bishops. A ninth-century writer called it 'the public school of the world this side of the ocean'.[2] Its Bibliothèque Municipale preserved thirteen manuscripts in uncial or half-uncial of the fifth to the eighth century, the most important homogeneous group in any city except Verona. Libri did not dare to take complete manuscripts of such celebrity. But most of the bindings were falling to pieces. All that was needed was to slit the sewing thread to remove complete gatherings. The stiletto must have come in handy. Libri took portions of six manuscripts, which afterwards became his MSS. 2, 3, 4, 5, 7 and 12. The most illustrious victim was a seventh-century Pentateuch, from which he abstracted the books of Leviticus and Numbers.

The manuscript holdings of the library of Tours were derived from the cathedral of Saint-Gatien, the collegiate church of St Martin of Tours and the abbey of Marmoutier. The library was in total disorder with many manuscripts uncatalogued. Here Libri's technique was different. There was no need to cut out gatherings. Complete manuscripts could be removed and their places on the shelves filled with uncatalogued works of lesser value. Libri took twenty-four. Among them was a seventh-century Pentateuch with nineteen large miniatures, known to scholars since the early eighteenth century when it was still the property of the cathedral.

Orléans was ravaged as severely as Tours. Libri both cut out gatherings and took complete volumes. Twenty-six manuscripts or parts of manuscripts were taken, dating from the seventh century onwards. The earliest had belonged to the ancient abbey of Fleury on the Loire.

The public library at Carpentras consisted of the collection formed and bequeathed by the eighteenth-century bibliophile bishop, Malachy d'Inguimbert. Mgr. d'Inguimbert had spent many years in Rome, had written the life of Pope Clement XI and been the confessor of Lorenzo Corsini, Pope Clement XII. His printed books aroused Libri's acquisitive instincts. The librarian, the learned but ineffectual Hyacinthe Olivier-Vitalis, impressed, in the royalist South of France, by Libri's title of Count, was only too willing to oblige him. Libri was anxious to obtain their uncut copy of the Aldine Theocritus, 1495, and offered to exchange it for his own copy plus a number of modern scientific books. Olivier-Vitalis was happy to agree. In fact Libri didn't own a copy and had quickly to obtain one from Payne and Foss. He also secured Castiglione's *Il Cortegiano*, 1528, bound for Jean Grolier, one of six copies Grolier had owned (it now belongs to Viscount Astor); the printer's manuscript of the same work, probably a present from the Torresano brothers to Grolier, who had it bound (now in Florence); fourteen other manuscripts, more fine printed books and 1,734 leaves for his autograph collection from the correspondence of the seventeenth-century savant, Nicolas-Claude Fabri de Peiresc. The historians of the Bibliothèque Inguimbertine observed with admirable moderation that Olivier-Vitalis 'did not have for the Library all the solicitude that it deserved'.[3]

Other libraries lost manuscripts to Libri, and probably also printed books, though little evidence of the latter class of losses has been identified.

Libri's next task was to conceal the origin of these French manuscripts by giving them Italian provenances. It was at that time fashionable among the nouveaux riches of the July Monarchy to claim descent from a Crusader. A class of forgers had emerged to satisfy this need by copying medieval charters but changing the name of the recipient. These shadowy performers were employed by Libri to wash out inconvenient marginalia, erase stamps and seals, and forge ownership inscriptions. Libri owned a genuine manuscript from the monastery of S. Pietro in Perugia. He had the inscription copied in other volumes. Early manuscripts were given Grottaferrata inscriptions. Those from Fleury were relocated to Florence by changing 'Floriacensis' to 'Florentinae'. Some forgeries were more ambitious. The 1472 Foligno Dante was doctored to make it appear a rare, or unique, variant. A fourteenth-century manuscript was inscribed with the ownership of Dante. Two eighth-century manuscripts bore the name of Charlemagne's father, Pippin, King of the Franks. The great Delisle himself could not decide whether both were forgeries or only one, and if so, which one.

Finally the manuscripts were sent to Florence to be rebound in Italian half-bindings of wooden boards and leather spines. Fine bindings were restored or improved nearer home. Libri kept a set of facsimiles of Renaissance binding tools for the purpose.

Alarm bells however were beginning to ring. In 1842 an anonymous denunciation reached the Prefect of Police that Professor Libri had stolen valuable manuscripts from French public libraries. Rumours began to be circulated by Chartistes — graduates of the École des Chartes, the national school of palaeography; Libri saw them as enemies, jealous at having been excluded from the work of cataloguing the nation's manuscripts. These rumours reached the press. Libri threatened to challenge the editor of *Le National* to a duel. For a time this threat was silenced. But Libri took great risks. He could not resist showing the Tours *Pentateuch* to a literary gathering in the house of the artist Paul Delaroche. Prosper Mérimée was amazed; he knew the manuscript well and had made tracings of the miniatures. He remarked that he had thought it was in Tours. Libri was not taken aback. He replied that his was the Italian original from which the Tours manuscript had been copied.

The time had come to begin realizing his most valuable asset, his library. Autograph letters and a few manuscripts had already been included anonymously in eleven auction sales in Paris. Towards the end of 1845 he decided to dispose of his medieval manuscripts. Since the origin of many was dubious, it was obviously prudent to offer them abroad. Through his friend Anthony Panizzi, another Italian political exile, he sent the list to the British Museum. Panizzi passed it to the Keeper of Manuscripts, Sir Frederic Madden. Madden was impressed. There were manuscripts that had belonged to Lorenzo de' Medici and Pope Leo X, fifteen Dantes, one of which was the earliest copy known, dated 1335, a 'Pentateuch … of the 3rd century', in uncial letters 'with many miniatures, executed by Roman artists, and resembling the style of the paintings at Pompeii'[4] (this was the manuscript from Tours), a Giulio Clovio signed by the artist, and an Ildephonsus 'believed to be the earliest specimen of Spanish art in existence'. More lists followed and finally a price, 250,000 francs, equivalent to £10,000. It was decided that the collections should be inspected.

In May 1846 Madden arrived in Paris, accompanied by his wife, his sister-in-law and his assistant, John Holmes. After a few days settling in and admiring the French capital, Madden and Holmes set out for Libri's apartment in the Sorbonne. They found the professor 'a rather corpulent person, of good humoured but broad features, but seeming as if he had never used soap and water or a brush. The room … was not more than about 16 feet wide, but filled with manuscripts on shelves up to the ceiling.'[5] The windows were closed, a fire was burning in the grate, and the heat, 'added to the smell of the piles of vellum around' caused Madden to gasp for breath. He and Holmes set to work, but found the task most laborious. The books were not only very dirty but were arranged in no kind of order. There were disappointments; Madden was uneasy about the date 1335 in the manuscript of Dante, and the Giulio Clovio turned out to be 'a mere *daub* and not worth £5'. Nevertheless, after nine days, Madden concluded that Libri was to be considered trustworthy and had not in general over-described his collection, which he estimated at between £8,000 and £9,000.

He was to be disabused. In London he saw the bookseller Thomas Rodd and learned not only that Libri was notorious as a dealer in books and manuscripts, but was suspected of having stolen part of his collection of manuscripts. This was later confirmed by the Berlin bookseller Asher. Worse was to follow. John Thomas Payne, of the great bookselling partnership of Payne & Foss, reported that in April, after the lists of manuscripts had been sent to the British Museum, Libri had held a sale of autograph material in Paris, including letters from collections he had told Madden were intact. By this time however the matter was out of Sir Frederic's hands, as the Trustees had applied to the Treasury for £9,000 to make the purchase. The Treasury, in those pre-Lottery days, refused and the sale fell through.

Libri next tried Turin, but with no more success. Meanwhile John Holmes had sent the catalogue to Bertram, fourth Earl of Ashburnham. Lord Ashburnham was a 'proud and autocratic nobleman',[6] the head of a family that claimed to be unique in having held its lands in a direct line since before the Norman Conquest. He was a passionate collector of fine manuscripts. He dispatched Thomas Rodd to Paris; the bookseller returned with a favourable report and two samples: the Tours Pentateuch and the Hours of Lorenzo the Magnificent. Ashburnham was persuaded to offer £8,000 for the collection. This was accepted and in April 1847 sixteen cases of manuscripts were delivered to Ashburnham Place.

Libri next began the dispersal of his printed books with an auction of Belles-Lettres in Paris in 1847 (fig. 2). The sale, described as 'la bibliothèque de M[onsieur] Lxxxx', began on 28 June and lasted into August. There were over 3,000 lots, including the uncut Theocritus and Grolier's copy of Castiglione, both from Carpentras, and the doctored Foligno Dante. The total was 106,000 francs, or about £4,000. There was a farcical incident. The *Galeomyomachia*, the 'war of cat and mouse', a Byzantine parody of the *Iliad*, printed by Aldus about 1494, was a work of considerable rarity, consisting of only ten leaves. The only known copy in

CATALOGUE

DE LA

BIBLIOTHÈQUE DE M. L****

Dont la vente se fera le lundi 28 juin 1847, et les vingt-neuf jours suivants à six heures de relevée, rue des Bons-Enfants, n° 30, maison Silvestre, salle du premier.

Les adjudications seront faites

Par Me COMMANDEUR, commissaire-priseur, rue Neuve-St-Augustin, 25.

BELLES-LETTRES

Parmi les livres rares et précieux de cette classe nous signalerons les suivants: **CATHOLICON**, de 1460. — **ANTHOLOGIA GRÆCA**, de 1494. — **HOMERUS**, de 1488. — **APOLLONIUS RHODIUS**, de 1496. — **MARTIALIS** d'Alde, 1501, sur **peau vélin**. — **SANNAZARIUS**, de 1526, sur **peau vélin**. — Opera **ALIONI** Astensis, de 1521 (*seul exemplaire complet*). — **DANTE**, de 1472. — **DANTE** (*circa* 1515), sur **peau vélin**. — **DANTE**, Quæstio fioruenta, de 1508. — **PETRARCA** d'Alde, de 1514, sur **peau vélin**. — **PETRARCA**, Triompho (*XVe siècle*), sur **peau vélin**.— **ARIOSTO**, de 1530 (*inconnu aux bibliographes*). — **LA BELLA MANO**, de 1474. — **BELINZONE**, de 1493. — **BOIARDO**, Sonetti, de 1499. — **CECCO D'ASCOLI**, de 1476. — **LA REGINA ANCROIA**, de 1510. — **TRABISONDA**, de 1492. — **BOIARDO**, Orlando innamorato, de 1543 (*inconnu aux bibliographes*). — **IL GIRONE**, de 1548 (*exempl. de Diane de Poitiers*), — **LA REGINA D'OCIENTE**, de 1620. — **DATI**, lettera di Colombo, de 1493.— **ALTRO MARTE**, de 1489. — **CANZONE A BALLO**, de 1568. — **FABRITII**, de 1527. — **TARIFFA**, de 1535. — **GALEOMYOMACHIA** d'Alde, (1494). — **ÆSOPUS**, de 1480 et de 1485. — **MORLINUS**, de 1520. — **GUERINO MESCHINO**, de 1477. — **BOCCACIO**, de 1483. — **NOVELLE ANTIKE**, de 1525, et *sans date*. — **IL PECORONE**, de 1558 — **DECOR PUELLARUM**, de 1461. — **L'ALCIBIADE**, de 1652 (*non rogné*). — **SANNAZARO** d'Alde, de 1514, en *papier bleu*. — **CASTIGLIONE**, il cortegiano, de 1528 (*exempl. de Grolier*). — **CICERO** ad familiares, de 1522 (*exempl. de Grolier*). — **CICERO**, ad Atticum, *Romæ*, 1470. — **GASPARINUS**, (*premier livre imprimé en France*). — **BEMBO**, lettere, de 1518, **sur peau vélin**. — **CATULLUS** d'Alde, 1515 (*exempl. de Grolier*). — **THEOCRITUS** d'Alde, 1495 (*non rogné*). — **ISOCRATES**, de 1493. — **RICCIUS** de imitatione, d'Alde, 1545, en *grand papier*. — **MUSÆUS** d'Alde, (1494). — **LIVRES ANNOTÉS** par Rabelais, Montaigne, Michel-Ange, Galilée, le Tasse, Alde Manuce, etc., etc.

SE DISTRIBUE A PARIS

CHEZ L. C. SILVESTRE ET P. JANNET, LIBRAIRES,

Rue des Bons-Enfants, 30.

1847

Fig. 2

France had been in the Bibliothèque Mazarine, bound with two other works, but a second, imperfect copy had recently appeared in a sale at Rouen. The librarian of the Mazarine, Silvestre de Sacy, had been horrified to discover in 1846 that the Library's copy of the *Galeomyomachia* was missing from its volume. When Libri's sale catalogue was published a year later Silvestre de Sacy noticed that it contained a perfect copy. He was naturally anxious to discover whether this was the stolen Mazarine copy and asked Libri if he might examine it. The professor arrived at the Library carrying the book and said at once, 'Are you thinking of bringing an action against me? If so, I refuse to provide any explanation.'[7] On being told that they only wanted to see whether it was the Mazarine copy, he handed it over. There were no marks to identify it. Thereupon Libri gave it to the Library, saying 'It will be a great pleasure to offer it to the Bibliothèque Mazarine to replace the one lost', and insisted that the donation should be reported in the *Journal des Débats*. It was afterwards remarked that the book had disappeared from a shelf close to where Libri normally sat.

Libri had carried off two successful sales, but calamity was imminent. M. Boucly, the Public Prosecutor, received two anonymous letters accusing Libri of thefts in Carpentras, Montpellier and Grenoble. Enquiries however failed to produce confirmation of the alleged thefts. When a third denunciation arrived in July 1847, Boucly renewed the investigation and this time books and manuscripts were reported to be missing from several locations. Troyes informed the magistrate that 'after M. Libri's visit the library of this town offers much less of interest to book lovers.'[8] Boucly continued his enquiries and uncovered other suspicious circumstances. On 4 February 1848, he submitted his report to the Minister of Justice, who passed it to the Prime Minister, Libri's friend Guizot. Libri was told and was able to convince Guizot that the charges were false. Guizot laid the report aside in a drawer of his private cabinet in the Ministry of Foreign Affairs.

Eighteen days later revolution broke out. Louis Philippe and Guizot took refuge in England. Libri had lost his protector. Boucly's report was discovered and at dinner on 27 February a puzzled high official of the Ministry of Foreign Affairs disclosed its existence to Terrien, a reporter on the newspaper *Le National*. The next day Terrien was listening to a lecture on the barometer at the Institut. Libri came in, beaming and wearing an enormous tricolour cockade; he advanced, shaking hands right and left with acquaintances. Terrien was shocked by this behaviour. He was convinced of Libri's guilt and tearing off a piece of paper he scribbled a note:

Monsieur, You are doubtless ignorant of the discovery in the Ministry of Foreign Affairs of a judicial report concerning your work as inspector of public libraries. Believe me, spare the new society reactions which they would find repugnant. Do not come again to the Institut.[9]

Libri's expression changed. He hurried from the room back to his apartment in the Sorbonne. Helped by his nephew Tito del Rosso he spent all night packing his most valuable books and manuscripts into eighteen chests and burning incriminating papers in the grate. The crates were hastily dispatched to England in the name of Tito del Rosso's girlfriend. A magistrate, sent to Le Havre to stop the consignment, arrived shortly after the boat had sailed. In the following days removal vans collected the remaining books and delivered them to other addresses. One chest, three baskets and three parcels of letters and autographs were given to an employee to burn; he neglected to do so and most were seized by the police. Meanwhile, on 29 February, Libri collected his salary from the Sorbonne, and using a friend's passport crossed the Channel in the company of Guizot's daughters, who were passing as English girls. Officials did not search the apartment until 22 March. They found every sign of a hurried departure: the bookcases empty, the drawers pulled out of the desk, the grate full of the ashes of burned papers.

In England Libri was welcomed by Panizzi and Guizot and was able to convince them that he was the object of a malicious persecution. Very cleverly he set about spreading the report that he was a political refugee, a supporter of the July Monarchy and of Guizot's government, forced to flee by the hostility of a strange combination of enemies: the Republican scientist Dominique François Jean Arago, the Jesuits and the Chartistes.

Boucly's judicial report was published, most irregularly, in the *Moniteur Universel* and articles appeared in the English papers. Libri was quick to reply. This was the beginning of a pamphlet war waged between his accusers and his supporters for the next four years. Libri's response took the form of a pamphlet published both in London and Paris. The English edition ran to 86 pages, the French one to 115; the text was the same.[10] It was dignified, authoritative, detailed and extremely effective. Libri had little difficulty in demolishing the Public Prosecutor's arguments. M. Boucly was not a bibliographer and his report was based on anonymous denunciations that did not specify which volumes had been stolen. Only two books were mentioned by name: the uncut Theocritus and Castiglione's *Libro del Cortegiano*, both from Carpentras. Libri proved that he had acquired the Theocritus by exchange, though he lied in saying that the copy he gave in exchange had been bought years earlier from Payne & Foss, whereas he had only bought it after the visit to Carpentras. Boucly's report did not give the date of the *Cortegiano*, nor did it say that the copy had been bound for Grolier. Libri must have gasped with relief when he read this evidence of his accuser's bibliographical ignorance. He was able to respond with perfect truth that the *Cortegiano* was a common book and had been published in more than one edition. There was nothing, he claimed, to connect the Carpentras copy with the one in his sale.

The *Réponse au Rapport de M. Boucly* succeeded in convincing English public opinion that he was an innocent victim, persecuted for his political opinions. In France too he had many supporters, notably the bibliographers Paul Lacroix and Gustave Brunet, the author Prosper Mérimée and the Montpellier professor Achille Jubinal. The note handed to him by Terrien at the Institut had disappeared. Libri cleverly altered it to make it sound like a threat to lynch him. His version ran: 'Spare the French people one of those acts of popular vengeance which are repugnant to the character of our nation … Disappear!'[11] Fear for his life had been the reason for his hurried departure.

Meanwhile in France legal proceedings had been started against him. The case was entrusted to a *juge d'instruction* called Hatton, assisted by an expert committee of six, all but one of them graduates of the École des Chartes. Their indictment was published in May 1850. It was a far more formidable document than Boucly's report. It detailed letters of Hevelius taken from the Bibliothèque de l'Observatoire, letters and documents of Peiresc removed from Carpentras, letters of scientists missing from the archives of the Institut and leaves missing from the manuscripts of Leonardo da Vinci which the French Revolutionary Government had seized from Milan and allotted to the Institut. Libri had been the only person to sell a Leonardo manuscript in Paris. In June 1850 he was tried in absentia. There was no defence and the accused was sentenced to ten years' imprisonment and the deprivation of his civil rights.

Libri remained safely in England and continued to publish pamphlets contesting the verdict. He was granted British nationality and married an old flame, Mélanie Collin. He transferred to her ownership the books left in Paris and appropriated by the Republic. She was eventually able to recover 15,000; the rest were sold to pay the expenses of the trial. In 1861, at the suggestion of Prosper Mérimée, Mélanie Collin petitioned the French Senate to set aside the verdict of the 1850 trial. The petition was refused.

In England Libri continued to buy manuscripts and books. In 1859 the first two of a series of sales were held at Sotheby's (fig. 3). The catalogues were very different in tone from the firm's normal understated style. Whereas the first of the great Hamilton Palace sales was merely described as 'The First Portion of the Beckford Library', Libri's first sale was called 'The extraordinary collection of SPLENDID MANUSCRIPTS, chiefly upon vellum, in various languages of Europe and the East, formed by M. Guglielmo Libri, The Eminent Collector, who is obliged to leave London in consequence of ill health, and for that reason to dispose of his Literary Treasures.' The catalogue, compiled of course by himself, contained an Introduction in English and French — a tedious affair of 38 pages, a list of works consulted in preparing the descriptions, and 37 plates of reproductions: the first to display these features that have since become commonplace in Sotheby and Christie catalogues. There were long notes to almost every lot, some of one or even two pages: another modern touch.

It must be admitted that this shrillness was perhaps to some extent justified. Collectors of the generation of William Beckford had been interested only in late medieval and Renaissance manuscripts. Libri belonged to a later generation that understood and appreciated the importance of early codices. The sale included 62 manuscripts earlier than the year 1200, a Koran in Kufic script, atlases of portulan charts, what were described as autograph manuscripts of Galileo, Kepler and Tasso and autograph letters of the Jesuit polymath Athanasius Kircher, together with less important and indeed trivial material. Sir Thomas Phillipps attended the first three days of the sale and bid voraciously, buying all but one of twenty manuscripts of Cicero. On the fourth, fifth and sixth days he was absent, no doubt to the auctioneer's dismay, as prices were less buoyant. Sir Frederic Madden appeared in person to buy a volume of designs for ships by Robert Dudley, the author of the *Arcano del Mare*, and bidding through Boone he obtained the Galileo and Kepler manuscripts. Sir Thomas returned on the seventh and last days, but in a more subdued mood, to buy nine manuscripts of the ninth to the thirteenth century. Altogether he

CATALOGUE

OF THE EXTRAORDINARY COLLECTION OF

SPLENDID MANUSCRIPTS,

CHIEFLY UPON VELLUM,

IN VARIOUS LANGUAGES OF EUROPE AND THE EAST, FORMED BY

M. GUGLIELMO LIBRI,

The Eminent Collector, who is obliged to leave London in consequence of ill health, and for that reason to dispose of his Literary Treasures.

Amongst these Manuscripts will be found:

BIBLIA LATINA, Sæc. XI, with Miniatures; EVANGELIA IV, Græce, Sæc. X-XI; several copies of the EVANGELISTS, in Latin, of Sæc. IX, with Miniatures in the Byzantine style; various LECTIONARIA of the IXth and Xth Centuries, with Miniatures; a large number of the FATHERS OF THE CHURCH, including S. Gregorius Nyssenus, Græce, Sæc. IX; S. Joannes Chrysostomus, Græce, Sæc. X, &c.; Two important MSS. OF SAINT CYPRIAN, one of the VIIth and the other of the IXth Century; different WORKS OF ST. AUGUSTIN, ST. JEROME, ST. GREGORY THE GREAT, ST. ISIDORE, &c. &c. all of the VIIIth, IXth, Xth, and XIth Centuries; BEDA IN MARCUM, Sæc. VIII, cotemporary with the Author; BEDÆ HISTORIA ANGLORUM, Sæc. XI; VITÆ SANCTORUM, Sæc. IX, X, and XI, with Ancient Designs or Miniatures of the Anglo-Saxon School; several Collections of LITURGIES, in Greek or in Latin, with the Ancient Music, written Sæc. IX, X, XI; JUSTINIANI DIGESTUM NOVUM, Sæc. XI-XII.

MANY OF THE GREEK WRITERS AND NEARLY ALL THE LATIN CLASSICS,

INCLUDING

Lucretius (Sæc. XIV.), **Lucanus** (Sæc. XIII.) Claudianus (Sæc. XII.), Vegetius (Sæc. XI), **Censorinus, Prudentius** (Sæc. X.), Donatus (Sæc. IX.), Priscianus (Sæc. XI), Boetius (Sæc. XI.) Cassiodorus (Sæc. IX.), Grammatici (Sæc. X.), &c. &c.

Mathematical, Medical, and other Scientific Works,

Including the earliest Manuscript in existence, containing modern numerical figures

ANCIENT ITALIAN POETS AND PROSE WRITERS;

Works in the Limousin Dialect; PORTULANI and Ancient Illuminated Maps;

Early French Poetry and Unpublished Romances of Chivalry; Old English Poetry;

AN EXTENSIVE COLLECTION OF ORIENTAL WORKS;

HORÆ AND OTHER DEVOTIONAL BOOKS, with magnificent Miniatures of the various Schools

AUTOGRAPH MSS. OF TASSO, GALILEO, KEPLER, LEIBNITZ, &c.

WHICH WILL BE SOLD BY AUCTION,

BY MESSRS.

S. LEIGH SOTHEBY & JOHN WILKINSON,

AUCTIONEERS OF LITERARY PROPERTY AND WORKS ILLUSTRATIVE OF THE FINE ARTS,

AT THEIR HOUSE, 3, WELLINGTON STREET, STRAND,

On MONDAY, 28th of MARCH, 1859, and SEVEN following Days,
(Sunday excepted), at ONE o'Clock precisely each Day.

MAY BE VIEWED THREE DAYS PRIOR, AND CATALOGUES HAD.

PRINTED BY J. DAVY AND SONS, 137, LONG ACRE, LONDON.

Fig. 3

had bought more than ten per cent of the sale, 133 lots at prices varying from one shilling to £60. Lord Crawford, bidding through Quaritch, secured 23 lots. Another substantial purchaser was the antiquary, Thomas Bateman.

The sale realized over £6,500 and could be considered a success for the vendor. The buyers were not so pleased. Madden complained that the 'Autographs of Galileo and Kepler … turn out not to be autographs at all! I have no remedy, except in a Court of Law…'.[12] Phillipps discovered that some of his purchases had been grossly misdescribed. He asked Sotheby's to approach Libri to request an adjustment of price on these lots. Libri refused, pointing to the conditions of sale that manuscripts were sold 'with all faults'. 'I have every reason to believe,' he wrote, 'that the manuscripts correspond with the Catalogue, but this is quite immaterial; the conditions of the sale being that no claim of the kind would be admitted.'[13]

What was described as 'The Choicer Portion of the Magnificent Library', consisting of printed books, was offered in August of the same year, a sale notable for the large number of fine bindings (fig. 4). The owner, after declaring that his state of health precluded writing an introduction, went on to do exactly that for fifteen pages. It was the first auction sale to include the Italian Renaissance bindings with the plaquette, subsequently famous, of Apollo and Pegasus. Libri did not know who the owner had been. In describing the 1544 Josephus he called him 'this unknown but celebrated collector', but later in the catalogue ventured an equally ridiculous guess: 'the celebrated collector by some called Mecenate (Maecenas), Physician to the Pope'. The sale realized £8,515.

There was a further sale, in two parts, of books and manuscripts in 1861. This again had a 28-page Introduction in English and French but fetched only £2,226 for 7,600 lots, scarcely more than £100 for each day's sale. Libri decided that the market required livening up and English collectors needed instruction in the merits of fine bindings. In 1862 there appeared his *Monuments inédits ou peu connus … du Cabinet de M. Guillaume Libri*, a large folio of illustrations in colour of over 150 bindings. The first eleven plates were of treasure bindings enriched with jewels or enamel. All were included in the relatively short sale of the 'Reserved Portion' in 1862. Sir Thomas Phillipps bought seven of the ten. Bidding in person, he had been run up by Libri's agents and had paid high prices. Though all seven contained medieval elements, it is doubtful whether any one would be

CATALOGUE

OF

THE CHOICER PORTION

OF THE

MAGNIFICENT LIBRARY,

FORMED BY

M. GUGLIELMO LIBRI,

SO EMINENT AS A COLLECTOR,

Who is leaving London in consequence of ill health, and solely for that reason disposing of his Literary Treasures;

AMONGST WHICH WILL BE FOUND:

UNKNOWN BLOCK-BOOKS;

Specimens of Early Typography and Art,

Comprising an unknown KALENDARIUM with the earliest Engravings on Copper;
AN UNRIVALLED COLLECTION OF WORKS PRINTED UPON VELLUM;
THE RAREST ALDINE AND JUNTA EDITIONS,
Embracing several printed on Vellum, Large Paper, or hitherto unknown;
EDITIONES PRINCIPES OF GREAT RARITY;

POEMS AND ROMANCES OF CHIVALRY,

In Italian, French, German, Spanish, and other Languages or Dialects of Europe;

AN EXTRAORDINARY SERIES OF ANCIENT ITALIAN LITERATURE,

IN WHICH ARE SEVERAL UNKNOWN RAPPRESENTAZIONI SACRE, NOVELLIERI, &c.;
EARLY AND PROBABLY UNIQUE MUSICAL COMPOSITIONS;
SCARCE WORKS RESPECTING AMERICA;
ELZEVIRS IN AN UNCUT STATE;

Early Productions of the English Press;

MANUSCRIPTS & BOOKS WITH AUTOGRAPH NOTES,

Containing among the former: PINDARUS, EUTROPIUS, PETRARCA, HORÆ AND BREVIARIA, WRITTEN UPON VELLUM, WITH SPLENDID ILLUMINATIONS; and among the latter: ANTHOLOGIA, *editio princeps with numerous manuscript annotations by the first* ALDUS—TASSO, GERUSALEMME, *with valuable additions in the autograph of* ALDO MANUZIO—RACINE, ATHALIE (1691), *with numerous corrections by the* AUTHOR—BOILEAU, SATIRES (Paris, 1668), *with numerous notes in the autograph of* THE SATIRIST HIMSELF, &c. &c.

AND ALSO INCLUDING

A MOST SUPERB, INTERESTING AND PERFECTLY UNIQUE

COLLECTION OF HISTORICAL BINDINGS,

Shewing the Progress of the Bibliopegistic Art from the Fifteenth Century

By means of about 1500 Volumes, in old ornamented Morocco or Calf, with arms or devices of former Possessors; amongst which will be found:—Eighteen Volumes formerly in the celebrated GROLIER COLLECTION; several Volumes in the splendid Bindings of MAJOLI, DIANE DE POICTIERS, DE THOU, COUNT D'HOYM, LONGEPIERRE, FOSCARINI, &c. &c.; Books with the arms of POPE PIUS V (and other Pontiffs), CARDINAL FARNESE, Members of the MEDICI and the D'ESTE Families, P. GIORDANO ORSINO, the Emperor CHARLES V, the DUKES OF BAVARIA, CHARLES VIII, FRANCIS I, HENRY II, FRANCIS II, CHARLES IX, HENRY III, HENRY IV, LOUIS XIII, LOUIS XIV, LOUIS XV, LOUIS XVI, MARIE ANTOINETTE, &c., of France; HENRY VII, HENRY VIII, EDWARD VI, QUEEN ELIZABETH, JAMES I, CHARLES I, OLIVER CROMWELL, CHARLES II, JAMES III (the Old Pretender), WILLIAM III, QUEEN ANNE, and succeeding Monarchs of England;

THE WHOLE OF THESE ANCIENT BINDINGS BEING

IN THE MOST PERFECT STATE OF PRESERVATION.

WHICH WILL BE SOLD BY AUCTION,

BY MESSRS.

S. LEIGH SOTHEBY & JOHN WILKINSON,

AUCTIONEERS OF LITERARY PROPERTY AND WORKS ILLUSTRATIVE OF THE FINE ARTS,

AT THEIR HOUSE, 3, WELLINGTON STREET, STRAND,

On MONDAY, 1st of AUGUST, 1859, and TWELVE following Days,

(SUNDAYS EXCEPTED), AT ONE O'CLOCK PRECISELY EACH DAY.

MAY BE VIEWED THREE DAYS PRIOR, AND CATALOGUES HAD.

PRINTED BY J. DAVY AND SONS, 137, LONG ACRE, LONDON.

Fig. 4

accepted by modern scholarship as being in original condition. The sale was the most successful of the series: £10,320 for 713 lots.

Libri was considered a scoundrel in France; in England there were few who still believed in his innocence; but in Italy he was regarded as an eminent man of science, unjustly accused.[14] In 1868, old and ill, he returned to a warm welcome from his remaining contemporaries in Florence. A year later he died in Fiesole.

At the time of his death none of the stolen manuscripts had been restored to its lawful owner. Lord Ashburnham rejected a request from the French ambassador to return the Libri collection against repayment of the purchase price. He was still convinced that the Professor had been traduced and that the manuscripts had been acquired legally. John Holmes prepared catalogues of the manuscripts at Ashburnham Place, though these did not become available in Paris until 1865. Ashburnham also published an album of nine facsimile plates.

Meanwhile a new protagonist had entered the scene, perhaps the only person to emerge from the whole affair with credit. Léopold Delisle, a Norman, like others who have subsequently held the same posts, was a scholar of outstanding intelligence and inexhaustible energy. He became Keeper of Manuscripts in 1847 in what was then the Bibliothèque Royale, and Administrateur-général of the Bibliothèque Nationale, as it had become, in 1874. It was not until his tenure as head of the Library that the vast accession of manuscripts during the Revolutionary period of the previous century was finally catalogued.

Lord Ashburnham's collection was derived from four distinct sources: the Libri manuscripts; the Stowe manuscripts, bought from the Duke of Buckingham and containing early Irish codices and Anglo-Saxon charters; the Barrois manuscripts, bought in 1849 from Joseph Barrois of Lille; and the so-called Appendix of manuscripts bought singly. Unluckily for Ashburnham the Barrois manuscripts included 64 stolen from the Bibliothèque Royale. After studying the Ashburnham catalogues Delisle published an article showing that some of the Barrois manuscripts had certainly been stolen, while those from Libri 'give rise to curious observations'. He was magnanimous in writing about their owner, observing that while he lamented the loss to France, it was a comfort to know that 'these manuscripts are in the gallery of an illustrious book lover, who appreciates their true value and to whom French erudition already owes so much.'[15] Ashburnham, on receiving a copy of the article, replied that he had already suspected that there had been fraudulent attempts to conceal the manuscripts' true provenances. At this stage neither side suggested restitution.

Lord Ashburnham's death in 1878 created a new set of circumstances. His son, the fifth Earl, had no literary interests and valued his father's collection solely for its monetary value. The fourth Earl had published the books of Leviticus and Numbers which Libri had abstracted from the seventh-century Lyons Pentateuch. On a visit to Lyons in the year of Lord Ashburnham's death Delisle was amazed to discover that the script of the Pentateuch was identical with that of the Ashburnham manuscript. Leviticus and Numbers were missing. A German scholar had seen the manuscript complete in 1834 and had published his report in 1837. Faced with this evidence, the fifth Earl capitulated and handed over his fragment to the French ambassador.

Complicated negotiations followed. The Earl offered the complete collection to the British Museum for £160,000, but the Treasury refused to advance so large a sum. Eventually Lord Ashburnham agreed to divide the collection, and the Museum acquired the Stowe manuscripts for £45,000. Meanwhile Delisle had inspected the manuscripts in London and had identified 166 as stolen. He valued them at 700,000 francs or £24,000. A stalemate followed, as the Earl refused to sell those manuscripts separately and thus to divide the Libri collection. At last he relented, and accepted an offer of £23,000 from Italy for the Libri manuscripts, less those claimed by France. Even then, when restitution seemed imminent, the French Government disgracefully refused the money.

A solution was found by the bookseller Karl Trübner, of Strasbourg, which since the 1870 War had been part of Germany. He offered to buy the 166 manuscripts and cede them to the French national library in return for the Manesse Codex and 150,000 francs or £6,000. The fourteenth-century Manesse Codex, originally in the Palatine Library in Heidelberg but in Paris since the seventeenth century, contained the largest surviving collection of poetry by the Minnesänger and 139 full-page illustrations. It had supplied some of the imagery in Gérard de Nerval's sonnet, 'El Desdichado'. However sad to lose this famous manuscript, Delisle agreed. The exchange was carried out, the Manesse Codex returned to Heidelberg and the lost manuscripts and fragments to the Bibliothèque Nationale. This was not quite the end of the story. The fragment of the Lyons Pentateuch, surrendered by the fifth Earl, had been reunited with its parent manuscript, but Delisle refused to return the other *membra disjecta* to the provincial libraries from which they had been removed. They had been lost through the librarians' negligence, he pointed out, and the provincial authorities had done nothing to assist in their recovery. They are still in Paris.

References

1. This paper is based principally on the following sources: Léopold Delisle, *Les manuscrits du comte d'Ashburnham*, Paris, 1883; *idem*, *Les manuscrits des Fonds Libri et Barrois à la Bibliothèque Nationale*, Paris, 1888; *idem*, *Catalogue des Fonds Libri et Barrois*, Paris, 1888; A. N. L. Munby, *The Earl and the thief*, Cambridge, Massachusetts, The Houghton Library, 1968; *idem*, 'The Triumph of Delisle', *Harvard Library Bulletin*, XVII, 3, July 1969, pp. 279–90; P. Alessandra Maccioni Ruju and Marco Mostert, *The life and times of Guglielmo Libri (1802–1869)*, Hilversum, 1995.
2. Heiric of Auxerre: cf. E. A. Lowe, 'Codices Lugdunenses antiquissimi', *Bibliothèque de la Ville de Lyon. Documents paléographiques, typographiques, iconographiques*, III–IV, Lyon, 1924, p. 7.
3. Robert et Maurice Caillet, *La Bibliothèque Inguimbertine de Carpentras*, Carpentras, 1929, p. 17.
4. Maccioni Ruju and Mostert, p. 219.
5. Munby, *The Earl*, p. 4.
6. cf. A. N. L. Munby, *Connoisseurs and medieval miniatures 1750–1850*, Oxford, 1972, p. 121.
7. Maccioni Ruju and Mostert, p. 208.
8. Paragraph 16 of Boucly's report, reprinted in Libri's *Réponse* (see note 10).
9. M. Terrien, *Aux lecteurs du Bulletin scientifique du National*, Paris, 1850, pp. 9–10.
10. G. Libri, *Réponse … au Rapport de M. Boucly publié dans le Moniteur Universel du 19 mars 1848*, London: Schulze et Cie., 1848; *idem*, Paris: chez tous les libraires, 1848.
11. Libri, *Réponse*, London edition, p. viii.
12. A. N. L. Munby, *Phillipps Studies no. 4*, Cambridge, 1956, p. 82.
13. *Ibid.*, p. 83.
14. E.g. Andrea Stiattesi, *Commentario storico-scientifico della vita e le opere del Conte Guglielmo Libri*, seconda edizione, Florence, 1880.
15. Maccioni Ruju and Mostert, pp. 322–3.

Bound for Botany Bay; or, what did the nineteenth-century convict read?

BILL BELL

> My name they say is Young Birdline,
> My fingers are fish-hooks, sirs;
> And I my reading learnt betime,
> From studying pocket-books, sirs.[1]

THAT THE ABILITY to purloin a purse was incompatible with the ability to read is an assumption that permeated nineteenth-century popular culture. Time and again the image of the Victorian felon as an unlearned and desperate character bore witness to the idea that the so-called criminal classes existed outside the world of polite books and reading. It was in relation to Britain's prison population, more than anywhere else in the nineteenth century, that the debate about literacy and morality would find its most explicit articulation.

In an age dominated by the idea of self-improvement, references to the encouragement of reading among the nation's convicts are to be found throughout government despatches and official reports. 'Silent meditation and the reading of the Bible', remarked one contemporary, was the surest means of producing in the prisoner 'a lasting reformation'.[2] 'If the men are not reading, they are almost certain to be in mischief', observed the chaplain at Dartmoor in 1857, and 'next to the pulpit, a suitable Library is our most powerful Engine for reclamation'.[3]

Of particular interest to reformers and government agencies in the early years of the century was the fate of the thousands of felons who were sentenced to penal servitude in the remote colony of New South Wales. This, and an almost obsessive attitude toward record-keeping within the penal system itself, has left us with a remarkably rich store of documentary evidence relating to official attitudes regarding the convict reader in the transportation period.

But what of the convicts themselves? Between the arrival of the First Fleet in 1788 and the last convict ship to Western Australia eight decades later, over 160,000 British prisoners would make the long journey south. Among the muster rolls are to be found individuals from every class and walk of life, from common labourers to clergymen, soldiers to clerks, bricklayers to schoolmasters. Consequently, the relationship of Australia's prison population to the printed word is as complex as the demography of convict life itself.

Books for a Captive Audience

For the majority of Australia-bound prisoners, the first few months, and in some instances years, after sentencing were spent in prison or on the hulks awaiting transportation. Originally conceived as a stop-gap measure, prison hulks had been in operation since the end of the American War of Independence, providing a place of containment for prisoners who could not be accommodated elsewhere. Sleeping and eating on board, their inhabitants spent weekdays labouring in the nearby docks on Admiralty and Ordnance work. The chief purpose of the hulks was as marshalling places where prisoners from all over Britain were made ready for transportation.

Well into the 1840s decommissioned naval vessels, moving between Woolwich, Chatham, Devonport, and Portsmouth, were home to over 70 per cent of the country's prison population.[4] Conditions on board were known from the start to have been notoriously bad. Calling the situation 'disgraceful and discreditable', the *Enquiry into the General Treatment and Condition of the Convicts in the Hulks at Woolwich* of 1847 observed that many ships were being used as repositories for prisoners considered undesirable by conventional prisons, the old and infirm, as well as the mentally ill. Under such conditions, the inspectors noted, such opportunities as there were for instruction in reading and writing had become matters of mere routine.[5]

After 1812, every prison ship was assigned a chaplain, who was responsible for creating a suitable moral atmosphere on board as well as providing rudimentary educational instruction. Chaplains' reports often make for depressing reading, and more than one comments on the general resistance to their efforts to improve hearts and minds. Faced with what he regarded as outright ignorance and obduracy, we find one chaplain in the 1830s persevering, spending every morning composing sermons for delivery to the prisoners in the evening. 'To transcribe discourses', he remarks optimistically, 'would allow them, who, although they are convicts, have been readers and remember, room to reflect.'[6]

Fig. 1. Convicts going on board the prison-ship *York* in Portsmouth Harbour, from E. W. Cooke, *Sixty Five Plates of Shipping and Craft*, 1829

An account of the daily routine on board the *Leviathan*, moored at Portsmouth in the 1830s, gives some indication of a typical weekday. Prisoners were mustered on deck at 5.45, after which breakfast was served. Work on shore began at 6.45 and continued until noon. Thereafter, a brief return to the ship for dinner, followed by a further six hours of labour. Only after a twelve-hour working day could an hour be found for educational instruction, before prayers and lights out.[7]

Reporting on a similar regime that was kept up at Gibraltar, the second largest hulking settlement at the time, the Governor remarked that it would be unfair, after a strenuous day's work, to make educational instruction compulsory, or to make the administration of rewards and punishments contingent on an individual's ability to read and write. Such a daily requirement, he feared, would not only be 'harsh' but might very well cause an outright rebellion.[8]

While chaplains would often find their charges unresponsive, as they strained to read and write by the light of dim candles in the damp and cold of the lower decks, there appear to have been some notable exceptions. In 1813 a school was successfully established on the *Captivity*, and that same year the chaplain on board the *Hardy* reported how, at the end of each day, prisoners were to be found 'mutually instructing each other in reading, writing, and manufacturing small articles.'[9] In 1815, we find an attempt by the chaplain of the *Retribution* to establish the first library for prisoners. By the 1820s, a collection of 100 volumes is known to have existed on the *Leviathan* while, in 1827, the *Dolphin* is said to have carried 'a small selection of the best religious publications'.[10]

In the years following the 1847 Enquiry the authorities seem to have made a concerted effort to relieve intellectual as well as the physical privation. By 1855 prison chaplains were receiving an annual allowance of 1*s*.6*d*. — or a maximum of three titles per head — for the purchase of library books. An impressive collection of a thousand titles was to be found in the same year on board the *Defence*. As well as a number of edifying works such as *First Sundays in Church* and the highly appropriate *Pursuit of Knowledge under Difficulties,* the ship's library included a number of more serious titles, including Marcel's *Conversations on Natural Philosophy* and Paley's *Moral Philosophy*.[11] It is difficult to determine whether such books were intended principally for the use of prisoners, or aimed at prison officers or for the personal use of the chaplain himself. What is clear however is that there were available on the *Defence* books to suit the intellectual tastes of almost every kind of reader.

While only scant information about the contents of other hulk libraries has survived, there is reason to believe that the literary fare on the *Defence* was unusual in its eclecticism. Such inventories as have survived suggest that the reading matter in most prison libraries was more 'instructive' than 'entertaining'. As late as 1857 we find one chaplain complaining that the religious texts available on the hulks were hardly calculated to appeal to 'men coming in tired from their outdoor labour'.[12]

By the mid-1850s, the tide of official opinion had begun to turn. As Patrick Brantlinger observes, 'despite the dominance among liberals of the wishful views that ignorance causes crime while education cured it, there were many reasons to believe the opposite.'[13] If the inculcation of reading and writing could induce the poor labourer to read his Bible with more devotion, so much to the good. But there was always a risk that a

Fig. 2. Illustration to accompany 'The Order of Prayer for The Visitation of Prisoners', *The Book of Common Prayer*, 1843

knowledge of the alphabet could open up the works of Tom Paine to the disaffected radical. As one prison administrator put it:

> Mere education cannot be received either as a panacea or preventative of serious crime; it is plainly a power which acts both ways, for evil and for good, according to the religious principles and moral habits of those who possess it.[14]

In the 1850s the debate surrounding the moral effect of education was to come to a head with a series of reforms in the prison system which tended to relegate the mental life of the convict to more explicit forms of organization, daily routines, and physical labour. If in the early years of the century religious instruction had been perceived as an essential element in penal reform, the 1852 *Report of the Directors of Convict Prisons* now observed 'that mere education does not produce moral elevation is too apparent', even going so far as to conclude that the conferring of 'a superior education on criminals [is] wrong in principle'.[15] It was a sentiment that was hardly likely to please educationists and religious leaders and served to ignite a struggle between the prison chaplaincy and the government that would continue for years to come.

Something of the priorities of the new regime can be detected from the dispatches exchanged throughout the 1850s between the HMSO, the Treasury, and the Prison Department. Coming to take a more direct interest in prison expenses, the Exchequer was soon issuing instructions to decline any requests for reading matter that could be considered 'unnecessary or extravagant'. By 1857, the book allowance was reduced to 1*s*.3*d*. a head. Reading was a luxury, as one official put it, and 'the Libraries of Hulks and Prisons should contain only plain elementary works'. Later that year, the Comptroller of the Stationary Office had no hesitation in declining an application from the chaplain of the prison hulk, *Stirling Castle*, for a number of titles, including copies of Lardner's *Cabinet Cyclopaedia* in 132 volumes, Forster's *Statesmen* in five volumes, Montgomery and Shelley's *Italian Authors* in three volumes, Bishop Thirkwall's *History of Greece* in eight volumes, and Swainson's *Natural History*. Should they accede to such ridiculous demands, it was argued, 'the public would eventually be called upon to supply all the Hulks, Prisons etc in the empire with Libraries equal or superior to those of the Athenaeum and the House of Commons'.[16]

At least half of the 463 books requested by Dartmoor Prison that same year were denied on the grounds that titles such as Nicholson's

Carpentry and *The Bridgewater Treatises* were thought unsuitable for a prison library.[17] Another hulk chaplain's request for multiple copies of Lady Wake's *Commentary*, Blair's *Lectures on Rhetoric*, and *The Women of Israel* was declined. While it was agreed that 'There cannot be too many religious, moral and instructive works of an inexpensive kind suitable for Convicts,' one copy of each would be enough for the purpose. Accompanying requests for copies of *The Beekeeper's Manual*, *The Cultivation of Winter Cucumber*, and *The Gardener's Dictionary* were declined on the basis that men in prison were in no position to cultivate gardens.[18]

While it is likely that such restrictions owed as much to budgetary constraints as other factors, it is also clear that some government officials felt a moral obligation to supply only the sort of literature that was suitable for the criminal classes. In 1855, the Chaplain of the Convict Prison at Portsmouth had requested the supply of a number of titles, which were deemed unacceptable. To his request for three copies of *The Internal Management of Country Banks*, and two copies of *A Treatise on the Law of Banker's Cheques*, back came the reply: 'Now one would naturally suppose that the majority of Convicts know a great deal too much of the internal arrangements of Country and other Banks, and that the less they are acquainted with these matters and with the law of cheques, the safer private property is likely to remain.' Eyebrows were similarly raised when, years later, a request for copies of *Jack Sheppard* and *Five Years of Penal Servitude* came from Chatham Prison. In that instance, the authorities were reassured to learn that these were meant principally for the officers and not for the use of prisoners.[19] It was a sentiment that would increase as the century progressed, so that by the 1870s 'education remained a privilege as well as a duty.' It was not until they had shown themselves worthy for at least a month that prisoners were considered to deserve visits from the educational instructor.[20]

Literacy in Chains

It is hardly surprising that the prospect of embarkation for Australia was greeted by many prisoners as something of a relief. Some would find shipboard provisions and medical care far better than those they had encountered during their previous months of incarceration. From the end of the eighteenth century every ship was assigned its own Surgeon Superintendent, whose main tasks were attendance to the medical care of his charges as well as the supervision of an adequate diet, open ventilation, and suitable hygiene on board. While the Captain had responsibility for the smooth running of the ship, all matters relating to the convicts came under the Surgeon's jurisdiction. With the assistance of prison guards and army officers, the Surgeon was therefore responsible for seeing that all regulations were observed and discipline appropriately administered.

Before 1846, when it became compulsory for there to be a religious instructor on board, surgeons were also expected to attend to the spiritual as well as temporal needs. As one official directive put it:

> It being highly desirable to keep the minds of the people on board convict ships as constantly and usefully employed as possible, you are to use your best endeavours to establish Schools, under such regulations as circumstances will permit. ... You are to read Church Service to the Convicts every Sunday and also a Sermon, or some well selected parts from the religious tracts which are supplied to you. You are to use every possible means to promote a religious and moral disposition in the Convicts ... and on arrival in New South Wales are to report the names of such ... as have been exemplary in their conduct during the voyage and who from proper use of the Books may deserve to have them as presents.[21]

While the *Eliza* was moored in Woolwich in the autumn of 1819, surgeon John Brydone kept an unusually detailed record of the prisoners he encountered as they awaited departure for Australia.[22] Throughout September we find him spending whole days visiting the hulk *Justitia*, interviewing his assigned prisoners, administering physical examinations, assessing their abilities to read and write, establishing their ages, occupations, crimes, and gathering detailed information from prison guards about their conduct on the hulks. The record reveals that on the *Eliza* skilled tradesmen outnumbered unskilled labourers and included in the musters are printers, engravers, locksmiths, tailors and cooks, two thirds of whom could read to some degree.[23]

With open berths and crowded decks, theft was a common occurrence and so the surgeon undertook to keep a faithful record of all belongings brought on board. One out of every six prisoners is known to have arrived on the *Eliza* with printed matter of some description. Of the 27 that came on board with books, most possessed at least a copy of the Bible or a Testament, some of which may have been distributed by a well-meaning religious visitor on the hulks. While in some cases the possession of the Scriptures could indicate that its owner had behaved well enough to warrant the favour of the chaplain, there seems to be no correlation in the

Fig. 3. The hulk *Justitia*, with convicts at work near Woolwich, from *The Malefactor's Register; or, New Newgate and Tyburn Calendar* [1779]

records between the ownership of a Bible and an individual's perceived moral state.

Despite the prevailing assumption that reading could serve as an ameliorating influence, some of the *Eliza*'s most literate prisoners had earned themselves bad reputations before coming on board. George Carr, a 23-year-old printer, who had been found guilty of highway robbery and who had subsequently proved troublesome in the hulks, brought with him a Bible and three other books. William Barlow, a 30-year-old labourer of 'very bad character' and 'disorderly' had been sentenced for burglary. When he stepped onto the *Eliza* he had in his possession no fewer than 21 books, though he appears not to have been in possession of any religious titles. James Fraser, an 18-year-old servant and housebreaker, having passed his time on the hulks in an 'orderly' fashion, brought with him a Bible and eighteen other books. Adam Murray, a 37-year-old shepherd who had been arrested for stealing livestock but had been relatively well behaved during his imprisonment, brought with him a Bible and four other volumes. Matthew Gillespie, a 17-year-old Scottish copperplate engraver, had received a sentence of fourteen years for housebreaking and had been classified as 'disorderly' on the hulks; he nevertheless had in his possession a Bible and twelve other books.

Even those prisoners who arrived on the *Eliza* without any reading matter would have been able to avail themselves of a number of religious books that were routinely distributed before anchors were weighed. Government regulations required that before departure a copy of the New Testament, two Books of Common Prayer, and two Psalters should be made available to every mess, with a ship's Bible to be provided for every sixteen persons. In between time-consuming medical obligations, we find the Surgeon taking time to distribute to each mess of six a New Testament and Book of Common Prayer, supplying over 100 religious books among the prisoners and crew, along with 160 tracts, an average of one for every man.

Brydone appears to have undertaken his duties with the utmost diligence and every Sabbath we find him reading the Divine Service throughout the ship and discoursing from Blair's *Sermons,* a text on which he relied heavily throughout the voyage. Apart from one or two minor incidents, behaviour on board seems to have been almost exemplary. As the ship approached Sydney Heads the Surgeon was gratified to receive a letter of thanks signed by all prisoners on board. While we know nothing of the identity of the man who drafted it, it is worth quoting as an indication of the level of articulacy that could sometimes be found among the convict population:

Respected Sir

The Prisoners under your charge feeling the good effects of your unrelenting care and attention to their interests and comfort, cannot pass it in silence without unanimously coming to the resolution of returning you their warm and sincere acknowledgement.

When any dispute arose as to the distribution of the necessaries allotted to their long but hitherto successful voyage, an application to you Sir was only necessary to put all to rights. And here we must beg leave to observe that in discharging this duty, it seemed to give you a secret satisfaction, and left a stamp on our minds that the goodness of your heart towards us could not be corrupted.

We have also to congratulate you on the successful termination of your professional labours as to the health of our number, where in the aggregate the hand of Death has only visited us in one solitary instance, and in this case, tho: much to be lamented, it seemed the finger of Providence had been long pointed.

Return therefore Sir to your Country to the bosom of your family, and friends, and take along with you the greetings & prayers of those unhappy beings who have been consigned to exile, by the Laws of their Country, but have yet their natural feelings, and cannot pass over such worth without thus expressing their unfeigned and heartfelt thanks.

We are Respected Sir, The Prison on board the Eliza your much obliged Servants.

While the voyage of the *Eliza* provides an unusually detailed amount of documentary evidence, we might well ask how typical it was of the convict ship in the early nineteenth century. Sailing from Cork in the same year, William Evans, Surgeon on board the *Bencoolen*, distributed Bibles and Prayer Books 'agreeably to Instructions from the Navy Board' a fortnight into the voyage. Two weeks later he observes with some satisfaction that, 'since the distribution of the Bibles and Prayer Books, the Prisoners, Guard & Crew are very attentive and seem to pay the most particular Observance to the Sacred Volumes.' The remaining months on board appear to have gone similarly well:

Voyages such as Ours have been usually characterized as Scenes of Gambling, immorality and impropriety of every kind, but it affords me a pleasure I cannot well describe, to have it in my power to state that the one We have just completed was of quite a different Character — as not a Single pack of Cards, or other gambling apparatus was to be found amongst the Prisoners since their Embarkation and their attention to their Prayer Books, and religious and moral tracts, which We from time to time supplied them with, coupled with their uniform decency and propriety of demeanour and submissiveness to all those placed over them, leads me to hope that they are sensibly affected & contrite for their past misdemeanours.[24]

Probably the most detailed account of educational instruction on board a convict ship is that left by Colin Arnott Browning, surgeon on board the *Earl Grey* as it made its way to Tasmania in the 1840s. *The Convict Ship; a Narrative of the Results of Scriptural Instruction and Moral Discipline* (1844) is from beginning to end a story of unalloyed success and pedagogical triumph in the face of adversity. In the weeks before the voyage, Browning had worked diligently to acquire supplies for the journey. As well as the standard government issue of Bibles, Prayer Books, and Psalters, he was gratified to acknowledge additional donations of 200 religious works from the British and Foreign Bible Society, 74 Bibles and Prayer Books from the SPCK, and a large number of donations from the Religious Tract Society.[25]

At the beginning of the voyage, literacy levels on board the *Earl Grey* appear to have been lower than most. On embarkation, estimated Browning, of a total 264 convicts 188 could 'neither read nor write'; 23 could 'only read', and only 53 could 'read and write'. When they arrived in Tasmania, according to the Surgeon, all but one could read with a degree of competence, while 60 could both 'read and write'. Early in the voyage, we are told, schools were established, overseen by the most competent of the prisoners:

An abundant variety of religious tracts, and of valuable little works published by the Tract Society were in constant circulation, and diligently perused; by the great body of the people who could read when they embarked, and by others when they acquired the ability, were the Scriptures studied in private; morning and evening they were read publicly to the whole of the people assembled, and always in the evening … and improved for solemn and faithful exhortation.

When they disembarked, claimed Browning, almost all had a copy of a Bible as well as a Prayer Book and other religious works, each having acquired 'a habit of application' and 'a love of useful knowledge'.[26]

It was with similarly unrestrained pride that J. S. Hampton, Surgeon Superintendent on board the *Sir George Seymour* in 1845, was to report the success of his efforts to improve the men under his care. Despite bad weather and widespread sickness, a Sunday School was established soon into the voyage, which we are told 198 prisoners attended with 'diligence':

> To improve the prisoners' minds, as well as to increase their self-respect and estimation of each other, a certain number of the most intelligent were selected, and encouraged to deliver lectures to their fellow-prisoners, in the evenings, on instructive and interesting subjects, and many of these lectures, as well as the attentive manner in which they were listened to, would have done credit to similar meetings of free men having much greater pretensions.

As well as lectures on worthy topics such as 'The Advantages of Education', 'The Use and Abuse of Music', and 'The Duties of Domestic Servants', prisoners also benefited from instruction on 'Poetry', 'Architecture', 'Ornithology' and 'The Circulation of the Blood'. In addition to which, a weekly newspaper was published throughout the voyage 'in a highly creditable manner'. Never in all of his years in the convict service, reported the Surgeon, had he encountered such 'uniform orderly good conduct'.[27]

So pleased was he with the outcome of the voyage of the *Hindostan*, in 1845, that Dr Andrew Henderson undertook to publish an account 'to show younger men in the service what has been done for Convicts' and to encourage other surgeons 'to use their utmost exertions to educate the unfortunate'. Henderson found that of the 200 'boy convicts' who embarked: 95 could 'read tolerably well, and write'; 27 could 'read indifferently … but could not write'; 31 'were just being initiated in the Primer, or first book of Lessons'; while 47 'did not even know the letters of the alphabet'. Dividing his charges into two divisions early in the voyage, Henderson recruited the help of one or two adult convicts, one of whom he refers to as 'a professional Schoolmaster', in the establishment of a school:

> The Junior Class … were arranged into sections of five each; over which were appointed Monitors, selected from the better Scholars of the Senior Division; to each Monitor was delivered two Primers for the use of his class, which were used by the boys in turns. … About 40 have been brought forward to read the Testament, of whom the number of those who had begun to be initiated in the Primer or alphabet, and those who had not are nearly equal. With regard, again, to the first or Senior Division, they were assembled in School on the afternoons … from 2 to 4; these were exercised according to their respective abilities in reading notable portions of the Old and New Testaments, in spelling, and in writing and Arithmetic. A marked improvement has been made by them in all these branches.[28]

Fig. 4. A team of Woolwich convicts, including boys and 'Specials', near Blackfriars Bridge, from *The Malefactor's Register; or, New Newgate and Tyburn Calendar* [1779]

Despite the optimistic tone of many of these accounts we should bear in mind that these are official reports, intended to convey a sense of a job well done. In the absence of corroborating evidence it is difficult to establish how many are accurate, and how many were the result of attempts to provide paymasters with a good impression.

The attitude of Ship's Surgeons towards the non-medical aspects of their duties could often in reality be perfunctory. Far from being committed to the spiritual or moral well-being of their flocks, some had little to do with religious instruction, apart from the obligatory reading of sabbath prayers. Scientific training was not always compatible with spiritual devotion, leading some to care little for the religious beliefs of their superiors in the Home Office. Others, despite the best of intentions, faced insurmountable obstacles, often finding it difficult to keep up with their punishing schedules. A prison hulk was sometimes a breeding ground for infection, and it was not unusual for a large proportion of its inmates to be severely ill on embarkation. Cases of pneumonia, tuberculosis, and syphilis were common and, where infectious disease was rife, the convict ship could look more like a field hospital than a prison. Where long hours of medical attention were required on the voyage, it could hardly be expected that an overworked surgeon would have the time, let alone the inclination, to teach spelling to recalcitrant prisoners.

In 1820 we find Robert Espie, who had been spending a considerable amount of time and energy organizing schools on board the *Dorothy*, putting two prisoners in chains for disrupting lessons. Despite frequent remarks on the progress that his scholars were making, we find him two months later putting yet another in irons for 'selling prayer books and various other things not his own property'.[29] Printed material would often have found its way onto the black market that operated on most convict ships, serving a number of uses for which it was not initially intended: it might be smoked, used in the privy, and recycled in other ways. It was reported in 1819 that, shortly into their voyage on the *Hibernia*, prisoners were found to have broken up Bibles and Prayer Books in order to make playing cards.[30] And, while it might have been an exemplary voyage in all other respects, one of Browning's schoolmasters on the *Earl Grey* was dismissed from his duties and kept in solitary confinement for repeated insubordination, accompanied by 'the most pernicious *levity*'.[31]

The Uses of Literacy

In Marcus Clarke's popular convict novel, *For the Term of His Natural Life*, the prisoner Rufus Dawes is told by Meekin, the chaplain, to be humble in his prayers and to allow his mind to be 'softened' by the teachings of the Word of God, saying that 'it would be better to read your Bible than to talk.' To Dawes's reply that he had read the Bible and that he doubted the existence of God, the chaplain responds by undertaking to mark up prescribed biblical passages in order for the prisoner to commit them to memory. When the book — which the guard tells him to keep clean — is finally delivered to his cell Dawes begins to read:

> He turned his eyes downwards to the texts. Good Meekin in the fullness of his stupidity, had selected the finest denunciations of bard and priest, the most notable of the Psalmist's curses upon his enemies, most furious of Isaiah's ravings anent the forgetfulness of the national worship, the most terrible thunderings of apostle and evangelist against idolatry and unbelief were grouped together and presented to Dawes to soothe him. All the material horrors of Meekin's faith — stripped, by force of dissociation from the context, of all poetic feeling and local colouring — were launched at the sinner by Meekin's ignorant hand.

When he returns the next morning, the chaplain finds the Bible on the floor, discarded, and Dawes as insubordinate as ever.

On his tour of Australia in the 1830s, the evangelical Reverend James Backhouse discovered some surprising attitudes towards official print culture. In 1833 he reported approvingly that 'several persons called upon us to receive tracts: some of these were reformed prisoners, who were diligent in distributing them, sticking up in cottages the broad sheets containing the Ten Commandments, &c.'[32] Yet the display of pious verses may not have been born of the high motives that Backhouse supposes: the use of printed sheets as a form of interior decoration was common among the illiterate poor in the nineteenth century. Any sense of convict piety was finally shattered when the minister later returned to the isolated settlement of Cock-Fighters Bridge on the Wollombi:

> Bibles were distributed among them about three years ago, but none are now to be found. Men in such a situation often take to card-playing, or other demoralizing occupations, to fill up vacant time. In some places in these Colonies, they have been known to convert the leaves of their Bibles into cards, and to mark the figures upon them with blood and soot![33]

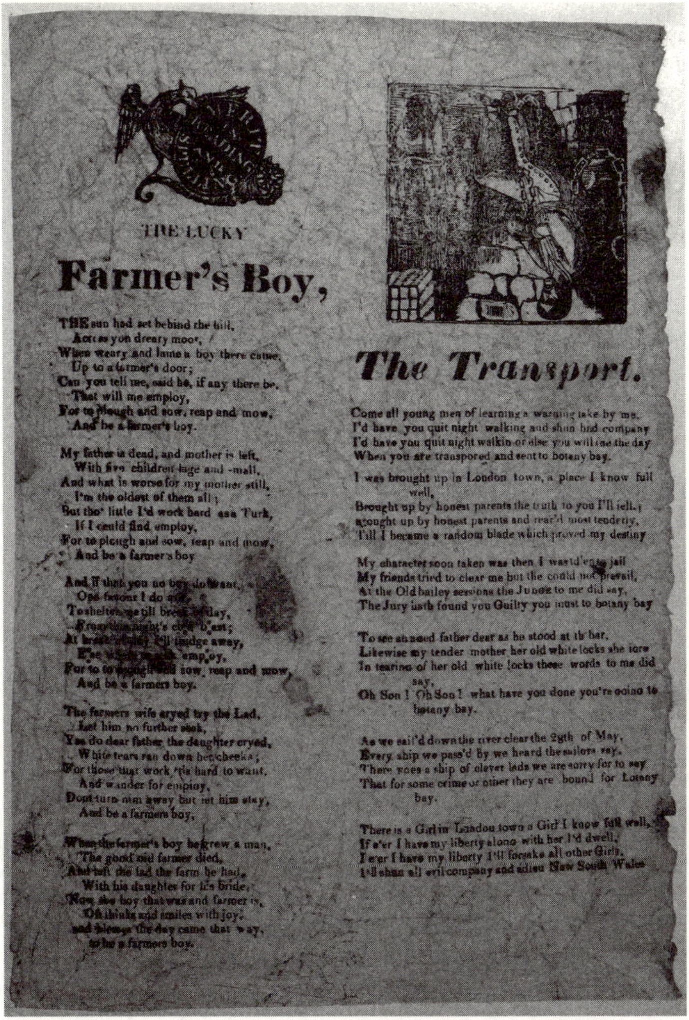

THE LUCKY

Farmer's Boy,

THE sun had set behind the hill,
Across yon dreary moor,
When weary and lame a boy there came,
Up to a farmer's door;
Can you tell me, said he, if any there be,
That will me employ,
For to plough and sow, reap and mow,
And be a farmer's boy.

My father is dead, and mother is left,
With five children large and small,
And what is worse for my mother still,
I'm the oldest of them all;
But tho' little I'd work hard as a Turk,
If I could find employ,
For to plough and sow, reap and mow,
And be a farmer's boy

And if that you no boy do want,
One favour I do ask,
To shelter me till break of day,
From this night's cold blast;
At break of day I'll trudge away,
Else where to seek employ,
For to to plough and sow, reap and mow,
And be a farmers boy.

The farmers wife cryed try the Lad,
Let him no further seek,
Yes do dear father the daughter cryed,
While tears ran down her cheeks;
For those that work 'tis hard to want,
And wander for employ,
Dont turn him away but let him stay,
And be a farmers boy,

When the farmer's boy he grew a man,
The good old farmer died,
And left the lad the farm he had,
With his daughter for his bride,
Now the boy that was and farmer is,
Oft thinks and smiles with joy,
and blesses the day came that way,
to be a farmers boy.

The Transport.

Come all young men of learning a warning take by me,
I'd have you quit night walking and shun bad company
I'd have you quit night walkin or else you will rue the day
When you are transpored and sent to botany bay.

I was brought up in London town, a place I know full well,
Brought up by honest parents the truth to you I'll tell,
Brought up by honest parents and rear'd most tenderly,
Till I became a random blade which proved my destiny

My character soon taken was then I was td'en to jail
My friends tried to clear me but the could not prevail,
At the Old bailey sessions the Judge to me did say,
The Jury hath found you Guilty you must to botany bay

To see an aged father dear as he stood at the bar,
Likewise my tender mother her old white locks she tore
In tearing of her old white locks these words to me did say,
Oh Son! Oh Son! what have you done you're going to botany bay.

As we sail'd down the river clear the 29th of May,
Every ship we pass'd by we heard the sailors say,
There goes a ship of clever lads we are sorry for to say
That for some crime or other they are bound for botany bay.

There is a Girl in London town a Girl I know full well,
If e'er I have my liberty along with her I'd dwell,
If e'er I have my liberty I'll forsake all other Girls,
I'll shun all evil company and adieu New South Wales

Fig. 5. Convict broadside (by kind permission of The University of Sheffield)

Resourcefulness born of necessity was an important part of everyday convict experience. While the emphasis of government agents and church organizations might have been on the Prayer Book and the Bible, there is evidence throughout the transportation period of the different uses to which print could be put. Outside official culture alternative forms of textuality proliferated, negotiating in complex ways the relationship between orality and literacy. Popular broadsides, playscripts, and songbooks, manuscript letters to be read aloud, seditious cartoons, and irreverent graffiti, were all regular features of everyday convict society.

Among the less literate, there was a proliferation of oral culture and story-telling; there are many references in official reports to the moral dubiety of the narratives that were in circulation, celebrating the exploits of famous criminals. In 1846 one chaplain was to remark on the fact that many prisoners who were bereft of moral values were 'familiar with, if not enamoured of' characters made famous by texts like the *Newgate Calendar*, in which criminal behaviour was 'held up for their sympathies and imitation'.[34] Scattered anecdotes relating to the presence of forbidden literature in prison cells would seem to suggest that there was a considerable clandestine market in illicit print that made its way past the gaze of the chaplain. Occasional observations by government inspectors bear witness to a hidden undergrowth of sensational and pornographic literature:

> We found several books, amongst them *Guthrie's Grammar*, the *Keepsake Annual* for 1836, and the ____ by ____, 18 plates, published by Stockdale, 1827. This last book is of the most disgusting nature, and the plates are obscene and indecent in the extreme. It was claimed as his property by a prisoner named ____, and was kept in the cupboard without any attempt at concealment.[35]

It is also likely that there was a vigorous trade in popular broadsides and chapbooks, many lamenting exile from home or telling the tragic stories of felons who had gone before. Titles like *The Convict's Farewell* and *The Prisoner's Lament* were bound to appeal to those who could identify with the unfortunate characters that filled their pages. Cheaply produced, these texts occupied a dynamic position between oral and literate culture, reflecting as well as perpetuating a rich proletarian musical tradition. One example, illustrated here, provides an example of print at the lowest end of the market. Poorly illustrated and full of typographical errors, it may have been produced by a semi-literate compositor.

Commenting on the significance of tattoos to convict identity, one historian remarks on the symbolic importance of the text imposed on that most personal of writing media, the prisoner's body. 'With the aid of a pin-prick artist's kit,' remarks Hamish Maxwell-Stewart, convicts were able 'to record their own tales of coercion.'[36] Found on the bodies of over 25 per cent of criminals tried in Britain, convict tattoos stood at once as symbols of freedom and defiance, serving to remind their owners and others of personal history and affiliation.

Among other forms of signification which convicts themselves used to memorialize experience were the hundreds of love tokens that were produced before departure for Australia. Fashioned from smoothed coins, and engraved with short poems, mottos, and personal information, these mementoes were often presented as parting gifts to loved ones left behind. While he was awaiting deportation for stealing a sheep, the nineteen-year-old bricklayer, Thomas Alsop, sought out the services of an engraver who provided him with a coin inscribed with the following poem for his mother (fig. 6a):

The rose
soon drupes
& dies, the brier
fades away, but
my fond heart
for you I love,
shall never
go astray

By all appearances, Alsop's token was the work of a professional engraver. Alsop was one of many convicts who, although themselves illiterate, were able to communicate with friends and family members through the intervention of their more educated peers.[37] Awaiting transportation for stealing a purse, the 22-year-old Mary Anne Whitlock left a token for her aunt in 1831. Bearing the simple motto 'ADIEU, DEAR AUNT, ADIEU', it is much cruder in appearance, and was possibly pricked out by herself (fig. 6b).[38]

While many Australia-bound convicts had only nominal levels of literacy, a significant proportion — commonly referred to as 'Specials' — were relatively well educated. Transported for white-collar crimes — such as embezzlement, forgery, and fraud — they brought with them the kind

Fig. 6a. Convict love tokens (by kind permission of Timothy Millett)

Fig. 6b

of skills that would serve them well in a new social context. Still others were relatively well-educated insurgents serving out sentences for political crimes. As recent historians have observed, while a 'surprisingly high proportion of [these] could read', some political prisoners were 'exceptionally rare in the sophistication of their literacy'.[39] Such was certainly the case on board the *Hougomont*, the last transport ship for Australia, which carried a large number of Fenian prisoners to Western Australia in 1867. The diary of one convict provides a fairly detailed account of life between decks, as it made its way from London to Freemantle, with entertainments including a debating society, recitations from Shakespeare, nightly theatricals, and the publication of a weekly journal containing original poetry, critical articles, and a lively correspondence column.[40]

It would be difficult to imagine a company of more erudite passengers than those responsible for the production of *The Voice of Our Exiles,* a weekly newspaper published in manuscript on board the *Clara,* the prospectus of which appeared in February 1864:

> In the works of Seneca composed in the evening of a brilliant tho' checquered career, we find the following aphorism — 'Si tempus in studium conferis, omne vitae fastidium effugeris.' 'You must devote your time to study — if you would escape all the weariness of life.' A Philosopher, a moralist and a man of the world, he had experienced the strangest vicissitudes of fortune. Of servile birth, he raised himself by the sheer force of his talents ... literary culture is able to mitigate the evils of servitude, and ... Rank and wealth without it, are no barrier against a monotonous and discontented existence.[41]

For several columns the editor continues in the same vein, drawing on a range of sources including Ovid, Boethius, Cervantes, and Bacon, presumably from memory. One of a series of highly sophisticated intellectual debates that went on throughout the journal's pages related to the penal code itself, the final editorial concluding:

> According to the principles laid down by Jeremy Bentham, and recognised in all modern Codes of Law, Secondary Punishment must contain two primary elements — the one of a reforming, the other of a deterring nature — both of them designed to act in an equal degree on the Criminal, and the latter also intended to operate on the mind of the Community to which he belongs. There is moreover involved in all Punishment, a third element — the idea of expiation.
>
> The question therefore resolves itself into the following ones. Does the present system, taken as a whole, contain these three indispensable conditions? Secondly —

Does any part of the present system contain them? Thirdly — Is it possible to devise a system which may contain them?

To their solution we believe that hitherto a wrong method has been applied.

In this most unlikely of cultural contexts, *conspicuous literacy* could apparently still confer a degree of social status in the face of other forms of deracination. Dickens's Magwitch was not the only one, it seems, to take revenge on the society that had condemned him by making himself a 'gentleman'.

The figure of the ignorant criminal was as familiar to the nineteenth-century prison reformer as it was to the patron of the *Police Gazette*, as natural to the reader of Dickens as it was to the music-hall audience. But, as historians now realize, it was an image informed by fiction rather than actuality. Over three decades ago, Charles Bateson observed that the average level of literacy on a convict ship was higher than among the free emigrant population of Australia during the period of transportation.[42] More recently, revisionist historians have provided more detailed evidence relating to the unusually high level of labour skills that convicts took with them to Australia in the nineteenth century. As Stephen Nicholas observes, 'three quarters of the English convicts who arrived in New South Wales could read and/or write, a significantly higher than the average for all English workers (58 per cent) who could sign the marriage register.'[43] While a minority of convicts would spend the rest of their lives outside literacy, for those who arrived with a level of education and a valuable trade there were fortunes to be made. Many of Australia's convicts would eventually come to distinguish themselves as schoolmasters, civil servants, and entrepreneurs; a minority would even take their places within the highest echelons of an emerging colonial elite.

In his now-famous critique of the post-Enlightenment penal code, Michel Foucault defines the 'carceral' as a place where the technologies of discourse and writing serve to restrain and define human subjectivity. Through statistical analysis, daily routine, bureaucratic categorization, and constant surveillance, argues Foucault, the human subject is constructed as a function of the systems of coercion in which it finds itself. In an attempt to offer an alternative to such a deterministic model, Michel de Certeau imagines a reading space outside the constraints of official regulation, where tactical resistance is evident among the most common practices of everyday life. In the act of reading, argues de Certeau, infinite possibilities can be found for the opportunistic, and often unpredictable, production of meaning.[44] In the face of official directives and prescriptive literacies, nineteenth-century convicts, from the most highly literate to the most meagrely educated, were to use a range of cultural practices to their own ends, of which reading and writing were among the most important.

References

1. Quoted in A. G. L. Shaw, *Convicts and the Colonies* (London: Faber, 1966), p. 162.
2. Shaw, *Convicts and the Colonies*, p. 19.
3. J. Jebb to H. Waddinton, 17 July 1857; Home Office Papers (The National Archives), PRO HO45/9455/7414/5.
4. Sean McConville, *A History of English Prison Administration*, vol. 1: 1750–1877 (London: Routledge and Kegan Paul, 1981), pp. 197–8.
5. Parliamentary Papers 1847, XVIII, pp. xiv–xix.
6. W. Branch Johnson, *The English Prison Hulks* (London: Phillimore, 1970), p. 126.
7. Johnson, *English Prison Hulks*, pp. 101–2.
8. R. Wilson to Lord Grey, 26 October 1846: PRO HO45/OS 1413.
9. Johnson, *English Prison Hulks*, p. 127.
10. *Ibid.*, p. 219.
11. *Ibid.*, pp. 129–30.
12. J. Jebb to H. Waddinton, 17 July 1857; Home Office Papers, PRO HO45/9455/7414.
13. Patrick Brantlinger, *The Reading Lesson: The Threat of Mass Literacy in Nineteenth Century Britain* (Bloomington: Indiana University Press, 1998), p. 75.
14. Parliamentary Papers, 1857, Sess. 2, XXIII, pp. 65, 73–4.
15. Parliamentary Papers, 1852–3, LI, p. 408.
16. Letter of 28 July 1856 to M. Wilson; Home Office Papers, PRO HO45/9455/7414.
17. Jebb to H. Waddinton, 17 July 1857; Home Office Papers, PRO HO45/9455/7414.
18. 14 April 1856; Home Office Papers, PRO H045/9455/7414.
19. Home Office Papers, PRO HO45/9455/7414.
20. McConville, pp. 410–11.
21. Surgeon Superintendent Regulations, quoted in Shaw, *Convicts and the Colonies*, p. 122.
22. Documents relating to the *Eliza* are held at the Mitchell Library, Sydney. The 40-year-old Brydone was himself educated and experienced: a brief autobiographical sketch reveals that he was classically trained in the town of Melrose and had qualified as a physician at Edinburgh University sixteen years before, since which time he had served the Navy in a number of countries, including extended periods in India.
23. The majority of the 26 illiterate prisoners being unskilled labourers or sailors. Only five of the 26 non-readers had skilled training including, quite surprisingly, a bookbinder.
24. William Evans, Journal on Board *Bencoolen*, 1819: PRO Adm 101/7/10.
25. Colin Arnott Browning, *The Convict Ship; a Narrative of the Results of Scriptural Instruction and Moral Discipline* (London: Smith, Elder, 1844), pp. 289–90.
26. Browning, *The Convict Ship*, pp. 33, 286, 292.
27. *British Parliamentary Papers, Crime and Punishment: Transportation*, no. 7 (Shannon: Irish University Press, 1969), p. 298.

28. Andrew Henderson, *Scraps and Facts of Convict Ships* (n.p.: 1845).
29. Robert Espie, Journal on Board *Dorothy*, 1820: PRO Adm 101/19/8.
30. Revd. Richard Hill to Macquarie, 8 July 1819, quoted in Shaw, p. 123.
31. Browning, *The Convict Ship*, p. 88.
32. James Backhouse, *A Narrative of a Visit to the Australian Colonies* (London: Hamilton, Adams, 1843), p. 138.
33. Backhouse, *Narrative of a Visit*, p. 395.
34. Janet Fyfe, *Books Behind Bars: the role of books, reading, and libraries in British prison reform, 1701–1911* (Westport, Connecticut, & London: Greenwood Press, 1992), pp. 177–8.
35. Quoted in *Books Behind Bars*, p. 177.
36. Hamish Maxwell-Stewart and James Bradley, 'Convict Tattoos: Tales of Freedom and Coercion', *Convict Love Tokens: The Leaden Hearts that the Convicts Left Behind*, ed. Michele Field and Timothy Millett (South Australia: Wakefield Press, 1998), pp. 47–52.
37. Although there is no documentary evidence to support the idea, it is sometimes believed that engravers were occasionally permitted onto the hulks in order to provide this service. It is just as likely that convicted engravers, of whom there are many in the lists, bartered their skills while they were in prison.
38. Field and Millett, *Convict Love Tokens*, pp. 95, 92.
39. David Kent and Norma Townsend, *Joseph Mason: Assigned Convict, 1831–1837* (Melbourne University Press, 1996), p. 8.
40. Denis Cashman, Diary, per *Hougoumont*, 1867: Australian National Maritime Museum MS Hou.
41. *Voice of our Exiles*, I (13 February 1864), National Library of Australia MS 6037.
42. Charles Bateson, *The Convict Ships 1787–1868* (Glasgow: Brown, Son & Ferguson, 1969).
43. Stephen Nicholas, ed., *Convict Workers: Reinterpreting Australia's Past* (Cambridge University Press, 1988), p. 9.
44. See especially Michel Foucault, *Discipline and Punish* (New York: Pantheon, 1977); Michel de Certeau, *The Practice of Everyday Life* (Berkeley, California: University of California Press, 1988).

Index

References to illustrations in *italic*